FROM RED TAPE TO RESULTS :

CREATING A GOVERNMENT THAT WORKS BETTER & COSTS LESS

Report of the National Performance Review

Vice President Al Gore

TIMES BOOKS

RANDOM HOUSE

*On September 7, 1993, Vice President Al Gore
and the National Performance Review
released a report, entitled "From Red Tape to
Results: Creating a Government That
Works Better and Costs Less." This edition,
published by Times Books, a division of
Random House, Inc., reproduces the
Government Printing Office document
in its entirety.*
NOT ONE WORD HAS BEEN OMITTED.

ISBN: 0-8129-2365-0

Manufactured in the United States of America

September 7, 1993

The President
The White House
Washington, DC

Dear Mr. President,

The National Performance Review, the intensive, 6-month study of the federal government that you requested, has completed its work. This report represents the beginning of what must be, and — with your leadership — will be, a long-term commitment to change. The title of this report reflects our goals: moving from red tape to results to create a government that works better and costs less.

Many talented federal employees contributed to this report, bringing their experience and insight to a difficult and urgent task. We sought ideas and advice from all across America: from other federal workers, from state and local government officials, from management experts, from business leaders, and from private citizens eager for change. This report benefitted greatly from their involvement, and we intend for them to benefit from the reforms we are proposing here.

It is your vision of a government that works for people, cleared of useless bureaucracy and waste and freed from red tape and senseless rules, that continues to be the catalyst for our efforts. We present this report to you confident that it will provide an effective and innovative plan to make that vision a reality.

Sincerely,

Al Gore
Vice President

CONTENTS

PREFACE

We can no longer afford to pay more for—and get less from—our government. The answer for every problem cannot always be another program or more money. It is time to radically change the way the government operates—to shift from top-down bureaucracy to entrepreneurial government that empowers citizens and communities to change our country from the bottom up. We must reward the people and ideas that work and get rid of those that don't.

Bill Clinton and Al Gore
Putting People First[1]

The National Performance Review is about change— historic change—in the way the government works. The Clinton administration believes it is time for a new customer service contract with the American people, a new guarantee of effective, efficient, and responsive government. As our title makes clear, the National Performance Review is about moving from red tape to results to create a government that works better and costs less.

These are our twin missions: to make government *work better* and *cost less*. The President has already addressed the federal deficit with the largest deficit reduction package in history. The National Performance Review can reduce the deficit further, but it is not just about cutting spending. It is also about closing the *trust* deficit: proving to the American people that their tax dollars will be treated with respect for the hard work that earned them. We are taking action to put America's house in order.

The National Performance Review began on March 3, 1993, when President Clinton announced a 6-month review of the federal government and asked me to lead the effort. We organized a team of experienced federal employees from all corners of the government—a marked change from past efforts, which relied on outsiders.

We turned to the people who know government best—who know what works, what doesn't, and how things ought to be changed. We organized these people into a series of teams, to examine both agencies and cross-cutting systems, such as budgeting, procurement, and personnel. The President also asked all cabinet members to create Reinvention Teams to lead transformations at their departments, and Reinvention Laboratories, to begin experimenting with new ways of doing business. Thousands of federal employees joined these two efforts.

But the National Performance Review did not stop there. From the beginning, I wanted to hear from as many Americans as possible. I spoke with federal employees at every major agency and at federal centers across the country—seeking their ideas, their input, and their inspiration. I visited programs that work: a Miami school that also serves as a community center, a Minnesota pilot program that provides

benefits more efficiently by using technology and debit cards, a Chicago neighborhood that has put community policing to work, a U.S. Air Force base that has made quality management a way of life.

We also heard from citizens all across America, in more than 30,000 letters and phone calls. We sought the views of hundreds of different organizations, large and small. We learned from the experience of state and local leaders who have restructured their organizations. And we listened to business leaders who have used innovative management practices to turn their companies around.

At a national conference in Tennessee, we brought together experts to explore how best to apply the principles of reinventing government to improving family services. In Philadelphia's Independence Square, where our government was born, we gathered for a day-long "Reinventing Government Summit" with the best minds

from business, government, and the academic community.

This report is the first product of our efforts. It describes roughly 100 of our most important actions and recommendations, while hundreds more are listed in the appendices at the end of this report. In the coming months, we will publish additional information providing more detail on those recommendations.

This report represents the beginning of what will be—what *must* be—an ongoing commitment to change. It includes actions that will be taken now, by directive of the President; actions that will be taken by the cabinet secretaries and agency heads; and recommendations for congressional action.

The National Performance Review focused primarily on *how* government should work, not on *what* it should do. Our job was to improve performance in areas where policymakers had already decided government should play a role.

We examined every cabinet department and 10 agencies. At two departments, Defense and Health and Human Services, our work paralleled other large-scale reviews already under way. Defense had launched a Bottom-Up Review to meet the President's 1994-1997 spending reduction target. In addition, comprehensive health and welfare reform task forces had been established to make large-scale changes in significant parts of Health and Human Services. Nevertheless, we made additional recommendations regarding both these departments and passed other findings on to the relevant task force for review.

The National Performance Review recommendations, if enacted, would produce savings of $108 billion over 5 years. As the table below indicates, $36.4 billion of these savings come from specific changes proposed in the agencies and departments of the government.

We also expect that the reinventions we propose will allow us to reduce the size of the civilian, non-postal workforce by 12 percent over the next 5 years. This will bring the federal workforce below two million employees for the first time since 1966. This reduction in the workforce will total 252,000 positions—152,000 over and above the 100,000 already promised by President Clinton.

Most of the personnel reductions will be concentrated in the structures of over-control and micromanagement that now bind the federal government: supervisors, headquarters staffs, personnel specialists, budget analysts, procurement specialists, accountants, and auditors. These central control structures not only stifle the

Clinton/Gore NPR Savings

(FY-1995-1999 $ in Billions)

AGENCIES	36.4
STREAMLINING THE BUREAUCRACY THROUGH REENGINEERING	40.4
PROCUREMENT 5% annual savings in total procurement spending	22.5
INFORMATION TECHNOLOGY Savings due to consolidation and modernization of the information infrastructure	5.4
INTERGOVERNMENTAL Offer fee-for-service option in lieu of existing administrative costs	3.3
TOTAL	108.0

(For a fuller description see Appendix A and Appendix B.)

creativity of line managers and workers, they consume billions per year in salary, benefits, and administrative costs. Additional personnel cuts will result as each agency reengineers its basic work processes to achieve higher productivity at lower costs—eliminating unnecessary layers of management and nonessential staff.

We will accomplish as much of this as possible through attrition, early retirement, and a time-limited program of cash incentives to leave federal service. If an employee whose job is eliminated cannot take early retirement and elects not to take a cash incentive to leave government service, we will help that employee find another job offer through out-placement assistance.

In addition to savings from the agencies and savings in personnel we expect that systematic reform of the procurement process should reduce the cost of everything the government buys. Our antiquated procurement system costs the government in two ways: first, we pay for all the bureaucracy we have created to buy things, and second, manufacturers build the price of dealing with this bureaucracy into the prices they charge us. If we reform the procurement system, we should be able to save $22 billion over 5 years.

As everyone knows, the computer revolution allows us to do things faster and more cheaply than we ever have before. Savings due to consolidation and modernization of the information infrastructure amount to $5.4 billion over 5 years.

Finally, by simplifying paperwork and reducing administrative costs, we expect to save $3.3 billion over 5 years in the cost of administering grant programs to state and local governments.

Many of the spending cuts we propose can be done by simplifying the internal organization of our departments and agencies. Others will require legislation. We recognize that there is broad support in Congress for both spending cuts and government reforms, and we look forward to working with Congress to pass this package of recommendations. As President Clinton said when he announced the National Performance Review:

This performance review is not about politics. Programs passed by both Democratic presidents and Republican presidents, voted on by members of Congress of both parties, and supported by the American people at the time, are being undermined by an inefficient and outdated bureaucracy, and by our huge debt. For too long the basic functioning of the government has gone unexamined. We want to make improving the way government does business a permanent part of how government works, regardless of which party is in power.

We have not a moment to lose. President Kennedy once told a story about a French general who asked his gardener to plant a tree. "Oh, this tree grows slowly," the gardener said. "It won't mature for a hundred years."

"Then there's no time to lose," the general answered. "Plant it this afternoon."

Al Gore
Vice President of the United States

INTRODUCTION

Our goal is to make the entire federal government both less expensive and more efficient, and to change the culture of our national bureaucracy away from complacency and entitlement toward initiative and empowerment. We intend to redesign, to reinvent, to reinvigorate the entire national government."

President Bill Clinton
Remarks announcing the National Performance Review
March 3, 1993

Public confidence in the federal government has never been lower. The average American believes we waste 48 cents of every tax dollar. Five of every six want "fundamental change" in Washington. Only 20 percent of Americans trust the federal government to do the right thing most of the time—down from 76 percent 30 years ago.[1]

We all know why. Washington's failures are large and obvious. For a decade, the deficit has run out of control. The national debt now exceeds $4 trillion—$16,600 for every man, woman, and child in America.

But the deficit is only the tip of the iceberg. Below the surface, Americans believe, lies enormous unseen waste. The Defense Department owns more than $40 billion in unnecessary supplies.[2] The Internal Revenue Service struggles to collect billions in unpaid bills. A century after industry replaced farming as America's principal business, the Agriculture Department still operates more than 12,000 field service offices, an average of nearly 4 for every county in the nation—rural, urban, or suburban. The federal government seems unable to abandon the

obsolete. It knows how to add, but not to subtract.

And yet, waste is not the only problem. The federal government is not simply broke; it is broken. Ineffective regulation of the financial industry brought us the savings and loan debacle. Ineffective education and training programs jeopardize our competitive edge. Ineffective welfare and housing programs undermine our families and cities.

We spend $25 billion a year on welfare, $27 billion on food stamps, and $13 billion on public housing—yet more Americans fall into poverty every year.[3] We spend $12 billion a year waging war on drugs—yet see few signs of victory. We fund 150 different employment and training programs—yet the average American has no idea where to get job training, and the skills of our workforce fall further behind those of our competitors.[4]

It is almost as if federal programs were *designed* not to work. In truth, few are "designed" at all; the legislative process simply churns them out, one after another, year after year. It's little wonder that when asked if "government always manages to mess things up," two-thirds of Americans say "yes."[5]

To borrow the words of a recent Brookings Institution book, we suffer not only a budget deficit but a performance deficit.[6] Indeed, public opinion experts argue that we are suffering the deepest crisis of faith in government in our lifetimes. In past crises—Watergate or the Vietnam War, for example—Americans doubted their leaders on moral or ideological grounds. They felt their government was deceiving them or failing to represent their values. Today's crisis is different: people simply feel that government doesn't work.[7]

In Washington, debate rarely focuses on the performance deficit. Our leaders spend most of their time debating policy issues. But if the vehicle designed to carry out policy is broken, new policies won't take us anywhere. If the car won't run, it hardly matters where we point it; we won't get there. Today, the central issue we face is not *what* government does, but *how* it works.

> We *need a federal government that delivers more for less. We need a federal government that treats its taxpayers as if they were customers and treats taxpayer dollars with respect for the sweat and sacrifice that earned them.*
>
> **Vice President Al Gore**
> May 24, 1993

We have spent too much money for programs that don't work. It's time to make our government work for the people, learn to do more with less, and treat taxpayers like customers.

President Clinton created the National Performance Review to do just that. In this report we make hundreds of recommendations for actions that, if implemented, will revolutionize the way the federal government does business. They will reduce waste, eliminate unneeded bureaucracy, improve service to taxpayers, and create a leaner but more productive government. As noted in the preface, they can save $108 billion over 5 years if those which will be enacted by the President and his cabinet are added to those we propose for enactment by Congress. Some of these proposals can be enacted by the President and his cabinet, others will require legislative action. We are going to fight for these changes. We are determined to create a government that works better and costs less.

A Cure Worse Than The Disease

Government is not alone in its troubles. As the Industrial Era has given way to the Information Age, institutions—both public and private—have come face to face with obsolescence. The past decade has witnessed profound restructuring: In the 1980s, major American corporations reinvented themselves; in the 1990s, governments are struggling to do the same.

In recent years, our national leaders responded to the growing crisis with traditional medicine. They blamed the bureaucrats. They railed against "fraud, waste, and abuse." And they slapped ever more controls on the bureaucracy to prevent it.

But the cure has become indistinguishable from the disease. The problem is not lazy or incompetent people; it is red tape and regulation so suffocating that they stifle every ounce of creativity. No one would offer a drowning man a drink of water. And yet, for more than a decade, we have added red tape to a system already strangling in it.

The federal government is filled with good people trapped in bad systems: budget systems, personnel systems, procurement systems, financial management systems, information systems. When we blame the people and impose more controls, we make the systems worse. Over the past 15 years, for example, Congress has created within each agency an independent office of the inspector general. The idea was to root out fraud, waste, and abuse. The inspectors general have certainly uncovered important problems. But as we learned in conversation after conversation, they have so intimidated federal employees that many are now afraid to deviate even slightly from standard operating procedure.

Yet innovation, by its nature, requires deviation. Unfortunately, faced with so many controls, many employees have simply given up. They do everything by the book—whether it makes sense or not. They fill out forms that should never have been created, follow rules that should never have been imposed, and prepare reports that serve no purpose—and are often never even read. In the name of controlling waste, we have created paralyzing inefficiency. It's time we found a way to get rid of waste and encourage efficiency.

The Root Problem: Industrial-Era Bureaucracies in an Information Age

Is government inherently incompetent? Absolutely not. Are federal agencies filled with incompetent people? No. The problem is much deeper: Washington is filled with organizations designed for an environment that no longer exists— bureaucracies so big and wasteful they can no longer serve the American people.

From the 1930s through the 1960s, we built large, top-down, centralized bureaucracies to do the public's business. They were patterned after the corporate structures of the age: hierarchical bureaucracies in which tasks were broken into simple parts, each the responsibility of a different layer of employees, each defined by specific rules and regulations. With their rigid preoccupation with standard operating procedure, their vertical chains of command, and their standardized services, these bureaucracies were steady—but slow and cumbersome. And in today's world of rapid change, lightning-quick information technologies, tough global competition, and demanding customers, large, top-down bureaucracies—public or private—don't

> *Our people, of course, work hard for their money.... They want quality in the cars they buy. They want quality in their local schools. And they want quality in their federal government and in federal programs.*
>
> **Senator John Glenn**
> Remarks introducing a hearing
> on federal planning and performance
> May 5, 1992

work very well. Saturn isn't run the way General Motors was. Intel isn't run the way IBM was.

Many federal organizations are also monopolies, with few incentives to innovate or improve. Employees have virtual lifetime tenure, regardless of their performance. Success offers few rewards; failure, few penalties. And customers are captive; they can't walk away from the air traffic control system or the Internal Revenue Service and sign up with a competitor. Worse, most federal monopolies receive their money without any direct input from their customers. Consequently, they try a lot harder to please Congressional appropriations subcommittees than the people they are meant to serve. Taxpayers pay more than they should and get poorer service.

Politics intensifies the problem. In Washington's highly politicized world, the greatest risk is not that a program will perform poorly, but that a scandal will erupt. Scandals are front-page news, while routine failure is ignored. Hence control system after control system is piled up to minimize the risk of scandal. The budget system, the personnel rules, the procurement process, the inspectors general—all are designed to prevent the tiniest misstep. We assume that we can't trust employees to make decisions, so we spell out in precise detail how they must do virtually everything, then audit them to ensure that they have obeyed every rule.

During Vice President Gore's town hall meeting with employees of the Department of Housing and Urban Development (HUD), the following exchange took place:

Participant: *We had an article in our newsletter several months ago that said — the lead story was "I'd rather have a lobotomy than have another idea." And that was reflecting the problem of our Ideas Program here in HUD.*

Many of the employees have wonderful ideas about how to save money and so on, but the way it works is that it has to be approved by the supervisor and the supervisor's supervisor and the supervisor's supervisor's supervisor before it ever gets to the Ideas Program ...

Many of the supervisors feel threatened because they didn't think of this idea, and this money is wasted in their office, and they didn't believe or didn't know it was happening and didn't catch it. So they are threatened and feel that it will make them look bad if they recognize the idea.

Vice President Gore: *So they strangle that idea in the crib, don't they?*

Participant: *And then they strangle the person that had the idea.*

The slightest deviation prompts new regulations and even more audits.

Before long, simple procedures are too complex for employees to navigate, so we hire more budget analysts, more personnel experts, and more procurement officers to make things work. By then, the process involves so much red tape that the smallest action takes far longer and costs far more than it should. Simple travel arrangements require endless forms and numerous signatures. Straightforward purchases take months; larger ones take years. Routine printing jobs take a dozen approvals.

This emphasis on process steals resources from the real job: serving the customer.

Indeed, the federal government spends billions of dollars paying people who control, check up on, or investigate others—supervisors, headquarters staffs, budget officers, personnel officers, procurement officers, and staffs of the General Accounting Office (GAO) and the inspectors general.[8] Not all this money is wasted, of course. But the real waste is no doubt larger, because the endless regulations and layers of control consume every employee's time. Who pays? The taxpayer.

Consider but one example, shared with Vice President Gore at a meeting of federal employees in Atlanta. After federal marshals seize drug dealers' homes, they are allowed to sell them and use the money to help finance the war on drugs. To sell the houses, they must keep them presentable, which includes keeping the lawns mowed.

In Atlanta, the employee explained, most organizations would hire neighborhood teenagers to mow a lawn for $10. But procurement regulations require the U.S. Marshals Service to bid out all work competitively, and neighborhood teenagers don't compete for contracts. So the federal government pays $40 a lawn to professional landscape firms. Regulations designed to save money waste it, because they take decisions out of the hands of those responsible for doing the work. And taxpayers lose $30 for every lawn mowed.

What would happen if the marshals used their common sense and hired neighborhood teenagers? Someone would notice—perhaps the Washington office, perhaps the inspector general's office, perhaps even the GAO. An investigation might well follow—hindering a career or damaging a reputation.

In this way, federal employees quickly learn that common sense is risky—and creativity is downright dangerous. They learn that the goal is not to produce results, please customers, or save taxpayers' money, but to avoid mistakes. Those who dare to innovate do so quietly.

This is perhaps the saddest lesson learned by those who worked on the National Performance Review: Yes, innovators exist within the federal government, but many work hard to keep their innovations quiet. By its nature, innovation requires a departure from standard operating procedure. In the federal government, such departures invite repercussions.

The result is a culture of fear and resignation. To survive, employees keep a low profile. They decide that the safest answer in any given situation is a firm "maybe." They follow the rules, pass the buck, and keep their heads down. They develop what one employee, speaking with Vice President Gore at a Department of Veterans Affairs meeting, called "a government attitude."

The Solution: Creating Entrepreneurial Organizations

How do we solve these problems? It won't be easy. We know all about government's problems, but little about solutions. The National Performance Review began by compiling a comprehensive list of problems. We had the GAO's 28-volume report on federal management problems, published last fall. We had GAO's *High-Risk Series*, a 17-volume series of pamphlets on troubled programs and agencies. We had the House Government Operations Committee's report on federal mismanagement, called *Managing the Federal Government: A Decade of Decline*. And we had 83 notebooks summarizing just the tables of contents of reports published by the inspectors general, the Congressional Budget Office, the agencies, and think tanks.

Unfortunately, few of these studies helped us design solutions. Few of the investigating bodies had studied success stories—organizations that had solved their problems. And without studying success, it is hard to devise real solutions. For years, the federal government has studied failure, and for years, failure has endured. Six of every ten major agencies have programs on the Office of Management and Budget's "high-risk" list, meaning they carry a significant

risk of runaway spending or fraud.

The National Performance Review approached its task differently. Not only did we look for potential savings and efficiencies, we searched for success. We looked for organizations that produced results, satisfied customers, and increased productivity. We looked for organizations that constantly learned, innovated, and improved. We looked for effective, entrepreneurial public organizations. And we found them: in local government, in state government, in other countries—and right here in our federal government.

At the Air Combat Command, for example, we found units that had doubled their productivity in 5 years. Why? Because the command measured performance everywhere; squadrons and bases competed proudly for the best maintenance, flight, and safety records; and top management had empowered employees to strip away red tape and redesign work processes. A supply system that had once required 243 entries by 22 people on 13 forms to get one spare part into an F-15 had been radically simplified and decentralized. Teams of employees were saving millions of dollars by moving supply operations to the front line, developing their own flight schedules, and repairing parts that were once discarded.[9]

At the Internal Revenue Service, we found tax return centers competing for the best productivity records. Performance on key customer service criteria—such as the accuracy of answers provided to taxpayers—had improved dramatically. Utah's Ogden Service Center, to cite but one example, had more than 50 "productivity improvement teams" simplifying forms and reengineering work processes. Not only had employees saved more than $11 million, they had won the 1992 Presidential Award for Quality.[10]

At the Forest Service, we found a pilot project in the 22-state Eastern Region that had increased productivity by 15 percent in just 2 years. The region had simplified its budget systems, eliminated layers of middle management, pared central headquarters

Americans voted for a change last November. They want better schools and health care and better roads and more jobs, but they want us to do it all with a government that works better on less money and that is more responsive.

President Bill Clinton
Remarks announcing the
National Performance Review
March 3, 1993

staff by a fifth, and empowered front-line employees to make their own decisions. At the Mark Twain National Forest, for instance, the time needed to grant a grazing permit had shrunk from 30 days to a few hours—because employees could grant permits themselves rather than process them through headquarters.[11]

We discovered that several other governments were also reinventing themselves, from Australia to Great Britain, Singapore to Sweden, the Netherlands to New Zealand. Throughout the developed world, the needs of information-age societies were colliding with the limits of industrial-era government. Regardless of party, regardless of ideology, these governments were responding. In Great Britain, conservatives led the way. In New Zealand, the Labor Party revolutionized government. In Australia and Sweden, both conservative and liberal parties embraced fundamental change.

In the United States, we found the same phenomenon at the state and local levels. The movement to reinvent government is as bipartisan as it is widespread. It is driven not by political ideology, but by absolute necessity. Governors, mayors, and legislators of both parties have reached the same conclusion: Government is broken, and it is time to fix it.

Where we found success, we found many common characteristics. Early on, we

articulated these in a one-page statement of our commitment. In organizing this report, we have boiled these characteristics down to four key principles.

1. Cutting Red Tape

Effective, entrepreneurial governments cast aside red tape, shifting from systems in which people are accountable for following rules to systems in which they are accountable for achieving results. They streamline their budget, personnel, and procurement systems—liberating organizations to pursue their missions. They reorient their control systems to prevent problems rather than simply punish those who make mistakes. They strip away unnecessary layers of regulation that stifle innovation. And they deregulate organizations that depend upon them for funding, such as lower levels of government.

2. Putting Customers First

Effective, entrepreneurial governments insist on customer satisfaction. They listen carefully to their customers—using surveys, focus groups, and the like. They restructure their basic operations to meet customers' needs. And they use market dynamics such as competition and customer choice to create incentives that drive their employees to put customers first.

By "customer," we do not mean "citizen." A citizen can participate in democratic decisionmaking; a customer receives benefits from a specific service. All Americans are citizens. Most are also customers: of the U.S. Postal Service, the Social Security Administration, the Department of Veterans Affairs, the National Park Service, and scores of other federal organizations.

In a democracy, citizens and customers both matter. But when they vote, citizens seldom have much chance to influence the behavior of public institutions that directly affect their lives: schools, hospitals, farm service agencies, social security offices. It is a sad irony: citizens own their government, but private businesses they do not own work much harder to cater to their needs.

3. Empowering Employees to Get Results

Effective, entrepreneurial governments transform their cultures by decentralizing authority. They empower those who work on the front lines to make more of their own decisions and solve more of their own problems. They embrace labor-management cooperation, provide training and other tools employees need to be effective, and humanize the workplace. While stripping away layers and empowering front-line employees, they hold organizations accountable for producing results.

4. Cutting Back to Basics: Producing Better Government for Less

Effective, entrepreneurial governments constantly find ways to make government work better and cost less—reengineering how they do their work and reexamining programs and processes. They abandon the obsolete, eliminate duplication, and end special interest privileges. They invest in greater productivity, through loan funds and long-term capital investments. And they embrace advanced technologies to cut costs.

These are the bedrock principles on which the reinvention of the federal bureaucracy must build—and the principles around which we have organized our actions. They fit together much like the pieces of a puzzle: if one is missing, the others lose their power. To create organizations that deliver value to American taxpayers, we must embrace all four.

Our approach goes far beyond fixing specific problems in specific agencies. Piecemeal efforts have been under way for years, but they have not delivered what Americans demand. The failure in Washington is embedded in the very systems by which we organize the federal bureaucracy. In recent years, Congress has

Principles of the National Performance Review

We will invent a government that puts people first, by:

- Cutting unnecessary spending
- Serving its customers
- Empowering its employees
- Helping communities solve their own problems
- Fostering excellence

Here's how. We will:

- Create a clear sense of mission
- Steer more, row less
- Delegate authority and responsibility
- Replace regulations with incentives
- Develop budgets based on outcomes
- Expose federal operations to competition
- Search for market, not administrative, solutions
- Measure our success by customer satisfaction

taken the lead in reinventing these systems. In 1990, it passed the Chief Financial Officers Act, designed to overhaul financial management systems; in July 1993, it passed the Government Performance and Results Act, which will introduce performance measurement throughout the federal government. With Congress's leadership, we hope to reinvent government's other basic systems, such as budget, personnel, information, and procurement.

Our approach has much in common with other management philosophies, such as quality management and business process reengineering. But these management disciplines were developed for the private sector, where conditions are quite different. In business, red tape may be bad, but it is not the suffocating presence it is in government. In business, market incentives already exist; no one need invent them. Powerful incentives are always at work, forcing organizations to do more with less. Indeed, businesses that fail to increase their productivity—or that tie themselves up in red tape—shrink or die. Hence, private sector management doctrines tend to overlook some central problems of government: its monopolies, its lack of a bottom line, its obsession with process rather than results. Consequently, our approach goes beyond private sector methods. It is aimed at the heart and soul of government.

The National Performance Review also shares certain goals with past efforts to cut costs in government. But our mission goes beyond cost-cutting. Our goal is not simply to weed the federal garden; it is to create a regimen that will *keep* the garden free of weeds. It is not simply to trim *pieces* of government, but to reinvent the way government does everything. It is not simply to produce a more efficient government, but to create a more *effective* one. After all, Americans don't want a government that fails more efficiently. They want a government that *works*.

To deliver what the people want, we need not jettison the traditional values that underlie democratic governance—values such as equal opportunity, justice, diversity, and democracy. We hold these values dear. We seek to transform bureaucracies precisely *because* they have failed to nurture these values. We believe that those who resist change for fear of jeopardizing our democratic values doom us to a government that continues—through its failures—to subvert those very values.

Our Commitment: A Long-Term Investment in Change

This is not the first time Americans have felt compelled to reinvent their government. In 1776, our founding fathers rejected the old model of a central power issuing edicts for all to obey. In its place, they created a

government that broadly distributed power. Their vision of democracy, which gave citizens a voice in managing the United States, was untried and untested in 1776. It required a tremendous leap of faith. But it worked.

Later generations extended this experiment in democracy to those not yet enfranchised. As the 20th century dawned, a generation of "Progressives" such as Teddy Roosevelt and Woodrow Wilson invented the modern bureaucratic state, designed to meet the needs of a new industrial society. Franklin Roosevelt brought it to full flower. Indeed, Roosevelt's 1937 announcement of his Committee on Administrative Management sounds as if it were written only yesterday:

The time has come to set our house in order. The administrative management of the government needs overhauling. The executive structure of the government is sadly out of date .... If we have faith in our republican form of government ... we must devote ourselves energetically and courageously to the task of making that government efficient.

Through the ages, public management has tended to follow the prevailing paradigm of private management. The 1930s were no exception. Roosevelt's committee—and the two Hoover commissions that followed—recommended a structure patterned largely after those of corporate America in the 1930s. In a sense, they brought to government the GM model of organization.

By the 1980s, even GM recognized that this model no longer worked. When it created Saturn, its first new division in 67 years, GM embraced a very different model. It picked its best and brightest and asked them to create a more entrepreneurial organization, with fewer layers, fewer rules, and employees empowered to do whatever was necessary to satisfy the customer. Faced with the very real threat of bankruptcy, major American corporations have revolutionized the way they do business.

Confronted with our twin budget and performance deficits—which so undermine public trust in government—President Clinton intends to do the same thing. He did not staff the Performance Review primarily with outside consultants or corporate experts, as past presidents have. Instead, he chose federal employees to take the lead. They consulted with experts from state government, local government, and the private sector. But as Vice President Gore said over and over at his meetings with federal employees: "The people who work closest to the problem know the most about how to solve the problem."

Nor did the effort stop with the men and women who staffed the Performance Review. President Clinton asked every cabinet member to create a Reinvention Team to redesign his or her department, and Reinvention Laboratories to begin experimenting immediately. Since April, people all across our government have been working full time to reinvent the federal bureaucracy.

The process is not easy, nor will it be quick. There are changes we can make immediately, but even if all of our recommendations are enacted, we will have only begun to reinvent the federal government. Our efforts are but a down payment—the first installment of a long-term investment in change. Every expert with whom we talked reminded us that change takes time. In a large corporation, transformation takes 6 to 8 years at best. In the federal government, which has more than 7 times as many employees as America's largest corporation, it will undoubtedly take longer to bring about the historic changes we propose.[12]

Along the way, we will make mistakes. Some reforms will succeed beyond our wildest dreams; others will not. As in any experimental process, we will need to monitor results and correct as we go. But we must not confuse mistakes with failure. As Tom Peters and Robert Waterman wrote in *In Search of Excellence,* any organization that is not making mistakes is not trying hard enough. Babe Ruth, the Sultan of Swat, struck out 1,330 times.

> I would invite those who are cynical about the possibility of this change to ask themselves this question: What would your reaction have been 10 years ago if someone had said that in the summer of 1993 American automobile companies would be making the highest quality, most competitively priced cars in the world?
>
> I know my reaction would have been, "No way. I am sorry, but I've bought too many clunkers. They can't do it. The momentum toward mediocrity is just too powerful."
>
> But that change has taken place. And if an industry as large and as stodgy as the automobile industry can undergo that kind of transformation, then the federal government can as well.
>
> **Vice President Al Gore**
> Town Hall Meeting,
> Department of Energy
> July 13, 1993

With this report, then, we begin a decade-long process of reinvention. We hope this process will involve not only the thousands of federal employees now at work on Reinvention Teams and in Reinvention Labs, but millions more who are not yet engaged. We hope it will transform the habits, culture, and performance of all federal organizations.

Some may say that the task is too large; that we should not attempt it because we are bound to make mistakes; that it cannot be done. But we have no choice. Our government is in trouble. It has lost its sense of mission; it has lost its ethic of public service; and, most importantly, it has lost the faith of the American people.

In times such as these, the most dangerous course is to do nothing. We must have the courage to risk change.

Chapter 1

CUTTING RED TAPE

About 10 years ago, two foresters returned from a hard day in the field to make plans for the coming week. Searching for a detail of agency policy, they found themselves overwhelmed by voluminous editions of policy manuals, reports, and binders filled with thousands of directives. One forester recalled the very first Forest Service manual—small enough to fit into every ranger's shirt pocket, yet containing everything foresters needed to know to do their jobs.

"Why is it that when we have a problem," the other forester asked, "the solution is always to add something—a report, a system, a policy—but never take something away?"

The first replied: "What if . . . we could just start over?" [1]

The federal government does at least one thing well: It generates red tape. But not one inch of that red tape appears by accident. In fact, the government creates it all with the best of intentions. It is time now to put aside our reverence for those good intentions and examine what they have created—a system that makes it hard for our civil servants to do what we pay them for, and frustrates taxpayers who rightfully expect their money's worth.

Because we don't want politicians' families, friends, and supporters placed in "no-show" jobs, we have more than 100,000 pages of personnel rules and regulations defining in exquisite detail how to hire, promote, or fire federal employees.[2] Because we don't want employees or private companies profiteering from federal contracts, we create procurement processes that require endless signatures and long months to buy almost anything. Because we don't want agencies using tax dollars for any unapproved purpose, we dictate precisely how much they can spend on everything from staff to telephones to travel.

And because we don't want state and local governments using federal funds for purposes that Congress did not intend, we write regulations telling them exactly how to run most programs that receive federal funds. We call for their partnership in dealing with our country's most urgent domestic problems, yet we do not treat them as equal partners.

Consider some examples from the daily lives of federal workers, people for whom red tape means being unable to do their jobs as well as they can—or as well as we deserve.

The district managers of Oregon's million-acre Ochoco National Forest have 53 separate budgets—one for fence maintenance, one for fence construction, one for brush burning—divided into 557 management codes and 1,769 accounting lines. To transfer money between accounts, they need approval from headquarters. They estimate the task of tracking spending in each account consumes at least 30 days of their time every year, days they could spend doing their real jobs.[3] It also sends a message: You are not trusted with even the simplest responsibilities.

Or consider the federal employees who repair cars and trucks at naval bases. Each time they need a spare part, they order it through a central purchasing office—a procedure that can keep vehicles in the shop for a month. This keeps one-tenth of the fleet out of commission, so the Navy buys 10 percent more vehicles than it needs.[4]

Or how about the new Energy Department petroleum engineer who requested a specific kind of calculator to do her job? Three months later, she received an adding machine. Six months after that, the procurement office got her a calculator—a tiny, hand-held model that could not perform the complex calculations her work required. Disgusted, she bought her own.[5]

Federal managers read the same books and attend the same conferences as private sector managers. They know what good management looks like. They just can't put it into practice—because they face constraints few managers in the private sector could imagine.

Hamstrung by rules and regulations, federal managers simply do not have the power to shape their organizations enjoyed

> *Never tell people how to do things. Tell them what you want to achieve, and they will surprise you with their ingenuity.*
>
> **General George S. Patton**
> 1944

by private sector managers. Their job is to make sure that every dollar is spent in the budget category and the year for which it was appropriated, that every promotion is consistent with central guidelines, and that every piece of equipment is bought through competitive bidding. In an age of personal computers, they are asked to write with quill pens.

This thicket of rules and regulations has layer upon layer of additional oversight. Each new procedure necessitates someone's approval. The result is fewer people doing real work, more people getting in their way. As management sage Peter Drucker once said, "So much of what we call management consists of making it difficult for people to work."[6]

As Robert Tobias, president of the National Treasury Employees Union, told participants at the Philadelphia Summit on Reinventing Government, "The regulations and statutes that bind federal employees from exercising discretion available in the private sector all come about as a response to the humiliations, mistakes, embarrassments of the past." Even though, as Tobias noted, "those problems are 15, 20, 30 years old," and "the regulations and the statutes don't change." The need to enforce the regulations and statutes, in turn, creates needless layers of bureaucracy.

The layers begin with "staff" agencies, such as the General Services Administration (GSA) and the Office of Personnel Management (OPM). These staff agencies were designed originally to provide specialized support for "line" agencies, such as the Interior and Commerce Departments, that do government's real work. But as rules and regulations began to proliferate, support turned into control. The Office of Management and Budget (OMB) which serves the President in the budget process, runs more than 50 compliance, clearance, and review processes. Some of this review is necessary to ensure budget control and consistency of agency actions—with each other and with the President's program—but much of it is overkill.

Line agencies then wrap themselves in even more red tape by creating their own budget offices, personnel offices, and procurement offices. Largely in response to appropriations committees, budget offices divide congressional budgets into increasingly tiny line items. A few years ago, for example, base managers in one branch of the military had 26 line items for housing repairs alone.[7] Personnel offices tell managers when they can and cannot promote, reward, or move employees. And procurement offices force managers to buy through a central monopoly, precluding agencies from getting what they need, when they need it.

What the staff agencies don't control, Congress does. Congressional appropriations often come with hundreds of strings attached. The Interior Department found that language in its 1992 House, Senate, and conference committee reports included some 2,150 directives, earmarks, instructions, and prohibitions.[8] As the federal budget tightens, lawmakers request increasingly specific report language to protect activities in their districts. Indeed, 1993 was a record year for such requests. In one appropriations bill alone, senators required the U.S. Customs Service to add new employees to its Honolulu office, prohibited closing any small or rural post office or U.S. Forest Service offices; and forbade the U.S. Mint and the Bureau of Engraving and Printing from even studying the idea of contracting out guard duties.

Even worse, Congress often gives a single agency multiple missions, some of which are contradictory. The Agency for International Development has more than 40 different objectives: Congress wants it to dispose of American farm surpluses, build democratic institutions, even strengthen the American land grant college system.[9] No wonder it has trouble accomplishing its real mission—promoting international development.

In Washington, we must work together to untangle the knots of red tape that prevent government from serving the American people well. We must give cabinet secretaries, program directors and line managers much greater authority to pursue their real purposes.

As Theodore Roosevelt said: "The best executive is the one who has the sense to pick good men [sic] to do what he wants

done, and self-restraint enough to keep from meddling with them while they do it."

Our path is clear: We must shift from systems that hold people accountable for process to systems that hold them accountable for results. We discuss accountability for results in chapter 3. In this chapter, we focus on six steps necessary to strip away the red tape that so engulfs our federal employees and frustrates the American people.

First, we will streamline the budget process, to remove the manifold restrictions that consume managers' time and literally force them to waste money.

Second, we will decentralize personnel policy, to give managers the tools they need to manage effectively—the authority to hire, promote, reward, and fire.

Third, we will streamline procurement, to reduce the enormous waste built into the process we use to buy $200 billion a year in goods and services.

Fourth, we will reorient the inspectors general, to shift their focus from punishing those who violate rules and regulations to helping agencies learn to perform better.

Fifth, we will eliminate thousands of other regulations that hamstring federal employees, to cut the final Lilliputian ropes on the federal giant.

Finally, we will deregulate state and local governments, to empower them to spend more time meeting customer needs—particularly with their 600 federal grant programs—and less time jumping through bureaucratic hoops.

As we pare down the systems of over-control and micromanagement in government, we must also pare down the structures that go with them: the oversized headquarters, multiple layers of supervisors and auditors, and offices specializing in the arcane rules of budgeting, personnel, procurement, and finance. We cannot entirely do without headquarters, supervisors, auditors, or specialists, but these structures have grown twice as large as they should be.

Counting all personnel, budget, procurement, accounting, auditing, and headquarters staff, plus supervisory personnel in field offices, there are roughly 700,000 federal employees whose job it is to manage, control, check up on or audit others.[10] *This is one third of all federal civilian employees.*

Not counting the suffocating impact these management control structures have on line managers and workers, they consume $35 billion a year in salary and benefits alone.[11] *If Congress enacts the management reforms outlined in this report,* we will dramatically cut the cost of these structures. We will reinvest some of the savings in the new management tools we need, including performance measurement, quality management, and training. Overall, these reforms will result in the net elimination of approximately 252,000 positions. (This will include the 100,000 position reduction the President has already set in motion.)

A reduction of 252,000 positions will reduce the civilian, non-postal work force by almost 12 percent—bringing it below two million for the first time since 1966.[12]

This reduction, targeted at the structures of control and micromanagement, is designed to improve working conditions for the average federal employee. We cannot empower employees to give us their best work unless we eliminate much of the red tape that now prevents it. We will do everything in the government's power to ease the transition for workers, whether they choose to stay with government, retire, or move to the private sector.

Our commitment is this: *If an employee whose job is eliminated cannot retire through our early retirement program, and does not elect to take a cash incentive to leave government service, we will help that employee find another job offer, either with government or in the private sector.*

Normal attrition will contribute to the reduction. In addition, we will introduce legislation to permit all agencies to offer cash payments to those who leave federal service voluntarily, whether by retirement or resignation. The Department of Defense (DOD) and intelligence community already have this "buy-out" authority; we will ask Congress to extend it to all agencies. We will also give agencies broad authority to offer early retirement and to expand their retraining, out-placement efforts, and other tools as necessary to accomplish the 12% reduction. Agencies will be able to use these tools as long as they meet their cost reduction targets.

These options will give federal managers the same tools commonly used to downsize private businesses. Even with these investments, the downsizing we propose will save the taxpayer billions over the next 5 years.

None of this will be easy. Downsizing never is. But the result will not only be a smaller workforce, it will also be a more empowered, more inspired, and more productive workforce.

As one federal employee told Vice President Gore at one of his many town meetings, "If you always do what you've always done, you'll always get what you always got." We can no longer afford to get what we've always got.

STEP 1: STREAMLINING THE BUDGET PROCESS

Most people can't get excited about the federal budget process, with its green-eyeshade analysts, complicated procedures, byzantine language, and reams of minutiae. Beyond such elements, however, lies a basic, unalterable reality. For organizations of all kinds, nothing is more important than the process of resource allocation: how much money they have, what strings are attached to it, and what hurdles are placed before managers who must spend it.

In government, budgeting is never easy. After all, the budget is the most political of documents. If, as the political scientist Harold D. Lasswell once said, politics is "who gets what, when, how," the budget answers that question.[13] By crafting a budget, public officials decide who pays what taxes and who receives what benefits. The public's largesse to children, the elderly, the poor, the middle class, and others is shaped by the budgets that support cities, states, and the federal government.

But if budgeting is inherently messy, such messiness is costly. Optimally, the budget would be more than the product of struggles among competing interests. It also would reflect the thoughtful planning of our public leaders. No one can improve quality and cut costs without planning to do so.

Unfortunately, the most deliberate planning is often subordinated to politics, and is perhaps the last thing we do in constructing a budget. Consider our process. Early in the year, each agency estimates what it will need to run its programs in the fiscal year that begins *almost 2 years later*. This is like asking someone to figure out not only what they will be doing, but *how much it will cost 3 years later*—since that's when the money will be spent. Bureau and program managers typically examine the previous year's activity data and project the figures 3 years out, with no word from top political leaders on their priorities, or even on the total amount that they want to spend. In other words, planning budgets is like playing "pin the tail on the donkey." Blindfolded managers are asked to hit an unknown target.

OMB, acting for the President, then crafts a proposed budget through back-and-forth negotiations with departments and agencies, still a year before the fiscal year it will govern. Decisions are struck on dollars Congress may never appropriate—dollars that, to agencies, mean people, equipment, and everything else they need for their jobs. OMB's examiners may question agency staff as they develop option papers, OMB's director considers the option during his Director's Review meetings, OMB "passes back" recommended funding levels for the agencies, and final figures are worked out during a final appeals process.

Early the next year, the President presents a budget proposal to Congress for the fiscal year beginning the following October 1. Lawmakers, the media, and interest groups pore over the document, searching for winners and losers, new spending proposals, and changes in tax laws. In the ensuing months, Congress puts its own stamp on the plan. Although House and Senate budget committees guide Congress' action, every committee plays a role.

Authorizing committees debate the merits of existing programs and the President's proposals for changes within their subject areas. While they decide which programs should continue and recommend funding levels, separate appropriations committees draft the 13 annual spending bills that actually comprise the budget.

Congressional debates over a budget resolution, authorization bills, and appropriations drag on, often into the fall. Frequently the President and Congress don't finish by October 1, so Congress passes one or more "continuing resolutions" to keep the money flowing, often at the previous year's level. Until the end, agency officials troop back and forth to OMB and to the Hill to make their case. States and localities, interest groups and advocates seek time to argue their cause. Budget staffs work non-stop, preparing estimates and projections on how this or that change will affect revenues or spending. All this work is focused on making a budget—not planning or delivering programs.

Ironies riddle the process.

• Uncertainty reigns: Although they begin calculating their budget 2 years ahead, agency officials do not always know by October 1 how much they will have to spend and frequently don't even receive their money until well into the fiscal year.

• OMB is especially prone to question unspent funds—and reduce the ensuing year's budget by that amount. Agency officials inflate their estimates, driving budget numbers higher and higher. One bureau budget director claims that many regularly ask for 90 percent more than they eventually receive.

• Despite months of debate, Congress compresses its actual decision-making on the budget into such a short time frame that many of the public's highest priorities—what to do about drug addiction, for example, or how to prepare workers for jobs in the 21st century—are discussed only briefly, if at all.

• The process is devoid of the most useful information. We do not know what last year's money, or that of the year before, actually accomplished. Agency officials devise their funding requests based on what they got before, not whether it produced results.

In sum, the budget process is characterized by fictional requests and promises, an obsession with inputs rather than outcomes, and a shortage of debate about critical national needs. We must start to plan strategically—linking our spending with priorities and performance. First, we must create a rational budgeting system.

Action: *The President should begin the budget process with an executive budget*

> *There are two ways to reduce expenditures. There is the intelligent way...going through each department and questioning each program. Then there is the stupid way: announcing how much you will cut and getting each department to cut that amount. I favor the stupid way.*
>
> **Michel Belanger**
> Chairman, Quebec National Bank
> May 7, 1992

resolution, setting broad policy priorities and allocating funds by function for each agency.[14]

Federal managers should focus primarily on the content of the budget, not on the process. A new executive budget resolution will help them do that. The President should issue a directive in early 1994 to mandate the use of such a resolution in developing his fiscal year 1996 budget. It will turn the executive budget process upside down.

To develop the resolution, officials from the White House policy councils will meet with OMB and agency officials. In those sessions, the administration's policy leadership will make decisions on overall spending and revenue levels, deficit reduction targets, and funding allocations for major inter-agency policy initiatives. The product of these meetings—a resolution completed by August—will provide agencies with funding ceilings and allocations for major policy missions. Then, bureaus will generate their own budget estimates, now knowing their agency's priorities and fiscal limits.

Our own Environmental Protection Agency (EPA) tried a similar approach in the 1970s as part of a zero-based budgeting trial run. Although zero-based budgeting fell short, participants said, two important advantages emerged: a new responsiveness to internal customer needs and a commitment to final decisions. When participants voted to cut research and development funds because they felt researchers ignored program needs, researchers began asking program managers what kind of research would support their efforts. EPA also found that, after its leaders had agonized over funding, they remained committed to common decisions.

Critics may view the executive budget resolution process as a top-down tool that will stifle creative, bottom-up suggestions for funding options. We think otherwise. The resolution will render top officials responsible for budget totals and policy decisions, but will encourage lower-level ingenuity to devise funding options within those guidelines. By adopting this plan, we will help discourage non-productive micro-management by senior department and agency officials.

Action: *Institute biennial budgets and appropriations.*[15]

We should not have to enact a budget every year. Twenty states adopt budgets for 2 years. (They retain the power to make small adjustments in off years if revenues or expenditures deviate widely from forecasts). As a result, their governors and legislatures have much more time to evaluate programs and develop longer-term plans.

Annual budgets consume an enormous amount of management time—time not spent serving customers. With biennial budgets, rather than losing months to a frantic "last-year's budget-plus-X-percent" exercise, we might spend more time examining which programs actually work.

The idea of biennial budgeting has been around for some time. Congressman Leon Panetta, now OMB director, introduced the first biennial budgeting bill in 1977, and dozens have been offered since. Although none have passed, the government has some experience with budget plans that cover 2 years or more. In 1987, the President and Congress drafted a budget plan for fiscal years 1988 and 1989 that set spending levels for major categories, enabling Congress to enact all 13 appropriations bills on time for the first time since 1977.

In addition, Congress directed the Defense Department to submit a biennial budget for fiscal 1988 and 1989 to give Congress more time for broad policy oversight. At the time, Congress asserted that a biennial budget would "substantially improve DOD management and congressional oversight," and that a two-year DOD budget was an important step toward across-the-board biennial budgeting. Administrations have continued to submit biennial budgets for DOD.

The 1990 Budget Enforcement Act and the 1993 Omnibus Budget Reconciliation Act set 5-year spending limits for discretionary spending and pay-as-you-go requirements for mandatory programs. With these multi-year caps in place, neither the President nor Congress has to decide the total level of discretionary spending each year. These caps provide even more reason for biennial budgets and appropriations. In Congress, 7 out of 10 members favor a biennial process with a 2-year budget resolution and multi-year authorizations. The time is ripe.

We recommend that Congress establish biennial budget resolutions and appropriations and multi-year authorizations. The first biennium should begin October 1, 1996, to cover fiscal years 1997 and 1998. After that, bienniums would begin October 1 of each even-numbered year. Such timing would allow President Clinton to develop the first comprehensive biennial federal budget, built on the new executive budget resolution. In off years, the President would submit only amendments for exceptional areas of concern, emergencies, or other unforeseen circumstances.

Biennial budgeting will not make our budget decisions easier, for they are shaped by competing interests and priorities. But it will eliminate an enormous amount of busy work that keeps us from evaluating programs and meeting customer needs.

Action: *OMB, departments, and agencies will minimize budget restrictions such as apportionments and allotments.*[16]

Congress typically divides its appropriations into more than 1,000 accounts. Committee reports specify thousands of other restrictions on using money. OMB apportions each account by quarter or year, and sometimes divides it into sub-accounts by line-item or object class—all to control over-spending. Departmental budget offices further divide the money into allotments.

Thus, many managers find their money fenced into hundreds of separate accounts. In some agencies, they can move funds among accounts. In others, Congress or the agency limits the transfer of funds, trapping the money. When that happens, managers must spend money where they have it, not where they need it. On one military base, for example, managers had no line item to purchase snowplow equipment, but they did have a maintenance account. When the snowplow broke down they leased one, using the maintenance account. Unfortunately, the 1-year lease cost $100,000—the same as the full purchase price.

Such stories are a dime a dozen within the federal bureaucracy. (They may be the only government cost that is coming down.) Good managers struggle to make things work, but, trapped by absurd constraints, they are driven to waste billions of dollars every year.

Stories about the legendary end-of-the-year spending rush also abound. Managers who don't exhaust each line item at year's end usually are told to return the excess. Typically, they get less the next time around. The result: the well-known spending frenzy. The National Performance Review received more examples of this source of waste—in letters, in calls, and at town meetings—than any other.

Most managers know how to save 5 or 10 percent of what they spend. But knowing they will get less money next year, they have little reason to save. Instead, smart managers spend every penny of every line item. Edwin G. Fleming, chief of the Resources Management Division of the Internal Revenue Service's Cleveland District, put it well in a letter to the Treasury Department's Reinvention Team:

Every manager has saved money, only to have his allocation reduced in the subsequent year. This usually happens only once, then the manager becomes a spender rather than a planner. Managing becomes watching after little pots of money that can't be put where it makes business sense because of reprogramming restrictions. So managers, who are monitors of these little pots of money, are rewarded for the ability to maneuver, however limitedly, through the baroque and bizarre world of federal finance and procurement.

Solutions to these problems exist. They have been tested in local governments, in state governments, even in the federal government. Essentially, they involve budget systems with fewer line items, more authority for managers to move money among line items, and freedom for agencies to keep some or all of what they save—thus minimizing the incentive for year-end spending sprees.

Typically, federal organizations experimenting with such budgets have found that they can achieve better productivity, sometimes with less money.

During an experiment at Oregon's Ochoco National Forest in the 1980s, when dozens of accounts were reduced to six, productivity jumped 25 percent the first year and 35 percent more the second. A 1991 Forest Service study indicated that the experiment had succeeded in bringing gains in efficiency, productivity, and morale, but had failed to provide the Forest Service region with a mechanism for complying with congressional intent. After 3 years of negotiations, Washington and Region 6, where the Ochoco Forest is located, couldn't agree. The region wanted to retain the initial emphasis on performance goals and targets so forest managers could shift money from one account to another if they met performance goals and targets. Washington argued that Congress would not regard such targets as a serious measure of congressional intent. The experiment ended in March 1993.[17]

When the Defense Department allowed several military bases to experiment with what was called the Unified Budget Test, base commanders estimated that they could accomplish their missions with up to 10 percent less money. If this experience could be applied to the entire government, it could mean huge savings.

Beginning with their fiscal year 1995 submissions to OMB, departments and agencies will begin consolidating accounts to minimize restrictions and manage more effectively. They will radically cut the number of allotments used to subdivide accounts. In addition, they will consider using the Defense Department's Unified Budget plan, which permits shifts in funds between allotments and cost categories to help accomplish missions.

OMB will simplify the apportionment process, which hamstrings agencies by dividing their funding into amounts that are available, bit by bit, according to specified time periods, activities, or projects. Agencies often don't get their funding on time and, after they do, must fill out reams of paperwork to show that they adhered to apportionment guidelines. OMB will also expedite the "reprogramming" process, by which agencies can move funds within congressionally appropriated accounts. Currently, OMB and congressional subcommittees approve all such reprogrammings. OMB should automatically approve reprogramming unless it objects within a set period, such as five days.

Action: *OMB and agencies will stop using full-time equivalent ceilings, managing and budgeting instead with ceilings on operating costs to control spending.*[18]

In another effort to control spending, both the executive and legislative branches often limit the number of each agency's employees by using full-time equivalent (FTE) limits. When agencies prepare their budget estimates, they must state how many FTEs they need in addition to how many dollars. Then, each department or agency divides that number into a ceiling for each bureau, division, branch, or other unit. Congress occasionally complicates the situation by legislating FTE floors.

Federal managers often cite FTE controls as the single most oppressive restriction on their ability to manage. Under the existing system, FTE controls are the only way to make good on the President's commitment to reduce the federal bureaucracy by 100,000 positions through attrition. But as we redesign the government for greater accountability, we need to use budgets, rather than FTE controls, to drive our downsizing.

FTE ceilings are usually imposed independently of—and often conflict with—budget allocations. They are frequently arbitrary, rarely account for changing circumstances, and are normally imposed as across-the-board percentage cuts in FTEs for all of an agency's units— regardless of changing circumstances. Organizations that face new regulations or a greater workload don't get new FTE ceilings. Consequently, they must contract out work that could be done better and cheaper in-house. One manager at Vice President Gore's town meeting at the State Department in May 1993 offered an example: his FTE limit had forced him to contract out for a junior programmer for the Foreign Service Institute. As it turned out, the programmer's hourly rate equaled the Institute Director's, so the move cost money instead of saving it.

The President should direct OMB and agency heads to stop setting FTE ceilings in fiscal year 1995.

For this transition, the agencies' accounting systems will have to separate true operating costs from program and other costs. Some agencies already have such systems in place; others must develop financial management systems to allow them to calculate these costs. We address this issue in a separate recommendation in chapter 3.

This recommendation fully supports the President's commitment to maintain a reduced federal workforce. Instead of controlling the size of the federal workforce by employment ceilings—which cause inefficiencies and distortions in managers' personnel and resource allocation decisions—this new system will control the federal workforce by dollars available in operating funds.

Action: *Minimize congressional restrictions such as line items and earmarks and eliminate FTE floors.*[19]

Congress should also minimize the restrictions and earmarks that it imposes on agencies. With virtually all federal spending under scrutiny for future cuts, Congress is increasingly applying earmarks to ensure that funding flows to favored programs and hometown projects.

Imagine the surprise of Interior Secretary Bruce Babbitt, who a few months after taking office discovered that he was under orders from Congress to maintain 23 positions in the Wilkes-Barre, Pennsylvania, field office of his department's anthracite reclamation program. Or that his department was required to spend $100,000 to train beagles in Hawaii to sniff out brown tree snakes. Edward Derwinski, former secretary of Veteran Affairs, was once summoned before the Texas congressional delegation to explain his plan to eliminate 38 jobs in that state.[20]

While understandable in some cases, congressional earmarks hamper agencies that seek to manage programs efficiently. Agencies should work with appropriations subcommittees on this problem.

Action: *Allow agencies to roll over 50 percent of what they do not spend on internal operations during a fiscal year.*[21]

As part of its 13 fiscal year 1995 appropriations bills, Congress should permanently allow agencies to roll over 50 percent of unobligated year-end balances in all appropriations for operations. It should allow agencies to use up to 2 percent of rolled-over funds to finance bonuses for employees involved. This approach, which the Defense Department and Forest Service have used successfully, would reward employees for finding more productive ways to work. Moreover, it would create incentives to save the taxpayers' money.

Shared savings incentives work. In 1989, the General Accounting Office (GAO) discovered that the Veterans Administration had not recovered $223 million in health payments from third parties, such as insurers. Congress then changed the rules, allowing the VA to hire more staff to keep up with the paperwork and also to keep a portion of recovered third-party payments for administrative costs. VA recoveries soared from $24 million to $530 million.[22]

If incentives to save are to be real, Congress and OMB will have to refrain from automatically cutting agencies' budgets by the amount they have saved when their next budget is prepared. Policy decisions to cut spending are one thing; automatic cuts to take back savings are quite another. They simply confirm managers' fears that they will be penalized for saving money. Agencies' chief financial officers should intervene in the budget process to ensure that this does not happen.

STEP 2: DECENTRALIZING PERSONNEL POLICY

Our federal personnel system has been evolving for more than 100 years—ever since the 1881 assassination of President James A. Garfield by a disappointed job seeker. And during that time, according to a 1988 Office of Personnel Management publication:

...anecdotal mistakes prompted additional rules. When the rules led to

new inequities, even more rules were added. Over time...a maze of regulations and requirements was created, hamstringing managers...often impeding federal managers and employees from achieving their missions and from giving the public a high quality of service.

Year after year, layer after layer, the rules have piled up. The U.S. Merit Systems

Catch-22

Our federal personnel system ought to place a value on experience. That's not always the case. Consider the story of Rosalie Tapia. Ten years ago, fresh from high school, she joined the Army and was assigned to Germany as a clerk. She served out her enlistment with an excellent record, landed a job in Germany as a civilian secretary for the Army, and worked her way up to assistant to the division chief. When the Cold War ended, Tapia wanted to return to the U.S. and transfer to a government job here.

Unfortunately, one of the dictates contained in the government's 100,000 pages of personnel rules says that an employee hired as a civil servant overseas is not considered a government employee once on home soil. Any smart employer would prefer to hire an experienced worker with an excellent service record over an unknown. But our government's policy doesn't make it easy. Ironically, Tapia landed a job with a government contractor, making more money— and probably costing taxpayers more—than a job in the bureaucracy would have paid.

Protection Board reports there are now 850 pages of federal personnel law—augmented by 1,300 pages of OPM regulations on how to implement those laws and another 10,000 pages of guidelines from the Federal Personnel Manual.

On one topic alone—how to complete a standard form for a notice of a personnel action—the Federal Personnel Manual contains 900 pages of instructions. The full stack of personnel laws, regulations, directives, case law and departmental guidance that the Agriculture Department uses—shown in the photo at right—weighs 1,088 pounds.

Thousands of pages of personnel rules prompt thousands of pages of personnel forms. In 1991, for example, the Navy's Human Resources Office processed enough forms to create a "monument" 3,100 feet tall—six times the height of the Washington Monument.

Costs to the taxpayer for this personnel quagmire are enormous. In total, 54,000 people work in federal personnel positions.[23] We spend billions of dollars for these staff to classify each employee within a highly complex system of some 459 job series, 15 grades and 10 steps within each grade.

Does this elaborate system work? No. After surveying managers, supervisors

and personnel officers in a number of federal agencies, the U.S. Merit Systems Protection Board recently concluded that federal personnel rules are too complex, too prescriptive, and often counterproductive.

Talk to a federal manager for 10 minutes: You likely will hear at least one personnel horror story. The system is so complex and rule-bound that most managers cannot even advise an applicant how to get a federal job. "Even when the public sector finds outstanding candidates," In 1989, Paul Volcker's National Commission on the Public Service explained, "the complexity of the hiring process often drives all but the most dedicated away." Managers who find it nearly impossible to hire the people they need sometimes flaunt the system by hiring people as consultants at higher rates than those same people would earn as federal employees. The average manager needs a year to fire an incompetent employee, even with solid proof. During layoffs, employees slated to be laid off can "bump" employees with less seniority, regardless of their abilities or performance—putting people in jobs they don't understand and never wanted.

Vice President Gore heard many stories of dissatisfaction as he listened to federal workers at meetings in their agencies. A supervisor at the Centers for Disease Control complained that it can take six to eight months and as many as 15 revisions to a job description in order to get approval for a position he needs to fill. A secretary from the Justice Department told the Vice President she was discouraged and overworked in an office where some secretaries were slacking off—with no system in place to reward the hard workers and take action against the slackers.

A worker from the Agency for International Development expressed her frustration at being so narrowly "slotted" in a particular GS series that she wasn't allowed to apply for a job in a slightly different GS series —even though she was qualified for the job. An Air Force lieutenant colonel told the vice president that her secretary was abandoning government for the private sector because she was blocked from any

more promotions in her current job series. The loss would be enormous, the colonel told Gore, because her secretary was her "right-hand person". One of the Labor Department's regional directors for unemployment insurance complained that even though he is charged with running a multimillion-dollar-a-year program, he isn't allowed to hire a $45,000-a-year program specialist without getting approval from Washington.

To create an effective federal government, we must reform virtually the entire personnel system: recruitment, hiring, classification, promotion, pay, and reward systems. We must make it easier for federal managers to hire the workers they need, to reward those who do good work, and to fire those who do not. As the National Academy of Public Administration concluded in 1993, "It is not a question of whether the federal government should change how it manages its human resources. It must change."

Action: *OPM will deregulate personnel policy by phasing out the 10,000-page Federal Personnel Manual and all agency implementing directives.*[24]

We must enable all managers to pursue their missions, freed from the cumbersome red tape of current personnel rules. The President should issue a directive phasing out the Federal Personnel Manual and all agency implementing directives. The directive should require that most personnel management authority be delegated to agencies' line managers at the lowest level practical in each agency. It should direct OPM to work with agencies to determine which FPM chapters, provisions, or supplements are essential, which are useful, and which are unnecessary. OPM will then replace the FPM and agency directives with manuals tailored to user needs, automated personnel processes, and electronic decision support systems.

Once some of the paperwork burden is eased, our next priority must be to give agency managers more control over who comes to work for them. To accomplish this, we propose to radically decentralize the government's hiring process.

Action: *Give all departments and agencies authority to conduct their own recruiting and examining for all positions, and abolish all central registers and standard application forms.*[25]

We will ask Congress to pass legislation decentralizing authority over recruitment, hiring, and promotion. Under the present system, OPM controls the examination system for external candidates and recruits and screens candidates for positions that are common to all agencies, with agencies then hiring from among candidates presented by OPM. Under the new system, OPM could offer to screen candidates for agencies, but agencies need not accept OPM's offer.

Under this decentralized system, agencies will also be allowed to make their own decisions about when to hire candidates directly—without examinations or rankings —under guidelines to be drafted by OPM. Agencies able to do so should also be permitted to conduct their own background investigations of potential candidates.

We will make sure the system is fair and easy for job applicants to use, however, by making information about federal job openings available in one place. In place of a central register, OPM will create a government-wide, employment information system that allows the public to go to one place for information about all job opportunities in the federal government.

Next, we must change the classification system, introduced in 1949 to create fairness across agencies but now widely regarded as time-consuming, expensive, cumbersome, and intensely frustrating—for both workers and managers.

After an exhaustive 1991 study of the system, the National Academy of Public Administration recommended a complete overhaul of the system. Classification standards, NAPA argued, are "too complex, inflexible, out-of-date, and inaccurate,"

> *First, we must cut the waste and make government operations more responsive to the American people. It is time to shift from top-down bureaucracy to entrepreneurial government that generates change from the bottom up. We must reward the people and ideas that work and get rid of those that don't.*
>
> **President Bill Clinton**
> February 17, 1993

creating "rigid job hierarchies that cannot change with organizational structure." They drive some of the best employees out of their fields of expertise and into management positions, for higher pay. And managers seeking to create new positions often fight the system for months to get them classified and filled.[26]

There is strong evidence that agencies given authority to do these things themselves can do better. Using demonstration authority under the 1978 Civil Service Reform Act, several agencies have experimented with simpler systems. In one experiment, at the Naval Weapons Center in China Lake, California, and the Naval Oceans Systems Center, in San Diego, the system was simplified to a few career paths and only four-to-six broad pay bands within each path. Known as the "China Lake Experiment," it solved many of the problems faced by the two naval facilities. It:

• classified all jobs in just five career paths—professional, technical, specialist, administrative and clerical;

• folded all GS (General Schedule) grades into four, five, or six pay bands within each career path;

• allowed managers to pay market salaries to recruit people, to increase the pay of

Recognizing the importance of attracting and retaining highly qualified professionals in government service, one of the demoralizing and frustrating aspects is the fact that we are retained to do a job but not allowed the flexibility to carry it out, assume the responsiblity, and reap the rewards or be accountable for out actions.

Edith Houston
Town Hall Meeting,
U.S. Agency for International Development
May 26, 1993

outstanding employees without having to reclassify them, and to give performance-based bonuses and salary increases;

• automatically moved employees with repeated marginal performance evaluations down to the next pay band; and

• limited bumping to one career path, and based it primarily on performance ratings, not seniority.

Another demonstration at McClellan Air Force Base, in Sacramento, California, involved "gainsharing"—allowing employees to pocket some of the savings they achieved through cooperative labor-management efforts to cut costs. It generated $5 million in productivity savings in four years and saw improved employee performance; fewer grievances; less sick leave and absenteeism; and improved labor-management relations.

A third demonstration at more than 200 Agriculture Department sites tested a streamlined, agency-based recruiting and hiring system that replaced OPM's register process. Under OPM's system, candidates are arrayed and scored based on OPM's written tests or other examinations. In USDA's demonstration, however, the agency grouped candidates by its own criteria, such as education, experience or ability, then picked from those candidates. A candidate might qualify for a job, for example, with a 2.7 college grade point average. Agencies could create their own recruitment incentives, do their own hiring, and extend the probationary period for some new hires. Managers were far more satisfied with this system than the existing one.

Action: *Dramatically simplify the current classification system, to give agencies greater flexibility in how they classify and pay their employees.*[27]

We will urge Congress to remove all the 1940s-era grade-level descriptions from the law and adopt an approach that is more modern. In addition, Congress should allow agencies to move from the General Schedule system to a broad-band system. OPM should develop such standard banding patterns, and agencies should be free to adopt one without seeking OPM's approval.

When agency proposals do not fit under a standard pattern, OPM should approve them as five-year demonstration projects that would be converted to permanent "alternative systems" if successful. OPM should establish criteria for broad-banding demonstration projects, and agencies' projects meeting those criteria should receive automatic approval.

These changes would give agencies greater flexibility to hire, retain, and promote the best people they find. They would help agencies flatten their hierarchies and promote high achievers without having to make them supervisors. They would eliminate much valuable time now lost to battles between managers seeking to promote or reward employees and personnel specialists administering a classification system with rigid limits. Finally, they would remove OPM from its role as "classification police."

To accompany agencies' new flexibility on classification and pay, they must also be given authority to set standards for their own workers and to reward those who do well.

Action: *Agencies should be allowed to design their own performance management and reward systems, with the objective of improving the performance of individuals and organizations.* [28]

The current government performance appraisal process is frequently criticized as a meaningless exercise in which most federal employees are given above-average ratings. We believe that agencies will be able to develop performance appraisals that are more meaningful to their employees. If they succeed, these new approaches will send a message that job performance is directly linked to workers' chances for promotion and higher pay.

Current systems to assess on-the-job performance were designed to serve multiple purposes: to enhance performance, to authorize higher pay for high performers, to retain high performers, and to promote staff development. Not surprisingly, they serve none of these purposes well.

Performance management programs should have a single goal: to improve the performance of individuals and organizations. Agencies should be allowed to develop programs that meet their needs and reflect their cultures, including incentive programs, gainsharing programs, and awards that link pay and performance. If agencies—in cooperation with employees—design their own systems, managers and employees alike should feel more ownership of them.

Finally, if performance measures are to be taken seriously, managers must have authority to fire workers who do not measure up. It is possible to fire a poor worker in the federal government, but it takes far too long. We believe this undermines good management and diminishes workers' incentives to improve.

> *There has to be a clear shared sense of mission. There have to be clearly understood goals. There have to be common values according to which decisions are made. There has to be trust placed in the employees who actually do the work, so that they will feel free to make decisions.*
>
> *They cannot be treated like automatons or children bound up in straightjackets and rules and regulations and told to do the same thing over and over and over again.*
>
> **Vice President Al Gore**
> August 4, 1993

Action: *Reduce by half the time required to terminate federal managers and employees for cause and improve the system for dealing with poor performers.* [29]

Agencies will reduce the time for terminating employees for cause by half. For example, agencies could halve the length of time during which managers and employees with unsatisfactory performance ratings are allowed to demonstrate improved performance.

To support this effort, we will ask OPM to draft and Congress to pass legislation to change the required time for notice of termination from 30 to 15 days. This legislation should also require the waiting period for a within-grade increase to be extended by the amount of time an employee's performance does not meet expectations. In other words, only the time that an employee is doing satisfactory work should be credited toward the required waiting period for a pay raise.

STEP 3: STREAMLINING PROCUREMENT

Every year, Washington spends about $200 billion buying goods and services. That's $800 per American. With a price tag like that, taxpayers have a right to expect prudent spending.

The federal government employs 142,000 workers dedicated to procurement.[30] The Federal Acquisition Regulation (FAR) controlling procurement runs 1,600 pages, with 2,900 more pages of agency-specific supplements.

These numbers document what most federal workers and many taxpayers already know: Our system relies on rigid rules and procedures, extensive paperwork, detailed design specifications, and multiple inspections and audits. It is an extraordinary example of bureaucratic red tape.

Like the budget and personnel systems, the procurement system was designed with the best of intentions. To prevent profiteering and fraud, it includes rigid safeguards. To take advantage of bulk purchasing, it is highly centralized. But the government wrote its procurement rules when retailing was highly stratified, with many markups by intermediaries. Today the game has changed considerably. Retail giants like Wal-Mart, Office Depot and Price Club are vertically integrated, eliminating the markups of intermediaries. Federal managers can buy 90 percent of what they need over the phone, from mail-order discounters. Bulk purchasing still has its advantages, but it is not always necessary to get the best price.

Our overly centralized purchasing system takes decisions away from managers who know what they need, and allows strangers—often thousands of miles away—to make purchasing decisions. The frequent result: Procurement officers, who make their own decisions about what to buy and how soon to buy it, purchase low-quality items that arrive too late.

This "secondhand" approach to purchasing creates another problem. When line managers' needs and experiences are not understood by the procurement officer, the government is unable to make decisions that reward good vendors and punish bad ones. As a result, vendors often "game" contracts—exploiting loopholes to require expensive changes. For example, in a major government contract for a computerized data network a few years ago, a vendor used slight underestimates of system demand in the contract specifications as an excuse to charge exorbitant prices for system upgrades. In the private sector, a manager could have used the incentive of future contracts to prevent such gaming; in the government, there is no such leverage.

The symptoms of what's wrong are apparent, too, from stories about small purchases.

One story that Vice President Gore has repeated in Washington over the past six months concerns steam traps. Steam traps remove condensation from steam lines in heating systems. Each costs about $100. But when one breaks, it leaks as much as $50 of steam a week. Obviously, a leaking steam trap should be replaced quickly.

When plumbers at the Sacramento Army Depot found leaking traps, however, their manager followed standard operating procedure. He called the procurement office, where an officer, who knew nothing about steam traps, followed common practice. He waited for enough orders to buy in bulk, saving the government about $10 per trap. There was no rule requiring him to wait— just a powerful tradition. So the Sacramento Depot didn't get new steam traps for a year. In the meantime, each of their leaking traps spewed $2,500 of steam. To save $10, the central procurement system wasted $2,500.

As the Vice President visited government agencies, he heard many more stories of wasteful spending—most of them

"Ash receivers, tobacco (desk type)..."

Our federal procurement system leaves little to chance.

When the General Services Administration wanted to buy ashtrays, it has some very specific ideas how those ashtrays—better known to GSA as "ash receivers, tobacco (desk type)," should be constructed.

In March 1993, the GSA outlined, in nine full pages of specifications and drawings, the precise dimensions, color, polish and markings required for simple glass ashtrays that would pass U.S. government standards.

A Type I, glass, square, $4^1/_2$ inch (114.3 mm) ash receiver must include several features: "A minimum of four cigarette rests, spaced equidistant around the periphery and aimed at the center of the receiver, molded into the top. The cigarette rests shall be sloped toward the center of the ash receiver. The rests shall be parallel to the outside top edge of the receiver or in each corner, at the manufacturer's option. All surfaces shall be smooth."

Government ashtrays must be sturdy too. To guard against the purchase of defective ash receivers, the GSA required that all ashtrays be tested. "The test shall be made by placing the specimen on its base upon a solid support (a 1 3/4 inch, 44.5mm maple plank), placing a steel center punch (point ground to a 60-degree included angle) in contact with the center of the inside surface of the bottom and striking with a hammer in successive blows of increasing severity until breakage occurs."

Then, according to paragraph 4.5.2., "The specimen should break into a small number of irregular shaped pieces not greater in number than 35, and it must not dice." What does "dice" mean? The paragraph goes on to explain: "Any piece 1/4 inch (6.4 mm) or more on any three of its adjacent edges (excluding the thickness dimension) shall be included in the number counted. Smaller fragments shall not be counted."

Regulation AA-A-710E, (superseding Regulation AA-A-710D).

---

produced by the very rules we have designed to prevent it. Take the case of government travel.

Because GSA selects a "contract airline" for each route, federal employees have few choices. If Northwest has the Washington-Tampa route, for instance, federal employees get routed through Detroit. If Northwest has the Boston-Washington route, employees have to use Northwest—even if USAir has more frequent flights at more convenient times. Workers told the Vice President of being routed through thousands of miles out of their way even if it cost them a day's worth of time—and a day's worth of taxpayers' money. Others told of being unable to take advantage of cheap "special fares" because they were not "government fares." And one worker showed the National Performance Review a memo from the Resolution Trust Corporation explaining that RTC workers would not be reimbursed for any travel expenses unless they signed their travel vouchers in blue ink!

Beyond travel, at every federal agency the Vice President visited, employees told stories about not getting supplies and equipment they needed, getting them late, or watching the government spend too much for them. At the Department of Health and Human Services, a worker told the Vice President that no matter how much his office needed a FAX machine—and how much time the machine would save workers—the purchase wouldn't be possible "without the signature of everyone in this room." An engineer from the National Institutes of Health added that in his agency, it takes more than a year to buy a computer, not a mainframe, but a personal computer! At the Transportation Department, a hearing-impaired employee told the Vice President of watching with dismay as her agency spent $600 to buy her a Telephone Device for the Deaf (TDD), when she knew she could buy one off the shelf for $300.

Anecdotes like these were documented in January 1993, when the Office of Federal Procurement Policy and the U.S. Merit Systems Protection Board collaborated on a survey of the procurement system's customers: federal managers. More than 1,000 responded. Their message: The system is not achieving what its customers want. It ignores its customers' needs, pays higher prices than necessary, is filled with peripheral objectives, and assumes that line managers cannot be trusted.

A study by the Center for Strategic and International Studies added several other conclusions. The procurement system adds costs without adding value; it impedes government's access to state-of-the-art commercial technology; and its complexity forces businesses to alter standard procedures and raise prices when dealing with the government.[31]

There is little disagreement that federal procurement must be reconfigured. We must radically decentralize authority to line managers, letting them buy much of what they need. We must radically simplify procurement regulations and processes. We must empower the system's customers by ending most government service monopolies, including those of the General Services Administration. As we detailed in

Chapter 1, we must make the system competitive by allowing managers to use any procurement office that meets their needs.

As we take these actions, we must embrace these fundamental principles: integrity, accountability, professionalism, openness, competition—and value.

Action: *Simplify the procurement process by rewriting federal regulations—shifting from rigid rules to guiding principles.[32]*

The Federal Acquisition Regulation (FAR), the government's principal set of procurement regulations, contains too many rules. Rules are changed too often and are so process-oriented that they minimize discretion and stifle innovation, according to a Merit Systems Protection Board survey.[33] As one frustrated manager noted, the FAR does not even clearly state the main goal of procurement policy: "Is it to avoid waste, fraud, and abuse? Is it to implement a social-economic agenda? Is it to procure the government's requirements at a fair and reasonable cost?"

This administration will rewrite the 1,600-page FAR, the 2,900 pages of agency supplements that accompany it, and Executive Order 12352, which governs federal procurement. The new regulations will:

• shift from rigid rules to guiding principles;

• promote decision making at the lowest possible level;

• end unnecessary regulatory requirements;

• foster competitiveness and commercial practices;

• shift to a new emphasis on choosing "best value" products;

- facilitate innovative contracting approaches;

- recommend acquisition methods that reflect information technology's short life cycle; and

- develop a more effective process to listen to its customers: line managers, government procurement officers, and vendors who do business with the government.

Action: *The GSA will significantly increase its delegated authority to federal agencies for the purchase of information technology, including hardware, software, and services.*[34]

In 1965, when "automated data processing" meant large, mainframe computers—often developed specifically for one customer—Congress passed the Brooks Act. It directed GSA to purchase, lease, and maintain such equipment for the entire federal government. The Act also gave GSA authority to delegate to agencies these same authorities. In 1986, Congress extended the requirement to software and support services.

Today, with most computer equipment commercially available in highly competitive markets, the advantages of centralized purchasing have faded and the disadvantages have grown. The federal government takes, on average, more than four years to buy major information technology systems; the private sector takes 13 months. Due to rapidly changing technology, the government often buys computers that are state-of-the-art when the purchase process begins and when prices are negotiated, but which are almost obsolete when computers are delivered. The phenomenon is what one observer calls "getting a 286 at a 486 price."

Currently, the GSA authorizes agencies to make individual purchases up to $2.5 million in equipment and services on their own. The GSA Administrator will raise authorization levels to $50 million, $20 million and $5 million. These levels will be calculated according to each agency's size, the size of its information technology budget, and its management record. In some cases, GSA may grant an agency greater or unlimited delegation.

GSA will also waive requirements that agencies justify their decisions to buy information technology items costing less than $500,000, if they are mass-produced and offered on the open market.

Action: *GSA will simplify the procurement process by allowing agencies to buy where they want and by testing a fully "electronic marketplace."*[35]

The government buys everything from forklifts and snowplows to flak jackets and test tubes through a system called the Multiple Award Schedule program, which includes more than one million separate items.

Under this program, GSA negotiates and awards contracts to multiple vendors of comparable products and services, at varying prices. GSA then creates a "supply schedule" for a particular good or service, identifying all vendors that have won contracts as well as the negotiated prices. Of GSA's 154 schedules, civilian agencies must must buy from 117. In ordering from schedules, agencies still must comply—in addition—with the Federal Acquisition Regulation, Federal Information Resources Management Regulation, and Federal Property Management Regulation.

In most cases, we should not limit managers to items on the supply schedules. If they can find the same or a comparable product for less, they should be free to buy it. Mandatory schedules should apply only when required by law, to ensure standardization, or when agencies voluntarily create team pools that buy in bulk for lower prices. In addition, GSA should revise regulations that currently limit agencies from buying more than $300,000 of information technology items on supply schedules, raise them to $500,000 and provide a higher limit for individual items costing more than $500,000.

To make supply schedules more user-friendly, GSA should conduct several pilot tests. One should test an "electronic marketplace," in which GSA would not negotiate prices. Instead, suppliers would list products and prices electronically, and agencies would electronically order the lowest-priced item that met their needs. Suppliers, at any time, would be able to add new products and change prices. Such a pilot would test whether visible price competition will cut prices and give line managers easier access to rapidly changing products.

Action: *Allow agencies to make purchases under $100,000 through simplified purchase procedures.*[36]

Under current law, agencies are allowed to make purchases of less than $25,000 on their own, using simple procurement procedures. These small purchases, on average, take less than a month to complete; purchases of more than $25,000 normally take more than three months. If Congress raised the threshold to $100,000, agencies could use simplified procedures on another 45,550 procurements—with a total value of $2.5 billion.

Congress should keep current rules that reserve small purchases for small businesses and should improve access to information on procurements of more than $25,000. To ensure that small business receives adequate notice of possible procurements, the federal government, with OMB as the lead agency, should adopt an electronic notification system.

Action: *Rely more on the commercial marketplace.*[37]

The government can save enormous amounts of money by buying more commercial products instead of requiring products to be designed to government-unique specifications. Our government buys such items as integrated circuits, pillows, and oil pans, designed to government specifications—even when there are equally good commercial products available.

We recommend that all agency heads be instructed to review and revise internal purchasing procedures and rules to allow their agencies to buy commercial products whenever practical and to take advantage of market conditions.

We will ask the Office of Management and Budget to draft a new federal commercial code with commercial-style procedures, and then ask Congress to adopt the new code and remove impediments to this money-saving approach to procurement.

Action: *Bring federal procurement laws up to date.*[38]

There are four federal labor laws implemented through the federal procurement process. Each was passed because of valid and well founded concerns about the welfare of working Americans. But as part of our effort to make the government's procurement process work more efficiently, we must consider whether those laws are still necessary—and whether the burdens they impose on the procurement system are reasonable ones.

The Davis-Bacon Act of 1931 requires that each repair or construction contract in excess of $2,000 for work on a public building specify that the prevailing area minimum wage be paid to workers on that contract. The law was passed because Congress feared that without it, federal contracts awarded through a sealed bid process could undermine local prevailing wages. While Congress shifted the government's focus to an open bidding process in 1984, we acknowledge that concerns about the impact of government contracts on prevailing wages are still valid.

Recognizing that the original $2,000 threshold in the law was set more than 60 years ago, we recommend that Congress modify the Davis-Bacon Act by raising the threshold for compliance to $100,000, a change similar to that proposed by Senator Kennedy in March 1993.

The Service Contract Act of 1965 has purposes similar to those of the Davis-Bacon Act, and applies to service contracts in excess of $2,500. It requires contractors to pay the minimum prevailing wage and specified fringe benefits. To keep contractors from "locking in" their wage agreements at low levels, the law imposes a five-year limit on service contracts and requires new wage determinations every two years.

We suggest that the five-year limit is inconsistent with the government's interest in entering into long-range contracts. We will urge Congress to increase the limit up to 10 years while retaining the two-year wage adjustment requirement.

The Copeland Anti-Kickback Act of 1934 regulates payroll deductions on federal and federally assisted construction. The law prohibits anyone from inducing employees to give up any part of their compensation and requires contractors to submit weekly statements of compliance and detailed weekly payroll reports to the Labor Department.

We suggest that such detailed reporting is an unreasonable burden on federal contractors, and we will urge Congress to modify the act. We suggest eliminating requirements for weekly reports and requiring contractors instead to certify with each payment that they have complied with the law. Contractors would also be required to keep records to prove their compliance for three years.

The Walsh-Healey Public Contracts Act requires contractors that supply materials to the federal government through contracts in excess of $10,000 to pay all workers the federal minimum wage, to agree that no employee is required to work more than 40 hours a week, and to avoid using convict labor or workers under the age of 16.

Over time, each of the requirements of the Walsh-Healey Act—with the exception of the provision relating to convict labor—has been superseded by other federal legislation. We therefore urge Congress to remove the burden of certifying compliance with redundant laws from federal contractors. Within 30 days of the repeal of that law, the President should amend Executive Order 11755 to include the convict labor provisions of the Walsh-Healey Act.

STEP 4: REORIENTING THE INSPECTORS GENERAL

Responding to growing concern about waste, fraud, and abuse in government, Congress passed the Inspector General Act in 1978. This act and subsequent amendments created the 60 Inspectors General offices that today employ 15,000 federal workers, including postal inspectors.

The act was broad in scope, requiring IGs to promote the efficiency, economy and integrity of federal programs with auditing program expenditures, and investigating possible fraud and abuse.

The inspectors general, who are independent of the agencies in which they operate, report to Congress twice a year.

These reports detail how much money IG audits have recovered or put to better use and the number of convictions resulting from their criminal investigations. The IGs also send the audit reports to the heads of their agencies and forward investigations for criminal prosecution to the U.S. Attorney General.

The Inspector General Act's two central mandates, combined with the last two administrations' eagerness to highlight "waste, fraud and abuse," have shaped the evolution of the IG offices. The standard by which they are evaluated is finding error or fraud: The more frequently they find mistakes, the more successful they are judged to be. As a result, the IG staffs often develop adversarial relations with agency managers—who, in trying to do things better, may break rules.

At virtually every agency he visited, the Vice President heard federal employees complain that the IGs' basic approach inhibits innovation and risk taking. Heavy-handed enforcement—with the IG watchfulness compelling employees to follow every rule, document every decision, and fill out every form—has had a negative effect in some agencies.

Action: *Broaden the focus of the Inspectors General from strict compliance auditing to evaluating management control systems.*[39]

In a government focused on results, the Inspectors General can play a key role not only in controlling managers' behavior by monitoring it, but in helping to improve it. Today, they audit for strict compliance with rules and regulations. In the future, they should help managers evaluate their management control systems. Today, they look for "waste, fraud, and abuse." In the future, they should also help improve systems to prevent waste, fraud and abuse and ensure efficient, effective service.

Many IGs have already begun to help their agencies this way. At the Justice

Department, for example, some offices were inefficient in completing background and security clearances. The Inspector General's office examined the problem, then recommended setting up a central database to manage the clearance process and warn officials automatically when they were about to miss deadlines for completing investigations. Similarly, the Inspector General of the Department of Health and Human Services has long been engaged in program evaluations to help agencies uncover inefficiencies. While the Inspector General's office retains the right to conduct formal audits and criminal investigations, it also uses its role as a neutral observer to collaborate on making programs work better.

Congress need pass no legislation to make this happen. Promoting the efficiency and integrity of government programs was part of the IGs' original mandate. But such change will require a cultural revolution within many IG offices, and we recommend two steps to help guide such a change. First, line managers, who are the IGs' front-line customers, should be surveyed periodically to see whether they believe the IGs are helping them improve performance. Second, criteria should be established for judging IG performance.

STEP 5: ELIMINATING REGULATORY OVERKILL

Reinventing our budget, personnel and procurement systems will strip away much—but not all—of the red tape that makes our governing processes so cumbersome. Thousands upon thousands of outdated, overlapping regulations remain in place. These regulations affect the people inside government and those who deal with it from the outside. Inside government, we have no precise measurement of how much regulation costs or how much time it steals from productive work. But there's no disagreement that the costs are enormous. And on the matter of external regulation, a

1993 study concluded that the cost to the private sector of complying with regulations is at least $430 billion annually—9 percent of our gross domestic product! [40]

We must clear the thicket of regulation by undertaking a thorough review of the regulations already in place and redesigning regulatory processes to end the proliferation of unnecessary and unproductive rules. We have worked closely with administration officials responsible for developing a new approach to regulatory review and incorporated that work into the following action.

Action: *The President should issue a directive requiring all federal agencies to review internal government regulations over the next 3 years, with a goal of eliminating 50 percent of those regulations.*[41]

Can regulations be eliminated? The answer is yes, as evidenced by promising experiments in several federal agencies.

In the Management Efficiency Pilot Program (MEPP) in five of the Department of Veterans' Affairs regional benefits offices, the offices were encouraged to do away with red tape.[42] At several benefits offices, 895 of 1,969 regulations were dropped, saving the staff more than 3,000 hours and $640,000 in one year. Productivity at MEPP centers increased by 35 percent in one year (1988-89), more than double the increase at other centers. A similar effort by five VA medical centers redirected $3.1 million to much-needed funding for acute care centers.

An even more sweeping example of a fresh start in internal regulations comes from the Air Force, where the Chief of Staff has established a servicewide program to streamline the organization and cut out bureaucracy. Under the Policy Review Initiative begun in 1992, the Air Force is replacing 1,510 regulations with 165 policy directives and 750 sets of instructions. This effort will cut 55,000 pages of intermingled policy and procedure to about 18,000 pages, clearly separating policy from procedure. This deregulation effort, managed by a staff of 10, is expected to be completed in fiscal year 1994.

Over the next 3 years, each federal agency will undertake a thorough and systematic review of its internal regulations. Agencies may choose their own strategies for reaching the goal of reducing internal regulations by 50 percent.

Action: *Improve inter-agency coordination of regulations to reduce unnecessary regulation and red tape.*[43]

In 1981, frustrated at the inconsistencies and duplication among federal regulatory efforts and their burden on government and the private sector, President Reagan required the Office of Management and Budget—specifically, the Office of Information and Regulatory Affairs (OIRA)—to review all regulations proposed by executive agencies.

With a limited staff, many of whom are also involved with paperwork reduction issues, the review process for proposed regulations can be lengthy. And while a lengthy review process may be appropriate for significant rules, it is a waste of time for others.

> We can lick gravity, but sometimes the paperwork is overwhelming.
>
> **Wernher von Braun**

In early 1993, Vice President Gore convened an informal working group to recommend changes in the regulatory review process. The working group and the National Performance Review coordinated their efforts closely. We endorse the recommendations of the working group and the President's executive order, which will implement those changes and streamline the regulatory review process.

The order will enhance the planning process and encourage agencies to consult with the public early in that process. In addition, in an effort to coordinate the regulatory actions of all executive agencies, the Vice President will meet annually with agency heads, and the Administrator of OIRA will hold quarterly meetings with representatives of executive agencies and the administration.

Improving the regulatory review process also means being selective in reviewing regulations. Through this order, the President will instruct OIRA to review only *significant* regulations—not, as under the current process, *all* regulations. The new review process, which will take into account a broad range of costs and benefits, will be more useful and realistic.

To ease the adverse effects of regulation on citizens, businesses, and the economy as a whole, the executive order also will require an ongoing review of existing regulations. Agencies will identify regulations that are cumulative, obsolete, or inconsistent, and, where appropriate, eliminate or modify them. They will also identify legislative mandates that require them to impose unnecessary or outdated regulations.

Action: *Establish a process by which agencies can more widely obtain waivers from regulations.*[44]

With the advent of the Government Performance and Results Act, which Congress passed in July 1993, we have begun to acknowledge the important principle of "flexibility in return for accountability."

Under the act, some agencies may apply for waivers from federal regulations if they meet specific performance targets. In other words, they will be exempt from some administrative requirements if they do their jobs better. The law applies only to internal regulations and government agencies, but it also urges wider waiver authority to test the potential benefits. In the spirit of that legislation, we seek to expand the concept of greater flexibility for greater accountability.

The President should direct each federal agency to establish and publish,in a timely manner, an open process through which other federal agencies can obtain waivers from that agency's regulations—with an expedited appeals process.

Rules adopting this new waiver process would state that all future agency regulations would be subject to the waiver process unless explicitly prohibited. We will also ask Congress to specify that legislation would be subject to waivers unless explicitly prohibited.

Action: *Reduce the burden of congressionally mandated reports.*[45]

Woodrow Wilson was right. Our country's 28th president once wrote that "there is no distincter tendency in congressional history than the tendency to subject even the details of administration" to constant congressional supervision.

One place to start in liberating agencies from congressional micromanagement is the issue of reporting requirements. Over the past decades, we have thrown layer upon layer of reporting requirements on federal agencies, creating an almost endless series of required audits, reports, and exhibits.

Today the annual calendar is jammed with report deadlines. On August 31 of each year, the Chief Financial Officers (CFO) Act requires that agencies file a 5-year financial plan and a CFO annual report. On September 1, budget exhibits for financial management activities and high risk areas are due. On November 30, IG reports are expected, along with reports required by the Prompt Payment Act. On January 31, reports under the Federal Civil Penalties Inflation Report Adjustment Act of 1990 come due. On March 31, financial statements are due, and on May 1 annual single-audit reports must be filed. On May 31 another round of IG reports are due. At the end of July and December, "high-risk" reports are filed. On August 31, it all begins again. And these are just the major reports!

In fiscal year 1993, Congress required executive branch agencies to prepare 5,348 reports.[46] Much of this work is duplicative. And because there are so many different sources of information, no one gets an integrated view of an agency's condition— least of all the agency manager who needs accurate and up to date numbers. Meanwhile, trapped in this blizzard of paperwork, no one is looking at results.

We propose to consolidate and simplify reporting requirements, and to redesign them so that the manager will have a clear picture of the agency's financial condition, the condition of individual programs, and the extent to which the agency is meeting its objectives. We will ask Congress to pass legislation granting OMB the flexibility to consolidate and simplify statutory reports and establishing a sunset provision in any reporting requirements adopted by Congress in the future.

STEP 6: EMPOWER STATE AND LOCAL GOVERNMENTS

What we usually call "government" is, in fact, a tangle of different levels of government agencies—some run from Washington, some in state capitals, and some by cities and towns. In the United States, in fact, some 80,000 "governments" run everything from local schools and water supply systems to the Defense Department and overseas embassies. Few taxpayers differentiate among levels of government, however. To the average citizen, a tax is a tax—and a service a service—regardless of which level of government is responsible. To reinvent government in the public's eyes, we must address the web of federal-state-local relations.

Washington provides about 16 percent of the money that states and localities spend and shapes a much larger share of such spending through mandates. Much of Washington's domestic agenda—$226 billion to be precise—consists of programs actually run by states, cities, and counties. But the federal government doesn't always distribute its money—or its mandates—wisely.

For starters, Washington allocates federal money through an array of more than 600 different grant programs. Many are small: 445 of them distribute less than $50 million a year nationwide; some 275 distribute less than $10 million. Through grants, Congress funds some 150 education and training programs, 100 social service programs, and more than 80 health care programs.

Considered individually, many categorical grant programs make sense. But together, they often work against the very purposes for which they were established. When a department operates small grant programs, it produces more bureaucracy, not more services. Thousands of public employees—at all levels of government—spend millions of hours writing regulations, writing and reviewing grant applications, filling out forms, checking on each other, and avoiding oversight. In this way, professionals and bureaucrats siphon money from the programs' intended customers: students, the poor, urban residents, and others. State and local governments find their money fragmented into hundreds of tiny pots, each with different—often contradictory—rules, procedures, and program requirements.

Henry Cisneros, Secretary of Housing and Urban Development, likens federal grants to a system of pipelines spreading out across the country. The "water," says Cisneros, reaches states and localities

Were we directed from Washington when to sow and when to reap, we should soon want for bread.

**Thomas Jefferson
1826**

through hundreds of individual pipelines. This means there is little chance for the water to be mixed, properly calibrated to local needs, or concentrated to address a specific problem, geographic area, or population.

In employment and training, for example, Washington funds training programs, literacy programs, adult education programs, tuition grant programs, and vocational education programs. Different programs are designed for different groups—welfare recipients, food stamp recipients, displaced homemakers, youth in school, drop-outs, "dislocated workers," workers displaced by foreign trade, and on and on.

At a plant in Pittsfield, Massachusetts, General Electric recently laid off a large group of workers. Some workers could get Trade Adjustment Assistance benefits, because their jobs were lost to foreign competition. Others could not; their jobs fell to defense cutbacks. Because they have a union, people working in one area began exercising their seniority rights and bumping people in other areas. Some workers bumped from trade-affected jobs to defense contracting jobs, then lost those a few weeks later. Under federal regulations, they could no longer get Trade Adjustment Assistance. Thus, friends who had spent years working side by side found themselves with very different benefits. Some got the standard 6 months of unemployment checks. Others got 2 years of unemployment checks and extensive retraining support. Try explaining that to people who have lost the only jobs they've ever held!

People who run such programs struggle to knit together funds from three, four, or five programs, hoping against hope that workers get enough retraining to land decent new jobs. But the task is difficult; each program has its own requirements, funding cycles, eligibility criteria, and the like. One employment center in Allegheny County, New York, has tried hard to bring several programs together and make them appear as seamless as possible to the customers. At the end of the day, to accommodate reporting requirements, the staff enters information on each customer at four different computer terminals: one for Job Training Partnership Act (JTPA) programs, one for the JOBS program, one for the Employment Service, and one for tracking purposes.

When Congress enacted JTPA, it sought to avoid such problems. It let local areas tailor their training programs to local needs. But federal rules and regulations have gradually undermined the good intentions. Title III, known as the Economic Dislocation and Worker Adjustment Assistance Act (EDWAA), helps states respond immediately to plant closings and large layoffs. Yet even EDWAA's most flexible money, the "national reserve fund," has become so tangled in red tape that many states won't use it. As Congress's Office of Technology Assessment put it, "the process is simply too obstacle ridden. ... many state EDWAA managers cannot handle the complexities of the grant application, and those that do know how are too busy responding to clients' urgent needs to write demanding, detailed grant proposals."

When Congress amended JTPA in 1993, targeting more funds to those with "multiple barriers" to employment, homeless advocates thought the change would help their clients. After all, who has more barriers to employment than someone without an address or phone number? But the new JTPA formula also emphasized training over job search assistance. So a local program in Washington, D.C. that had won a Labor Department award for placing 70 percent of its clients in jobs—many of them service sector jobs paying more than the minimum wage—lost its JTPA funding. Why? It didn't offer training. It just helped the homeless find jobs.[47]

But federal programs rarely focus on results. As structured by Congress, they pay more attention to process than outcomes—in this case, more to training than to jobs. Even in auditing state and local programs, federal overseers often do little more than check to see whether proper forms are filed in proper folders.

The rules and regulations behind federal grant programs were designed with the best of intentions—to ensure that funds flow for the purposes Congress intended. Instead, they often ensure that programs don't work as well as they could—or don't work at all.

Virtually every expert with whom we spoke agreed that this system is fundamentally broken. No one argued for marginal or incremental change. Everyone wants dramatic change—state and local officials, federal managers, congressional staff. As in managing its own affairs, the federal government must shift the basic paradigm it uses in managing state and local affairs. It must stop holding programs accountable for process and begin holding them accountable for results.

The task is daunting; it will take years to accomplish. We propose several significant steps on the journey:

• Establish a cabinet-level Enterprise Board to oversee new initiatives in community empowerment;

• Cut the number of unfunded mandates that Washington imposes;

• Consolidate 55 categorical grants into broader "flexible grants;"

• Increase state and local flexibility in using the remaining categorical grants;

• Let all agencies waive rules and regulations when they conflict with results; and

• Deregulate the public housing program.

The likely benefits are clear: administrative savings at all levels; greater flexibility to design solutions; more effective concentration of limited resources; and programs that work for their customers.

Action: *The President should establish a cabinet-level Enterprise Board to oversee new initiatives in community empowerment.*[48]

The federal government needs to better organize itself to improve the way it works with states and localities. The President should immediately establish a working group of cabinet-level officials, with leadership from the Vice President, the Domestic Policy Council, and the National Economic Council.

The Board will look for ways to empower innovative communities by reducing red tape and regulation on federal programs. This group will be committed to solutions that respect "bottom-up" initiatives

> *Sometimes we need to start out with a blank slate and say, "Hey, we've been doing this for the last 40, 50 years. It doesn't work." Let's throw out everything, clear out minds...Let's have as a goal doing the right thing for the right reasons, even if it entails taking risks.*
>
> **Vincent Lane,**
> Chairman, Chicago Housing Authority,
> Reinventing Government Summit
> Philadelphia, June 25, 1993

rather than "top-down" requirements. It will focus on the administration's community empowerment agenda, beginning with the 9 Empowerment Zones and 95 Enterprise Communities that passed Congress as part of the President's economic plan.

In participating communities, for example, federal programs could be consolidated and planning requirements could be simplified; waivers would be granted to assure maximum flexibility; federal funding cycles would be synchronized; and surplus federal properties could be designated for community use.

Action: *The President should issue a directive limiting the use of unfunded mandates by the administration.*[49]

As the federal deficit mounted in the 1980s, Congress found it more and more difficult to spend new money. Instead, it often turned to "unfunded mandates"— passing laws for the states and localities to follow, but giving them little or no money to implement those policies. As of December 1992, there were at least 172 separate pieces of federal legislation in force that imposed requirements on state and local governments. Many of these, such as clean water standards and increased public access for disabled citizens, are unquestionably noble goals.

But the question remains: How will state and local governments pay to meet those goals? We recommend that Congress refrain from this practice and that the President's directive establish that the executive branch will similarly limit its use of unfunded mandates in policies, legislative proposals and regulations.

The directive would narrow the circumstances under which departments and agencies could impose new unfunded burdens on other governments. It also would direct federal agencies to review their existing regulations and reduce the number of mandates that interfere with effective service delivery. OMB's Office of Information and Regulatory Affairs (OIRA) should review all major regulations or legislation proposed by the executive branch for possible adverse impacts on states and localities. Finally, OIRA's director should

create a forum in which federal, state, and local officials could develop solutions to problems involving unfunded mandates.

Action: *Consolidate 55 categorical grant programs with funding of $12.9 billion into six broad "flexible grants"—in job training, education, water quality, defense conversion, environmental management, and motor carrier safety.*[50]

This proposal came from the National Governors Association (NGA) and National Conference of State Legislatures (NCSL), which describe it as "a first step toward broader, more ambitious reforms." It would consolidate some 20 education, employment and training programs, with a combined $5.5 billion in fiscal year 1993 spending; roughly 10 other education programs ($1.6 billion); 10 small

How Much Do You Get for a 1983 Toyota?

What does the price of a used car have to do with the federal government's family policies?

More than it should. Caseworkers employed by state and local government to work with poor families are supposed to help those families become self-sufficient. Their job is to understand how federal programs work. But as it turns out, those caseworkers also have to know something about used cars. Used cars? That's right. Consider this example, recounted to Vice President Gore at a July 1993 Progressive Foundation conference on family policy in Nashville, Tennessee:

Agencies administering any of the federal government's programs for the poor must verify many details about people's lives. For instance, they must verify that a family receiving funds

under Aid to Families with Dependent Children (AFDC) does not own a car worth more than $1,500 in *equity value*. To give a poor family food stamps, it must verify that the family doesn't own a car worth more than $4,500 in *market value*. Medicaid specifies a range that it allows for the value of a recipient's car, depending on the recipient's Medicaid category. But under food stamp rules, the car is exempt if it is used for work or training or transporting a disabled person. And under AFDC, there is no exemption for the car under any circumstances.

Recounting that story to a meeting of the nation's governors, the Vice President asked this simple question: "Why can't we talk about the same car in all three programs?"

environmental programs ($392 million); six water quality programs ($2.66 billion); and six defense conversion programs ($460 million).

Action: *Congress should allow states and localities to consolidate separate grant programs from the bottom up.*[51]

Recognizing the political and administrative obstacles to wholesale reform of more than 600 existing categorical grants in the short term, the National Performance Review focused on an innovative solution to provide flexibility and to encourage result-oriented performance at the state and local levels.

Our proposal calls for Congress to authorize "bottom-up" grant consolidation initiatives. Localities would have authority to mix funding from different programs, with simple notification to Washington, when combining grants smaller than $10 million each. For a consolidation involving any program funded at more than $10 million, the federal awarding office (and state, if applicable), would have to approve it before implementation. In return for such consolidation, the state and local governments would waive all but one of the programs' administrative payments from the federal government.

When different grants' regulations conflict, the consolidating agency would select which to follow. States and localities that demonstrated effective service integration through consolidation would receive preference in future grant awards.

Each of the partners in the intergovernmental system must work collaboratively with others—federal, state, and local—to refine this recommendation. The details will be negotiated with important state and local organizations, such as the NGA, the NCSL, the U.S. Conference of Mayors, and the National League of Cities, before legislation is drafted.

Bottom-up consolidation will be given a high priority by the administration. It represents a way to improve state and local

performance without tackling the thorny political problem involved in consolidating 600 grant programs, reconciling thousands of rules and regulations, and anticipating every possible instance when flexibility might be necessary. It puts the burden of identifying obstacles and designing the best solution where it belongs—on those who must make the programs work.

Action: *Give all cabinet secretaries and agency heads authority to grant states and localities selective waivers from federal regulations or mandates.*[52]

> *The National Performance Review is not intended to be the final word on reinventing government but rather a first step. This long overdue effort will require continuing commitment from the very top to truly change the way government does business.*
>
> **U.S. Rep. John Conyers (D. Mich.)**
> August 28, 1993

For federal grant programs to work, managers must have flexibility to waive rules that get in the way. Some departments have this authority; others don't. Federal decisions on most waivers come very slowly, and states often must apply to a half-dozen agencies to get the waivers they need. Florida, for example, has a two-year waiver allowing it to provide hospice care to AIDS patients under Medicaid. Its renewal takes 18 months. So state officials have to reapply after only six months.

Waiver legislation should grant broad waiver authority, with the exception of fair housing, non-discrimination, environmental, and labor standards. We will ask Congress to grant such authority to cabinet officers. These waivers should be granted under limited circumstances, however. They must be time-limited and designed to include performance measures. When each experiment is concluded, the granting agency should decide whether the new way of doing things should be included in standard practice.

Action: *Give control of public housing to local public housing authorities with histories of excellent management and substantially deregulate the rest.*[53]

Public housing is a classic story of good intentions gone awry. When the program began in the 1930s, it was hailed as an enlightened response to European immigrants' squalid living conditions in cities across the country. Through an enormous bureaucracy stretching from Washington into virtually every city in America, the public housing program brought clean, safe, inexpensive living quarters to people who could not afford them otherwise.

Now, however, public housing is even more troubled than our categorical grant programs. With its tight, centralized control, it epitomizes the industrial-era program: hierarchical, rule-bound, and bureaucratic. HUD's Washington, regional, and local offices rigidly control local public housing authorities, who struggle to help the very poor.

Frustrated by the failure of public housing, innovative state and local governments began to experiment with new models of developing, designing, financing, managing, and owning low-income housing. Successful efforts tailored the housing to the characteristics of the surrounding community. Local public housing authorities began to work with local governments and non-profit organizations to create innovative new models to serve low-income people.

HUD recognizes that local authorities with proven records of excellence can serve their customers far better if allowed to make their own decisions. We and the secretary recommend that Congress give HUD authority to create demonstration projects in which local housing authorities would continue to receive operating subsidies as long as they met a series of performance targets, but would be free from other HUD control. Individual demonstrations could vary, but all federal rules would be open for waivers as long as HUD could measure performance in providing long-term, affordable housing to those poor enough to be eligible for public housing.

In addition, HUD should work closely with local housing authorities, their national organizations, public housing tenant organizations, and state and local officials to eliminate unnecessary rules, requirements, procedures, and regulations. In particular, HUD should replace its detailed procurement and operating manuals and design and site selection requirements with performance measures, using annual ranking of local housing authorities to encourage better service and greater accountability. It should eliminate the annual budget review, an exercise in which HUD field staff spend thousands of hours reviewing and approving detailed budgets from local housing authorities —even though the reviews do not influence federal funding decisions. And it should work with Congress to change current rent rules, which create strong incentives for people to move from public housing as soon as they find jobs.

Conclusion

The changes described above are ambitious. They will take enormous effort and enormous will. It will be many years before all of them take root. But if they succeed, the American people will have a government capable of attacking their problems with far more energy, and far less waste, than they can today imagine.

We must move quickly, because the bureaucracy, by its nature, resists change. As Tom Peters wrote in *Thriving on Chaos,* "Good intentions and brilliant proposals will be dead-ended, delayed, sabotaged, massaged to death, or reversed beyond recognition or usefulness by the overlayered structures...."[54]

But the changes we propose will produce their own momentum to overcome bureaucratic resistance. As the red tape is being cut, federal workers will become more and more impatient with the red tape that remains. They will resist any reversal of the process. And they will be strengthened in their resistance by the steps we propose in the next chapters.

Chapter 2

PUTTING CUSTOMERS FIRST

We are going to rationalize the way the federal government relates to the American people, and we are going to make the federal government customer friendly. A lot of people don't realize that the federal government has customers. We have customers. The American people.

Vice President Al Gore
Town Meeting,
Department of Housing
and Urban Development,
March 26, 1993

All of us—bureaucrat or business owner, cabinet secretary or office clerk—respond to incentives. We do more of what brings us rewards and recognition, less of what brings us criticism. But our government, built around a complex cluster of monopolies, insulates both managers and workers from the power of incentives.

We must change the system. We must force our government to put the customer first by injecting the dynamics of the marketplace.

The best way to deal with monopoly is to expose it to competition. Let us be clear: this does *not* mean we should run government agencies exactly like private businesses. After all, many of government's functions are public responsibilities precisely because the private sector cannot, should not, or would not manage them. But we *can* transplant some aspects of the business world into the public arena. We can create an environment that commits federal

managers to the same struggle to cut costs and improve customer service that compels private managers. We can imbue the federal government—from top to bottom—with a driving sense of accountability.

Is it really possible to reinvent government in this way? Horror stories about government waste are so abundant that many doubt its ability to change. For some, the only solution is to cut or abolish programs wholesale. In some instances those cuts make sense and we are recommending them. But alone they do not address the problem we face or move us decidedly toward a government that works better and costs less.

We propose a different approach. We must make cuts where necessary; we also must make our government effective and efficient. Some programs clearly should be eliminated, others streamlined. We will offer many proposals to do both in chapter 4. But reinventing government isn't just about trimming programs; it's about fundamentally changing the way government does business. By forcing public agencies to compete for their customers—between offices, with other agencies, and with the private sector—we will create a permanent pressure to streamline programs, abandon the obsolete, and improve what's left.

This process will be neither quick nor easy. But as it unfolds, a very different type of government will emerge, one that is accountable to its true customers— the public.

We propose four specific steps to empower customers, break federal monopolies, and provide incentives for federal employees to better serve their customers.

First, we will require that all federal agencies put customers first by regularly asking them how they view government services, what problems they encounter, and how they would like services improved. We will ensure that all customers have a voice, and that every voice is heard.

Second, we will make agencies compete for their customers' business. Wherever feasible, we will dismantle government's monopolies, including those that buy goods and services, acquire and maintain office space, and print public documents. These internal monopolies serve their customers— government workers—so poorly, it's no wonder those workers have such trouble serving customers *outside* government.

Third, where competition isn't feasible, we will turn government monopolies into more businesslike enterprises—enterprises in closer touch with both customers and market incentives.

Fourth, we will shift some federal functions from old-style bureaucracies to market mechanisms. We will use federal powers to structure private markets in ways that solve problems and meet citizens' needs—such as for job training or safe workplaces—without funding more and bigger public bureaucracies.

Together, these strategies will enable us to create a responsive, innovative, and entrepreneurial government. If we inject market mechanisms into federal agencies as we are cutting red tape, we will create new dynamics—and a new dynamism— throughout the federal government.

STEP 1: GIVING CUSTOMERS A VOICE— AND A CHOICE

Setting Customer Service Standards

Long lines, busy signals, bad information, and indifferent workers at front counters—these are all too common occurrences when customers come in contact with their government. Quite simply, the quality of government service is below what its customers deserve.

We propose to set a goal of providing customer services *equal to the best in business.*

Too many agencies have learned to overlook their customers. After all, most of government's customers can't really take their business elsewhere. Veterans who use veterans' hospitals, companies that seek environmental permits, or retirees applying for social security benefits must deal with public agencies that hold monopolies. And monopolies, public or private, have little sensitivity to customer needs.

So government agencies must do what many of America's best businesses have done: renew their focus on customers. Some are already trying. The Internal Revenue Service (IRS) and Social Security Administration (SSA) have taken major steps to improve their telephone services to customers. SSA, the U.S. Postal Service (USPS), and the Department of Veterans Affairs are developing a combined government services kiosk, providing a single point of access for services offered by the three agencies. The Library of Congress, the Energy Department, the National Aeronautics and Space Administration, the

National Science Foundation, and other federal agencies have placed their materials on Internet, a worldwide computer network.[1]

Good service means giving people what they need. To do that, however, one must first find out what they want—a step few federal agencies have taken. In the future, federal agencies will ask their customers what they want, what problems they have, and how the agencies can improve their services.

Knowing what customers want, public agencies must set clear and specific customer service standards. When Federal Express promises to deliver a package the next day by 10:30 a.m., both customers and employees understand precisely what that means. Similarly, when the Air Force's Tactical Air Command discarded its thick set of specifications about living quarters for visiting pilots and adopted a simple standard—equivalent to "a moderately priced hotel, like Ramada"—employees understood exactly what it meant.[2]

Several federal agencies that frequently interact with citizens have launched aggressive customer service initiatives. We endorse strengthening these initiatives—described below—and expanding them across the federal government.

Internal Revenue Service. The IRS, the federal agency most citizens prefer to avoid, might seem the least likely to develop a customer focus. But it's working hard to do just that.

Four years ago, the General Accounting Office (GAO) discovered that IRS staff gave a wrong answer to one of every three taxpayers who called with a question. Since then, the agency has improved its accuracy rate to 88 percent.[3] And—in a switch that signals a basic change in attitude—agency employees now refer to taxpayers as customers.

In IRS pilot projects across the country, employees now have authority to change work processes on their own in order to improve productivity. Front-line workers also have more authority to resolve issues one-on-one with individual taxpayers. The agency is fostering competition among its tax return centers, based on customer service levels and efficiency at handling the 1.7 billion pieces of paper the IRS receives each year. Centers that perform better get higher budgets and workloads, and employees get promotion opportunities. The IRS was among the first government agencies to use 800 numbers and automated voice mail systems to increase customer access to information. Today, the IRS is beginning to survey its customers.

Customer Service Standards: IRS

*A*s part of the National Performance Review, the IRS is publishing customer service standards, including these:

- If you file a paper return, your refund due will be mailed within 40 days.

- If you file an electronic return, your refund due will be sent within 14 days when you specify direct deposit, within 21 days when you request a check.

- Our goal is to resolve your account inquiry with one contact; repeat problems will be handled by a Problem Resolution Office in an average of 21 days.

- When you give our tax assistors sufficient and accurate information and they give you the wrong answers, we will cancel related penalties.

- With your feedback, by 1995 IRS forms and instructions will be so clear that 90 percent of individual tax returns will be error-free.

In addition, some centers are serving customers in truly astonishing ways. One anecdote makes the point. At the Ogden, Utah Service Center—a winner of the Presidential Award for Quality—a down-

Customer Service Standards: Social Security Administration

As part of its participation in the National Performance Review, the Social Security Administration will publish nationally, and post in each of its offices, these performance standards:

• You will be treated with courtesy every time you contact us.

• We will tell you what benefits you qualify for and give you the information you need to use our programs.

• We will refer you to other programs that may help you.

• You will reach us the first time you try on our 800 number.

pensions, survivors' and disability insurance, and the supplemental security income (SSI) program. The agency has 1,300 field offices and receives 60 million calls a year on its toll-free lines. As the nation's population ages, the agency faces an ever-increasing workload. Recently, an inspector general's report showed that customer satisfaction had fallen 4 years in a row due to longer waiting times in offices and increasing problems in reaching someone on the phone.[5]

Fortunately, the Social Security Administration is strengthening its customer orientation. When Hurricane Andrew struck South Florida, where 367,000 people collect social security and SSI, agency workers took steps to ensure that senior citizens would know how to get their checks despite the devastation. Local offices used television, radio, and loudspeaker trucks touring the area with messages in English, Spanish, and Creole. The agency also hired an airplane to tow a banner with SSA's toll-free 800 telephone number over the hard-hit Homestead area.

More generally, the Social Security Administration recently adopted a customer-oriented strategic plan, which includes objectives such as issuing social security numbers orally within 24 hours of an application. Besides pinpointing some of their objectives as standards to reach today, SSA is publishing all 34 of its objectives and seeking customer feedback on whether it set the right targets for service.

U.S. Postal Service. The Postal Service, which delivered 166 billion pieces of mail in 1992, has begun improving customer service for a good reason: It has competition. While most people still use the Postal Service to deliver first class mail, the use of private delivery services and electronic mail is rising quickly.

The Postal Service has decided to meet its competition head-on. Using focus groups, the agency identified service areas where its customers wanted improvement. It found that people wanted shorter waiting lines at counters, better access to postal information, and better responses to their

on-his-luck man hitchhiked from out of state to get his refund check. As it turns out, this center doesn't issue checks. But IRS employees there discovered that a disbursing center had sent a check to the hitchhiker's old address and that it had been returned. They ordered a new check sent to Ogden and helped the hitchhiker make ends meet until the check arrived.

In the end, the IRS's efforts could affect all of us, not only as filers of tax returns but as taxpayers. If IRS forms are easier to understand and use, more taxpayers might file on time. If the IRS develops an image as a more effective, user-friendly agency, more taxpayers might decide to file in the first place. A mere 1-percent increase in voluntary compliance would add $7 billion in government revenue each year.[4]

Social Security Administration. Every year, more than 47 million Americans come in contact with the Social Security Administration, which administers old-age complaints. Using these standards to measure performance, the agency set a long range goal of "100-percent satisfaction" and developed a customer satisfaction index to measure progress toward it.

The agency also is providing incentives for employee performance: In cooperation with two postal unions, managers now use customer satisfaction data to help determine employee bonuses.

Action: *The President should issue a directive requiring all federal agencies that deliver services to the public to create customer service programs that identify and survey customers. The order will establish the following standard for quality: Customer service equal to the best in business.*[6]

The President's directive will lay out principles to govern the provision of customer services. For example, organizations should:

- survey their customers frequently to find out what kind and quality of services they want;

- post standards and results measured against them;

- benchmark performance against "the best in business";

- provide choices in both source of service and delivery means;

- make information, services, and complaint systems easily accessible;

- handle inquiries and deliver services with courtesy;

- provide pleasant surroundings for customers; and

- provide redress for poor services.

The order will direct all federal agencies that deal with the public to:

Customer Service Standards: USPS

As part of its participation in the National Performance Review, the USPS will expand its plans to display these standards in post offices:

- Your first class mail will be delivered anywhere in the United States within 3 days.

- Your local first class mail will be delivered overnight.

- You will receive service at post office counters within 5 minutes.

- You can get postal information 24 hours a day by calling a local number.

- immediately identify who their customers are;

- survey their customers on services and results desired, and on satisfaction with existing services;

- survey front-line employees on barriers to, and ideas for, matching the best in business;

- in 6 months, report results on these three steps to the President; and

- develop and publish a customer service plan—including an initial set of customer service standards—within 1 year.

The customer service plans will address the need to train front-line employees in customer service skills. They will also identify companies that agencies will use to judge how they compare to the "best in business." The directive will ask cabinet secretaries and agency heads to use improvement in customer satisfaction as a primary criterion in judging the performance of agency managers and front-line employees.

Action: *For voluntary customer surveys, the Office of Management and Budget will delegate its survey approval authority under the Paperwork Reduction Act to departments that are able to comply with the act.*[7]

The public's input is crucial to improving customer service. But current law gives the Office of Management and Budget (OMB) power to decide on virtually all agency requests to solicit information from the public (OMB can delegate this authority). This law was designed to minimize onerous paperwork burdens the federal government imposes on businesses and citizens. But it also minimizes the number of times agencies ask customers about their needs. It often slows agencies down so much that they abandon the idea of doing a survey altogether.

For many agencies, customer surveys are the single most useful way to measure performance. If OMB has to approve every request for a customer survey, however, neither the directive described above nor the Government Performance and Results Act, which the President signed in August 1993, will work. Citizens do not like to be forced to fill out forms by their government. But most Americans would be pleased to receive a *voluntary* survey asking how their post office or social security office could improve its customer service.

We propose to delegate approval of voluntary customer surveys to departments with the ability to comply with the law, and ensure that they create rapid approval processes so bottlenecks don't develop at lower levels.

Customer-driven programs rarely cost more than others; indeed, productivity gains in past federal experiments have more than offset cost increases. At the Ogden Service Center, the IRS office's new approach helped workers process 5 percent more tax returns. When organizations shift their focus to customers, they act like Avis—they try harder.

Crossing Agency Boundaries

Unfortunately, even agencies that try harder find very real obstacles in the way of putting their customers first. Perhaps the worst is Washington's organizational chart. Time and again, agencies find it impossible to meet their customers' needs, because organizational boundaries stand in the way.

Sometimes, programs housed in the same agency are only tangentially related. While most Agriculture Department programs relate to food, for instance, its customers range from farmers who grow it to poor children whose families use food stamps. At other times, programs dealing with the same customers are located in a dozen different agencies. Rather than make people jump over organizational boundaries on their own, we must remove the boundaries at the point of customer contact. We must make the delivery of services "seamless."

The traditional solution is to shuffle the organizational chart. But in Washington, such proposals set off monumental turf wars between agencies in the executive branch, and between committees in Congress. After years of struggle, one or two agencies are reorganized — or a new department is created. Meanwhile, the nation's problems keep changing, so the new structure is soon out of date.

In a rapidly changing world, the best solution is not to keep redesigning the organizational chart; it is to melt the rigid boundaries between organizations. The federal government should organize work according to customers' needs and anticipated outcomes, not bureaucratic turf. It should learn from America's best-run companies, in which employees no longer work in separate, isolated divisions, but in project- or product-oriented teams.

To do so, the government must make three changes. It must give federal workers greater decision making authority, allowing them to operate effectively in cross-cutting ventures. It must strip federal laws of prohibitions against such cooperation. And it must order agencies to reconsider their own regulations and tradition-bound thinking. For example, the Forest Service found that 70 percent of its regulatory barriers to new, creative ways of doing business were self-imposed.[8]

Despite these barriers, some noteworthy initiatives are underway. Rural Development Councils, under the Agriculture Department's direction, work with several federal departments as well as states and localities to better coordinate rural aid programs. At the Federal Aviation Administration (FAA), a systems manager helps coordinate the activities of the FAA, Defense Department, international aviation organizations, and various private interests on matters involving satellites, data links, and traffic flow management.[9]

We should bring the same approach to other parts of government. The following examples illustrate the problems we face and the solutions we must create.

Action: *Create a system of competitive, one-stop, career development centers open to all Americans.*[10]

Our nation's economic future depends on the quality of our workforce. Our individual futures, too, depend on whether we have marketable, flexible skills with which to adapt to the changing demands of new technologies. In a country where the average worker changes jobs seven times in a lifetime, those skills are more than desirable; they are crucial.

Our government invests heavily in education and training. Together, 14 separate government departments and agencies invest $24 billion a year, through 150 employment and training programs.[11] But we do not invest this money well enough. For one thing, our system is organized for the convenience of those who deliver services, not those who use them. For another, the system lacks competition and incentives for improvement.

"The United States has a worldwide reputation for providing its youth extensive opportunity to attend college," the General Accounting Office noted recently. "However, our country falls short in employment preparation of many noncollege-youth." Unlike our competitors, GAO said, we have no national policy to systematically prepare non-college educated youth for jobs.[12]

Our system is badly fragmented. Each service — from job referral to retraining — is designed for different people, with different rules, regulations, and reporting requirements. Bewildered, often dispirited, job seekers must trudge from office to office, trying to fit themselves into a program. When they find a program, they may find that they aren't eligible, that it's all filled up, or that the classroom is across town.

American workers deserve a better deal. Nowhere on the government reinvention front is action more urgently needed or are potential rewards greater. We envision a new workforce development system, focused on the needs of workers and employers. We will organize it around the customer — whether an individual or a business — then provide that customer with good information about the performance of different providers and plenty of choices. If we do this, career centers and training providers will have to compete for their customers' business, based on the quality of their services.

Specifically, we propose one-stop career management centers across the country, open to all Americans — regardless of race, gender, age, income, employment experience, or skills. (One-stop centers are also a key feature of the Workforce Investment Strategy the Labor Department is developing.) Our centers would offer skills assessment, information on jobs, access to education and training — everything people needed to make career decisions. The centers would be linked to all federal, state, and local workforce development programs, and to many private ones (which are, after all, the source of most job-training money). Core services such as labor market information and job search help would be offered free. Some centers might offer other services, from comprehensive testing to career counseling and workshops, on a fee-for-service basis.

These centers would help their customers get access to funds from any of the 150 programs for which they qualified. To make this possible, the federal government would eliminate or waive many rules and regulations that keep our workforce development programs separate. The centers would also be allowed to generate their own revenues, including fees collected from employers and employees would could afford to pay. Any organization, public or private, would be allowed to seek a charter to operate one or more one-stop career centers. The process would be performance-driven, with contracts renewed only if centers met customers' demands. The federal government would establish national chartering standards for the centers, but states and local employment boards would decide which organizations met the standards.

Today, local organizations such as state employment services get most of their federal funds almost as a matter of entitlement. They account for the money, but we do not hold them accountable for whether they spend it effectively. We would make funding for these new centers more competitive, opening the process to public and private, nonprofit and for-profit, entities.

We would judge these centers in part by how many people sought help at them — on the theory that centers attracting the most customers were clearly doing something right. But we would focus as well on what happened after the customers left. Did they enroll in meaningful training programs? Did they find jobs? Did they keep their jobs? Did they increase their incomes? Finally, we would give customers the necessary information to decide the same thing for themselves: Which training program would meet their needs best?

We believe that the central problem in the Employment Service is not the line workers, but the many rules and regulations that prevent them from doing their jobs. Waiver of these antiquated rules will free up these workers to perform well. In order for state employment services to compete on a level playing field—particularly after the negative effects of the last decade of spending cuts and over-regulation—line workers must be given the opportunity to retool. The Labor Department should ensure that they receive the necessary training to enable them to participate in the process.

The biggest single barrier to creating an integrated system of one-stop career centers is the fragmented nature of federal funds. The 150 federal programs have different rules, different reporting requirements, even different fiscal years. To synchronize these —and to break down the walls between categorical programs—the National Economic Council should convene a Workforce Development Council, with members from the Departments of Labor, Education, and Health and Human Services; the Office of Management and Budget; and other departments and agencies with employment and training programs. This council should standardize fiscal and administrative procedures, develop a standard set of terms and definitions between programs, develop a comprehensive set of results-oriented performance standards, and improve the qualitative evaluation of program performance.

Action: *The President shoud issue a directive that requires collaborative efforts across the government to empower communities and strengthen families.*[13]

At Vice President Gore's recent conference on family policy in Nashville, experts agreed that effective family policy requires new approaches at the federal, state, and local levels. We should stop dividing up families' needs into health, education, welfare, and shelter, each with its own set of agencies and programs, many of which contradict one another and work at cross-purposes. Instead, across all levels of government, we need collaborative, community-based, customer-driven approaches through which providers can integrate the full network of services.

For instance, we spend about $60 billion a year on the well-being of children. But we have created at least 340 separate programs for families and children, administered by 11 different federal agencies and departments.[14] Thus, a poor family may need to seek help from several departments—Agriculture for food stamps, Housing and Urban Development for rental support, Health and Human Services for health care and chasing down dead-beat parents. For each program, they will have to visit different offices, learn about services, fill out forms to establish eligibility—and wait.

The system is fragmented and illogical. In Texas, where the immunization rate among poor children is about 30 percent, the state Health Department sought permission to have nurses who run the Agriculture Department's Women, Infants and Children supplemental food program also give immunizations. The Agriculture Department said no—unless Texas developed an elaborate cost allocation plan. Consequently, mothers and children will have to continue visiting more than one agency.[15]

A few years ago, *Governing* magazine described a teenage girl who was pregnant, had a juvenile record, and was on welfare. Between the three problems, she had more than six caseworkers—each from a different agency. As one put it: "The kid has all these people providing services, and everybody's doing their own thing and Tasha's not getting better. We need to have one person who says, 'Now look, let's talk about a plan of action for Tasha.'"[16] President Clinton's directive will help remove obstacles that agencies face in trying to serve Tasha and others like her.

Action: *The President should issue a directive and propose legislation to reconstitute the Federal Coordinating Council for Science, Engineering, and Technology as the National Science and Technology Council, giving it a broader role in setting science and technology policy.[17]*

Progress in science and technology is a key ingredient of national economic success. President Clinton's *A Vision of Change for America*, released in February, cites studies showing that "investments in research and development (R&D) tend to be the strongest and most consistent positive influence on productivity growth."[18] In an increasingly competitive world economy, the American people need the best possible return on federal R&D investments.

The Federal Coordinating Council for Science, Engineering, and Technology (FCCSET) is a White House-managed team that helps set policy for technology development. With representatives from more than a dozen agencies, it develops interagency projects, such as biotechnology research and the high-performance computing initiative. Unfortunately, FCCSET lacks the teeth to set priorities, direct policy, and participate fully in the budget process. It can't compel agencies to participate in its projects, nor can it tell agencies how to spend funds. Its six funded projects will account for just 16 percent of Washington's $76 billion R & D budget in 1994. At a time of declining federal resources, experts in business, academia, and government recognize the need for one-stop shopping for science and technology policy.

A new National Science and Technology Council would direct science and technology policy more forcefully, and would streamline the White House's advisory apparatus by combining the functions of FCCSET, the National Space Council, and the National Critical Materials Council.

Action: *The President should issue a directive to give the Trade Promotion Coordinating Committee greater authority to control federal export promotion efforts.*[19]

Unlike most of our economic competitors, the United States has no national export strategy. Our export programs are fragmented among 19 separate organizations—including the Agriculture and Commerce Departments and the Small Business Administration. The U.S. and Foreign Commercial Service, in Commerce's International Trade Administration, is the lead agency for trade promotion overseas. But dozens of other entities—many within Commerce—also have trade promotion roles.

Our export programs provide little benefit to all but our nation's largest businesses. The economic implications of such selective assistance are serious. Exports are among our most effective job-creating tools. They create about 20,000 new jobs for every $1 billion in exports. Thousands of small and mid-sized companies make products attractive for overseas markets, but are discouraged by high transaction costs and a lack of information. According to trade experts, the United States may be the "world's biggest export underachiever."[20]

The President's directive will give the Trade Promotion Coordinating Committee (TPCC), chaired by the Commerce Secretary and including representatives from 19 departments, agencies, and executive offices, broader authority to create performance measures and set allocation criteria for the nation's export promotion programs. Working with the National Economic Council, TPCC will ensure that such programs better serve the exporting community.

Action: *The President should issue a directive to establish ecosystem management policies across the government.*[21]

"For too long, contradictory policies from feuding agencies have blocked progress, creating uncertainty, confusion, controversy, and pain throughout the region," President Clinton declared at the Forest Conference held in Portland, Oregon in April 1993. Shortly thereafter, the President announced his Forest Plan—a proactive approach to ensuring a sustainable economy and a sustainable environment through ecosystem management. We recommend extending the concept of ecosystem management across the federal government.

Although economic growth has strained our ecological systems, our government lacks a coordinated approach to ecosystem management. A host of agencies have jurisdiction over individual pieces of our natural heritage. The Bureau of Land Management oversees more than 60 percent of all public lands; the Forest Service manages our national forests and grasslands; the Fish and Wildlife Service manages our National Wildlife Refuge System; the National Park Service oversees the national parks; the Environmental Protection Agency implements laws to regulate air and water quality; the National Oceanic and Atmospheric Administration (NOAA) manages marine resources; and various other agencies run programs that affect the environment. Different agencies, with jurisdictions over the same ecosystem, do not work well together. Even within the same agency, bureaus fight one another.

At the local level, a hodge podge of government agencies control activities that affect the environment. Consider, for instance, the San Francisco Bay delta estuary. One of the most human-altered estuaries on the west coast of North or South America, it is governed by a complex array of agencies, plans, and laws. One mile of the delta may be affected by decisions of more than 400 agencies.[22]

The White House Office on Environmental Policy has convened an interagency task force of appropriate assistant secretaries to develop and implement cross-agency ecosystem management projects. The Office of Management and Budget will review the plans as part of the fiscal 1995 budget process. In 1994, the assistant secretaries will establish cross-agency teams to develop initial ecosystem management plans for implementation in fiscal year 1995. Also in 1994, the President should issue a directive that will declare sustainable ecosystem management across the federal government.

Action: *The President should create a Federal Coordinating Council for Economic Development.*[23]

The federal government has no coherent policy for regional development and community dislocation. Instead, it offers a fragmented and bureaucratic system of seven programs to assist states and localities. The major programs are the Commerce Department's Economic Development Administration, the Housing and Urban Development Department's Community Development Block Grant Program, and the Agriculture Department's Rural Development Administration and Rural Electrification Administration. The Defense Department, Tennessee Valley Authority, and Appalachian Regional Commission run smaller programs. Thus, states and communities must turn to many different agencies and programs, rather than a single coordinated system. Communities find it hard to get help, and the dispersion of effort limits overall funding.

Washington's economic and regional development activities should be reconfigured to suit its customers—states and communities. We propose a Federal Coordinating Council for Economic Development, comprising the appropriate cabinet secretaries and agency heads, to coordinate such activities and provide a central source of information for states and localities. The council will provide a unifying framework for economic and regional development efforts, develop a governmentwide strategic plan and unified budget to support the framework, prevent duplication in the various programs, and assess appropriate funding levels for the agencies involved.

Action: *Eliminate statutory restrictions on cross-agency activities that are in the public interest.*[24]

A series of legislative restrictions make it particularly difficult to pursue solutions to problems that span agency boundaries. For instance, to put together a working group on an issue that cuts across agency lines, one agency has to fund all costs for the group. Several agencies cannot combine their funds to finance collaborative efforts. Rather than discourage cross-agency operations, the federal government should encourage them. Congress should repeal the restrictions that stand in the way of cross-agency collaboration, and refrain from putting future restrictions in appropriations bills. In addition, Congress should modify the Intergovernmental Personnel Act to give cabinet members and those working for them greater authority to enter into cooperative agreements with other federal, state, and local agencies.

STEP 2: MAKING SERVICE ORGANIZATIONS COMPETE

While our federal government has long opposed private monopolies, it has deliberately created public ones. For instance, most federal managers must use monopolies to handle their printing, real estate, and support services. Originally, this approach was supposed to offer economies of scale and protect against profiteering and corruption. In an earlier time—of primitive

The Air Combat Command—Flying High With Incentives and Competition

The military: the most conservative, hierarchical and traditional branch of the government and the bureaucracy least likely to behave like a cutting-edge private company, right? Wrong.

One of Washington's most promising reinvention stories comes from the Air Combat Command. With 175,000 employees at 45 bases across the country, the ACC owns and operates all of the Air Force's combat aircraft. Says its commander, General John Michael Loh, "We manage big, but we operate small."

How? The ACC adopted overall performance standards, called quality performance measures. Each ACC unit decides for itself how to meet them. General Loh then provides lots of incentives and a healthy dose of competition.

The most powerful incentive is the chance to do creative work, General Loh told the National Performance Review's Reinventing Government Summit in Philadelphia. For instance, the Air Combat Command allows maintenance workers to fix parts that otherwise would have been discarded or returned to the depot for repair "under the thesis that our people aren't smart enough to repair parts at the local level." The

results have been astonishing. Young mechanics are taking parts from B-1s, F-15s, and F-16s—some of which cost $30,000 to $40,000—and fixing them for as little as $10. The savings are expected to reach $100 million this year. ACC managers have an incentive, too: Because they control their own operating budgets, these savings accrue to their units.

General Loh instilled competition by using benchmarking, which measures performance against the ACC standard and shows commanders exactly how their units compare to others. The ACC also compares its air wings to similar units in the Army, Navy, and Marine Corps; units in other air forces; and even the private sector. Before competition, the average F-16 refueling took 45 minutes. With competition, teams cut that time to 36 minutes, then 28.

The competition is against a standard, not a fellow ACC unit. "If you meet the standard, you win," says General Loh. "There aren't 50 percent winners and 50 percent losers. We keep the improvement up by just doing that—by just measuring. If it doesn't get measured, it doesn't get improved."

recordkeeping, less access to information, and industrial-era retail systems—it may have offered some advantages.

But not today. Economists don't agree on much, but they do concur that monopolies provide poorer service at higher prices than competitive companies. Our public monopolies have brought us higher costs, endless delays, and reduced flexibility.

Monopolies don't suffer the full costs of their inefficiency. With nowhere else to go, customers absorb them. A monopoly's managers don't even know when they are providing poor service or failing to take advantage of new, cost-cutting technologies, because they don't get signals from their customers. In contrast, competitive firms get instant feedback when customers go elsewhere. No wonder the bureaucracy defends the status quo, even when the quo has lost its status.

As for economies of scale, the realities have changed. The philosophy when these procurement systems were set up was that if the government bought in bulk, costs would be lower, and taxpayers would get the savings. But it no longer works that way.

As we discuss more fully in chapter 1, we no longer need to buy in bulk to buy cheaply. The last decade has brought more and more discount stores, which sell everything from groceries to office supplies to electronic equipment at a discount. The Vice President heard story after story from federal workers who had found equipment and supplies at discount stores—even local hardware stores—at two-thirds the price the government paid.

Not all federal operations should be forced to compete, of course. Competition between regulatory agencies is a terrible idea. (Witness the regulation of banks, which can decide to charter with the state or federal government, depending on where they can find the most lenient regulations.) Nor should policy agencies compete. In the development of policy, cooperation between different units of government is essential. Competition creates turf wars, which get in the way of creating rational policies and programs. It is in *service delivery* that

> "It is better to abolish monopolies in all cases than not to do it in any."
>
> **Thomas Jefferson**
> Letter to James Madison, 1788

competition yields results—because competition is the one force that gives public agencies *no choice* but to improve.

The Government Printing Office

Perhaps the oddest federal monopoly is the Government Printing Office.

In 1846, Congress established a Joint Committee on Printing (JCP) to promote efficiency and protect agencies from profiteering and abuse by commercial printers. The JCP sets standards for all agency activities—including printing, photocopying, and color and paper quality. When the Naval Academy wants to use parchment paper for graduation certificates, for instance, the JCP must approve the decision.

The JCP also supervises the Government Printing Office, the mandatory source of most government printing—a whopping $1 billion a year. Along with printing federal publications, the GPO must approve all privately contracted government printing jobs. This even includes printing orders less than $1,000—of which there were 270,000 in 1992. Simply for processing orders to private companies, GPO charges 6 to 9 percent.

Such oversight doesn't work in an age of computers and advanced telecommunications. Desktop publishing has replaced the traditional cutting and pasting with computer graphics and automated design. In private business, in-house printing flourishes. Small printing companies specialize in strategic market niches.

The "government look"

Here's a sad story about the Government Printing Office, multiple signatures, and $20,000 of wasted taxpayer money.

Vice President Gore heard it from an employee at the Transportation Department's National Highway Traffic Safety Administration, which promotes highway safety. Hoping to convey safety messages to young drivers, her office tries to make its materials "slick"—to compete with sophisticated advertising aimed at that audience. Sound simple? Read on.

After the agency decides what it wants, it goes through multiple approvals at the GPO and the Department of Transportation. In the process, the material can change substantially. Orders often turn out far differently than NHTSA wanted. But under the GPO's policy, agencies must accept any printing order that the GPO deems "usable."

"I can cite one example where more than $20,000 has been spent and we still do not have the product that we originally requested," the employee explained, "because GPO decided on its own that it did not have a `government' look. We were not attempting to produce a government look. We were trying to produce something that the general public would like to use."

Action: *Eliminate the Government Printing Office's monopoly.*[25]

For all executive branch printing, Congress should end the JCP's oversight role. Congressional control of executive branch printing may have made sense in the 1840s, when printing was in its infancy, the government was tiny, there was no civil service, and corruption flourished. But it makes much less sense today. We want to encourage competition between GPO, private companies, and agencies' in-house publishing operations. If GPO can compete, it will win contracts. If it can't, government will print for less, and taxpayers will benefit.

The General Services Administration

Among government's more cumbersome bureaucracies is the General Services Administration (GSA), which runs a host of federal support services—from acquiring and managing more than 270 million square feet of office space to brokering office furniture and supplies to disposing of the government's car and truck fleets.

With its monopoly, GSA can pass whatever costs it wants on to tenants and customers. Often it rents the cheapest space it can find, then orders federal agencies to occupy it—regardless of location or quality. (Occasionally an agency with enough clout refuses, and GSA ends up paying to rent empty space.) This is not all GSA's fault. Frequently, the agency is hemmed in by federal budget and personnel rules. GSA admits that many of its customers are unhappy. It has already permitted some agencies to make their own real estate deals. We propose to open that door farther.

Action: *The President should end GSA's real estate monopoly and make the agency compete for business. GSA will seek legislation, revise regulations, and transfer authority to its customers, empowering them to choose among competing real estate management enterprises, including those in the private sector.[26]*

Specifically, GSA will create one or more property enterprises, with separate budgets. The enterprises will compete with private companies—real estate developers and rental firms—to provide and manage space for federal agencies. Agencies, in turn, will lease general purpose space and procure, at the lowest cost, real property services—acquisition, design, management, and construction. Such competition should lower costs for federal office space.

All other federal agencies with real estate holdings, including the Defense and Veterans Affairs Departments, will adopt similarly competitive approaches.

Competition in Support Services

Every federal agency needs "support services"—accounting, property management, payroll processing, legal advice, and so on. Currently, most managers have little choice about where to get them; they must use what's available in-house. But no manager should be confined to an agency monopoly. Nor should agencies provide services in-house unless the services can compete with those of other agencies and private companies.

Over the past decade, a few federal entrepreneurs have created support service enterprises, which offer their expertise to other agencies for a fee. Consider the Center for Applied Financial Management, in the Treasury Department's Financial Management Service. A few years ago, Treasury officials realized that many agencies reporting to their central accounting system

Dialing for Dollars: How Competition Cut the Federal Phone Bill

In the mid 1980s, a long-distance call on the federal system, which the General Services Administration manages, cost 30 to 40 cents a minute, the "special government rate." AT&T's regular commercial customers normally paid 20 cents a minute. The Defense Department, citing GSA's rates, would not use the government-wide system.

Spurred by complaints about high costs and the loss of customers, GSA put the government's contract up for bid among long-distance phone companies. It offered 60 percent of the business to the winner, 40 percent to the runner up.

Today, the government pays 8 cents a minute for long-distance calls. More agencies—including the Defense Department—are using the system. And taxpayers are saving a bundle.

had problems meeting the Treasury's reporting standards. Rather than send nasty letters, they decided to offer help.

The Treasury established a consulting business. The center includes a small group of people who offer training, technical assistance, and even a system for accounting programs so that agencies need not own the software. The center markets its services to government agencies, aggressively and successfully, competing with accounting and consulting firms for agency business and dollars. Its clients include the Small Business Administration and the Nuclear Regulatory Commission. Already, the center's work has reduced the errors in reports submitted to the Treasury and reduced agencies' accounting costs. Opened 2 years ago, the center plans to be profitable by 1995; if not, the Treasury will close it.

Action: *The administration should encourage operations of one agency to compete for work in other agencies.*[27]

We want to expand the approach exemplified by Treasury's Center for Applied Financial Management throughout government. Just as in business, competition is the surest way to cut costs and improve customer service.

Competing with the Private Sector

Forcing government's internal service bureaus to compete to please their customers is one strategy. Forcing government's external service organizations to do the same is another. In a time of scarce public resources, we can no longer afford so many service monopolies. Many federal organizations should begin to compete with private companies. Consider the National Oceanic and Atmospheric Administration.

Action: *The National Oceanic and Atmospheric Administration (NOAA) will experiment with a program of public-private competition to help fulfill its mission.*[28]

NOAA, a part of the Commerce Department, maintains a fleet of ships to support its research on oceans and marine life and its nautical charting. But its fleet is reaching the end of its projected life expectancy. And even with the fleet, NOAA has consistently fallen far short of the 5,000 days at sea that it claims to need each year to fulfill its mission. NOAA faces a basic question—whether to undertake a total fleet replacement and modernization plan, estimated to cost more than $1.6 billion in the next 15 years, or charter some privately owned ships.

The experience of the U.S. Army Corps of Engineers, which contracts out 30 to 40 percent of its ocean floor charting to private firms, shows that the private sector can and will do this kind of work. Competition among private companies for these services also might reduce NOAA's costs.

Action: *The Defense Department will implement a comprehensive program of contracting non-core functions competitively.*[29]

The Defense Department is another agency in which necessity is becoming the mother of invention. Facing a swiftly falling budget, the department literally can't afford to do things in its usual way—especially when private firms can perform DOD's non-core functions better, cheaper, and faster. Functions such as command, deployment, or rotation of troops cannot be contracted, of course. But data processing, billing, payroll, and the like certainly can.

Private firms—including many defense contractors—contract out such functions. General Dynamics, for instance, has contracted with Computer Services Corporation to provide all its information technology functions, data center operations, and networking. But at the Pentagon, a bias against out-sourcing remains strong. Only a commitment by senior leaders will overcome that bias.

In addition to the cultural barriers at the Pentagon, numerous statutory roadblocks exist. In section 312 of the fiscal year 1993 DOD Authorization Act, for example, Congress stopped DOD from shifting any more in-house work to contractors. Another law requires agencies to obtain their construction and design services from the Army Corps of Engineers or Naval Facilities Engineering Command. The administration should draft legislation to remove both of these roadblocks. It will also make contracting easier by rescinding its orders on the performance of commercial activities and issuing a new order, to establish a policy supporting the acquisition of goods and services in the most economical manner possible. OMB will review Circular A-76, which governs contracting out, for potential changes that would simplify the contracting process and increase the flexibility of managers.

Action: *Amend the Job Training Partnership Act to authorize public and private competition for the operation of Job Corps Civilian Conservation Centers.*[30]

The Labor Department's Employment and Training Administration (ETA) supervises 108 Job Corps Centers, which provide training and work experience to poor youth. The ETA contracts with for-profit and non-profit corporations to operate 78 of the centers. The department has long sought to contract out the other 30, now run by the Agriculture and Interior Departments as Civilian Conservation Centers. But Congress under the Job Training Partnership Act, has passed legislation barring such action.

Because they are insulated from competition, CCC managers have few incentives to cut costs and boost quality. For the past 5 years, average per-trainee costs at a CCC have run about $2,000 higher than at centers run by contractors. Competition would force the Interior and Agriculture Departments to operate the rural centers more efficiently—or risk losing their operations to private competitors.

Truth in Budgeting

If federal organizations are to compete for their customers, they must do so on a level playing field. That means they must include their full costs in the price they charge customers. Businesses do this, but federal agencies hide many costs in overhead, which is paid by a central office. Things like rent, utilities, staff support, and the retirement benefits of employees are often assigned to the overall agency rather than the unit that incurred them. In this way, governmental accounting typically understates the true cost of any service.

With a new accounting system that recognizes full costs—and assigns rent, utilities, staff support, retirement benefits, and all other costs to the unit that actually incurs them—we can determine the true costs of what government produces. At that point, we can compare costs across agencies, make agencies compete on a level playing field, and decide whether we are getting what we pay for.

Action: *By the end of 1994, the Federal Accounting Standards Advisory Board will issue a set of cost accounting standards for all federal activities. These standards will provide a method for identifying the true unit cost of all government activities.*[31]

Some government agencies have already moved in this direction. Others have gone even further. The Defense Department is experimenting with what it calls a Unit Cost Budget. It calculates the costs of delivering a unit of service, then budgets for the desired service levels.

The Defense Logistics Agency (DLA) began this experiment, hoping to ease pressures to contract out its supply depots to private companies. DLA examined the cost of receiving and delivering shipments, then attached a dollar figure to each item received and another to each item delivered. All money was then appropriated according to the number of items shipped or received. Line items disappeared, incentives grew. The more boxes a depot shipped or received, the more money that depot brought in. For the first time, DLA could calculate its true costs, compare those of various installations, and pinpoint problems. This approach, which enables managers to set productivity targets, is now spreading to other military installations.

STEP 3: CREATING MARKET DYNAMICS

Not all public activities should be subject to competition, as noted above. In some cases, even service delivery operations are better off as monopolies. In the private sector, we call these utilities and regulate them to protect the consumer. They are run in a businesslike fashion, and they respond to the market. (For instance, they have stockholders and boards, and they can borrow on the capital markets.) They simply don't face competition.

Many governments, including our federal government, do something very similar. They create government-owned corporations to undertake specific tasks. The Postal Service and Tennessee Valley Authority are two examples. Such corporations are free from many restrictions and much of the red tape facing public agencies, but most of them remain monopolies—or, as with the Postal Service, partial monopolies.

At other times governments subject public organizations to market dynamics, stimulate the creation of private enterprises, or spin off public enterprises to the private sector. To get the best value for the taxpayer's dollar, the federal government needs to use these options more often.

Consider the National Technical Information Service (NTIS), a once-failing agency in the Commerce Department that turned itself around in a brief year's time. Established to disseminate federally funded scientific and technical information, NTIS was, until recently, not meeting its mission. The agency, which receives no congressional appropriations, was suffering serious financial problems, selling fewer documents each year to its mostly private sector customers, and charging higher and higher prices on those it did sell.

Commerce—not surprisingly—considered abolishing the agency. A year earlier, the department's inspector general had concluded that NTIS's reported earnings of $3.7 million were vastly overstated, that it suffered $674,000 in additional operating losses in 1989, and that its procedures in handling such losses and cash shortfalls violated government accounting principles and standards.

Commerce instead decided to turn the agency around. The effort worked. NTIS's revenues and sales are both up. Why? Because the agency was forced to respond to its customers' unhappiness. NTIS reduced the turnaround time on its orders, cut complaints about incorrect orders, and dramatically slashed the percentage of unanswered phone calls. Consequently, most business customers who turned away in the 1980s have returned. NTIS's turnaround shows what can happen when public organizations face the pressure of customer demands.[32]

Other agencies may require a structural change to enhance their customer service. Because it's run as a public agency, for instance, the Federal Aviation Administration's air traffic control (ATC) system is constantly hamstrung by budget, personnel, and procurement restrictions. To ensure the safety of those who fly, the FAA must frequently modernize air traffic control technology. But this has been virtually impossible, because the FAA's money comes in annual appropriations. How can the FAA maintain a massive, state-of-the-art, nationwide computer system when it doesn't know what its appropriation for next year or the years beyond will be?

As a result, the 10-year National Airspace Plan, begun in 1981, is now 10 years behind schedule and 32 percent over budget. Federal personnel rules aggravate the problems: The FAA has trouble attracting experienced controllers to high-cost cities. With no recent expansion, the system lacks the capacity to handle all air travel demands. Consequently, airlines lose about $2 billion annually in costs for additional personnel, equipment, and excess fuel. Passengers lose an estimated $1 billion annually in delays.

America needs one seamless air traffic control system from coast to coast. It should be run in a businesslike fashion—able to borrow on the capital markets, to do long-term financial planning, to buy equipment it needs when it needs it, and to hire and fire in reasonable fashion. The solution is a government-owned corporation.

Action: *Restructure the nation's air traffic control system into a corporation.*[33]

"There is an overwhelming consensus in the aviation community that the ATC system requires fundamental change if aviation's positive contribution to trade and tourism is to be sustained," one study concluded earlier this year.[34]

The ATC's problems can't be fixed without a major reorganization. Under its current structure, the system is subject to federal budget, procurement, and personnel rules designed to prevent mismanagement and the misuse of funds. The rules, however, prevent the system from reacting quickly to events, such as buying the most up-to-date technology. In its recent report, *Change, Challenge, and Competition,* the National Commission to Ensure a Strong Competitive Airline Industry, chaired by former Virginia Governor Gerald Baliles, recommended the creation of an independent federal corporate entity within the Transportation Department. We agree.

We should restructure the ATC into a government-owned corporation, supported by user fees and governed by a board of directors that represents the system's customers. As customer use rises, so will revenues, providing the funds needed to answer rising customer demands and finance new technologies to improve safety. Relieved of its operational role, the FAA would focus on regulating safety. With better, safer service, we all would benefit. This approach has already worked in Great Britain, New Zealand, and other countries.

Action: *The General Services Administration will create a Real Property Asset Management Enterprise, separating GSA's responsibility for setting policy on federally owned real estate from that of providing and managing office space.*[35]

In asset management, too, government could take a few lessons from business. We must begin to manage assets based on their rates of return. A good place to start is in the General Services Administration.

The federal government owns assets—land, buildings, equipment—that are enormous in number and value. But it manages them poorly. Like several other agencies, GSA wears two hats: with one, it must provide office space to federal agencies. With the other, it serves as manager and trustee of huge real estate holdings for American taxpayers. It cannot do both—at least not well. Should it maximize returns for taxpayers by selling a valuable asset? Or, as the office space provider, should it require an agency to occupy one of its own buildings when less expensive leased space is available?

GSA will create a Real Property Asset Management Enterprise, solely responsible for managing federally owned real estate to optimize the rate of return for taxpayers, while competing with the private sector and better serving tenants' needs.

Action: *The Department of Housing and Urban Development will turn over management of its "market rate" rental properties and mortgage loans to the private sector.*[36]

The Department of Housing and Urban Development (HUD) has a growing workload of problem multi-family loans and foreclosed properties. In addition, restrictive rules and outdated practices hamper its management of these assets. Rather than more staff, HUD needs a new approach.

HUD, which oversees the Federal Housing Administration, owns many loans and properties it acquired from the FHA when owners defaulted on their loans.

These "market-rate" assets—which were never set aside for low-income people—have fewer restrictions on disposal than most HUD-subsidized properties. But in trying to sell the assets, HUD still faces a variety of legal and political pressures. If the department entered into limited partnerships with real estate firms, it could retain most profits from any sales and let a private business entity perform the sales in the most economically beneficial way.

STEP 4: USING MARKET MECHANISMS TO SOLVE PROBLEMS

Government cannot create a program for every problem facing the nation. It cannot simply raise taxes and spend more money. We need more than government programs to solve our problems. We need *governance*.

Governance means setting priorities, then using the federal government's immense power to steer what happens in the private sector. Governance can take many forms: setting regulations, providing financial incentives, or ensuring that consumers have the information they need to drive the market.

When the Roosevelt administration made home ownership a national priority, the government didn't build millions of homes or distribute money so families could buy them. Instead, the Federal Housing Administration helped to create a new kind of mortgage loan. Rather than put down 50 percent, buyers could put down just 20 percent; rather than repay mortgages in 5 years, borrowers could stretch the payments over 30 years. The government also helped to create a secondary market for mortgages, helping even more Americans buy homes.

As we reinvent the federal government, we, too, must rely more on market incentives and less on new programs.

Worker Safety and Health

Today, 2,400 inspectors from the Occupational Safety and Health Administration (OSHA) and approved state programs try to ensure the safety and health of 93 million workers at 6.2 million worksites. The system doesn't work well enough. There are only enough inspectors to visit even the most hazardous workplace once every several years. And OSHA has the personnel to follow up on only 3 percent of its inspections.

Action: *The Secretary of Labor will issue new regulations for worksite safety and health, relying on private inspection companies or non-management employees.*[37]

Government should assume a more appropriate and effective role: setting standards and imposing penalties on workplaces that don't comply. In this way, OSHA could ensure that all workplaces are regularly inspected, without hiring thousands of new employees. It would use the same basic technique the federal government uses to force companies to keep honest financial books: setting standards and requiring periodic certification of the books by expert financial auditors. No army of federal auditors descends upon American businesses to audit their books; the government forces them to have the job done themselves. In the same way, no army of OSHA inspectors need descend upon corporate America. The health and safety of American workers could be vastly improved—without bankrupting the federal treasury.

The Labor Secretary already is authorized to require employers to conduct certified self-inspections. OSHA should give employers two options with which to do so: They could hire third parties, such as private inspection companies; or they could authorize non-management employees, after training and certification, to conduct inspections. In either case, OSHA would set inspection and reporting standards and conduct random reviews, audits, and inspections to ensure quality.

Within a year or two of issuing the new regulations, OSHA should establish a sliding scale of incentives designed to encourage workplaces to comply. Worksites with good health, safety, and compliance records would be allowed to report less frequently to the Labor Department, to undergo fewer audits, and to submit less paperwork. OSHA could also impose higher fines for employers whose health and safety records worsened or did not improve.

Environmental Protection

As governments across the globe have begun to explore better ways to protect the environment, they have discovered that market mechanisms—fees on pollution, pollution trading systems, and deposit-rebate systems—can be effective alternatives to regulation. But while the idea of "making the polluter pay" is widely accepted in this country, our governments have not widely applied it. Many federal, state, and local regulations rely on an earlier approach to environmental control: stipulating treatment, not outcomes. Their wholesale shift to a new approach will take time.

Action: *Encourage market-based approaches to reduce pollution.*[38]

Many federal agencies, lawmakers, and environmental groups endorse using market-based incentives to meet environmental goals. We propose that both EPA and Congress use administrative and legislative measures—for example, the Clean Water Act—to promote market mechanisms to stop pollution.

One route is allowing polluters to "trade" pollution rights. This would reward companies that not only meet legal requirements–but go the extra mile to reduce

pollution by more than the law requires.

Rather than dictating exactly which technologies industry should use to reduce pollution, the government would set standards and let the market handle the details. The government could also assess fees based on the amount and nature of pollution emissions or discharges. Fees could reflect the quality, toxicity, and other adverse characteristics of pollutants.

The federal government has used this approach before. In the 1970s, the Environmental Protection Agency (EPA) distributed credits to companies that cut air pollution and let them trade credits between different sources of their own pollution or sell them to other companies located nearby. In the 1980s, the EPA used a similar approach as it forced industry to remove lead from gasoline. Both efforts were successful: industry met its targets, while spending billions of dollars less than otherwise would have been required. Then, as part of the 1990 Clean Air Act, the President and Congress agreed to give credits to coal-burning electric power plants for their allowable emissions of sulfur dioxide, to cut down on acid rain. Power plants that cut their emissions below a certain level can sell unused credits to other plants. Experts estimate that this will cut the cost of reducing sulfur dioxide emissions by several billion dollars a year.[39]

Public Housing

For two decades, public housing was a success. But by the 1970s, it had come to symbolize everything wrong with the "liberal" approach to social problems. Inflexible federal standards, an overly centralized administrative structure, and local political pressures combined to produce cookie-cutter high-rise projects in our worst urban areas. Over time, many projects degenerated into hopeless concentrations of welfare families beset by violence and crime.

We spend $13 billion a year on public housing, but we create few incentives for better management. In local housing agencies, managers are hamstrung by endless federal regulations that offer little flexibility. Any savings they generate are simply returned to the government.

Tenants enjoy even less flexibility. With housing subsidies attached to buildings, not people, the program's clients have no choice about where to live. They, therefore, have absolutely no leverage—as customers—over the managers.

Action: *Authorize the Department of Housing and Urban Development to create demonstration projects that free managers from regulations and give tenants new market powers, such as freedom of choice to move out of old public housing buildings.[40]*

We want to let public housing authorities, through not-for-profit subsidiaries, compete for new construction and modernization funds that they would use to create market-rate housing. The managers would manage this new housing free of most regulations, provided they met performance standards set by HUD. They would rent to a mix of publicly subsidized and market-rate tenants. The rents of unsubsidized tenants would help to finance the subsidies of assisted tenants.

With portable subsidies, publicly assisted tenants could look for housing wherever they could find it. Rather than dependent beneficiaries, forced to live where the government says, they would become "paying customers," able to choose where to live. Thus, public housing managers would no longer have guaranteed tenants in their buildings; they would have to compete for them.

Conclusion

We know from experience that monopolies do not serve customers well. It is an odd fact of American life that we attack monopolies harshly when they are businesses, but embrace them warmly when they are public institutions. In recent years, as fiscal pressures have forced governments at all levels to streamline their operations, this attitude has begun to break down. Governments have begun to contract services competitively; school districts have begun to give their customers a choice; public managers have begun to ask their customers what they want.

This trend will not be reversed. The quality revolution sweeping through American businesses—and now penetrating the public sector—has brought the issue of customer service front and center. Some federal agencies have already begun to respond: the IRS, the Social Security Administration, and others. But there is much, much more to be done. By creating competition between public organizations, contracting services out to private organizations, listening to our customers, and embracing market incentives wherever appropriate, we can transform the quality of services delivered to the American people.

In our democratic form of government, we have long sought to give people a voice. As we reinvent government, it is time we also gave them a choice.

Chapter 3

EMPOWERING EMPLOYEES TO GET RESULTS

Take two managers and give to each the same number of laborers and let those laborers be equal in all respects. Let both managers rise equally early, go equally late to rest, be equally active, sober, and industrious, and yet, in the course of the year, one of them, without pushing the hands that are under him more than the other, shall have performed infinitely more work.

George Washington

When Nature has work to be done, she creates a genius to do it.

Ralph Waldo Emerson

Two hundred years ago, George Washington recognized the common sense in hiring and promoting productive managers—and taking authority away from unproductive ones. One hundred years ago, Emerson observed that we all share a common genius, ignited simply by the work at hand. These American originals defined the basic ingredients of a healthy, productive work environment: managers who innovate and motivate, and workers who are free to improvise and make decisions.

Today, our federal government's executive branch includes 14 cabinet departments, 135 agencies and hundreds of boards and commissions. These entities employ more than 2.1 million civilians (not counting the Postal Service), and 1.9 million members of the military, spend $1.5 trillion a year, and, directly or indirectly, account for one third of our national economy[1]. Their tasks are both massive and difficult. As the National

Academy of Public Administration wrote not long ago, "The federal government now manages ... some of the most important and complex enterprises in the world."[2] But it does not manage them well.

Admittedly, "management" is a fuzzy concept, hard to recognize or define. But poor management has real consequences. Money is wasted. Programs don't work. People aren't helped. That's what taxpayers and customers see.

Inside government, bad management stifles the morale of workers. The "system" kills initiative. As Vice President Gore, responding to the concerns of Transportation Department employees, put it:

One of the problems with a centralized bureaucracy is that people get placed in these rigid categories, regulations bind them, procedures bind them, the organizational chart binds them to the old ways of the past...The message over time to...employees becomes: Don't try to do something new. Don't try to change established procedures. Don't try to adapt to the new circumstances your office or agency confronts. Because you're going to get in trouble if you try to do things differently."[3]

Cutting red tape, organizing services around customers, and creating competition will start to generate an environment that rewards success. Now, we must encourage those within government to change their ways. We must create a culture of public entrepreneurship.

*O*ur *long-term goal is to change the very culture of the federal government... A government that puts people first, puts its employees first, too. It empowers them, freeing them from mind-numbing rules and regulations. It delegates authority and responsibility. And it provides for them a clear sense of mission.*

Vice President Al Gore
Speech to National Performance Review members
May 24, 1993

But changing culture is a lot harder than changing rules and regulations. An attitude of powerlessness and complacency pervades the federal workplace. As one veteran of many government reform initiatives observed, "Changing government is a bit like moving the town cemetery. It's much harder to deal with the feelings it arouses than with the relocation itself."

The Quality Imperative

Of course, many thought that turning General Motors around would be impossible. If you talked to their employees, the same undoubtedly was true of General

Electric, Motorola, Harley-Davidson, and scores of leading corporations before they embraced a new management philosophy. In the 1970s and 1980s, as technology began to revolutionize everything and global competitors began to take away market share, firms that had grown fat and happy had to face the facts: This wasn't the 1950s anymore.

These firms quickly discovered that economists can be wrong: *More* isn't always better: *better* is better. One by one, they began to pursue a new goal—*quality*—and to reorganize their entire businesses around it.

The quality imperative is simple: *Do everything smarter, better, faster, cheaper.* It is not simple, however, to obey. It means dismantling the old ways of doing business. The same tired command hierarchies that continue to bind government are being scrapped daily by companies on the rise. In their place, firms seek new ways to manage and organize work that develop and use the full talents of every employee. They want everyone to contribute to the bottom line— that is, to produce goods and services that match customer needs at the lowest cost and fastest delivery time.

The quality movement has spawned many proven methods and mantras, each with its loyal fans: management by results; total quality management; high-performance organization; business process reengineering. But the quest for quality—in performance, product, and service—unifies them all.

Government has recognized the quality imperative. In 1987, the U.S. Department of Commerce instituted the Malcolm Baldrige National Quality Award. Now the object of fierce competition, it recognizes private firms that achieve excellence by pursuing quality management. In 1988, the Federal Quality Institute began awarding the Presidential Award for Quality to federal agencies that do the same. The Presidential Award criteria, modeled on Baldrige, set new standards for federal government performance. The President should encourage all department and agency heads to manage with these criteria in mind.

Changing the Culture: Power and Accountability

Companies do not achieve high quality simply by announcing it. Nor can they get to quality by hiring the services of the roving bands of consultants who promise to turn businesses around overnight. They do it by turning their entire management systems upside down—shedding the power to make decisions from the sedimentary layers of management and giving it to the people on the ground who do the work. This rewrites the relationship between managers and the managed. The bright line that separates the two vanishes as everyone is given greater authority over how to get their job done.

But with greater authority comes greater responsibility. People must be accountable for the results they achieve when they exercise authority. Of course, we can only hold people accountable if they know what is expected of them. The powerless know

The Federal Quality Imperative

The Presidential Quality Award sets forth seven principles to identify excellent government agencies:

- *Leadership:* Are your top leaders and managers personally committed to creating and sustaining your organization's vision and customer focus? Does your effort extend to the management system, labor relations, external partnerships, and the fulfillment of public responsibilities?

- *Information and Analysis:* Do your data, information, and analysis systems help you improve customer satisfaction, products, services, and processes?

- *Strategic Quality Planning:* Do you have short-term and long-term plans that address customer requirements; the capabilities necessary to meet key requirements or technological opportunities; the capacities of external suppliers; and changing work processes to improve performance, productivity improvement, and waste reduction?

- *Human Resource Development and Management:* Is your agency's entire workforce enabled to develop its full potential and to pursue performance goals? Are you building and maintaining an environment for workforce excellence that increases worker involvement, education and training, employee performance and recognition systems, and employee well-being and satisfaction?

- *Management of Process Quality:* Does your agency systematically and continually improve quality and performance? Is every work unit redesigning its process to improve quality? Are internal and external customer-supplier relationships managed better?

- *Quality and Operational Results:* Are you measuring and continuously improving the trends and quality of your products and services, your business processes and support services, and the goods and services of your suppliers? Are you comparing your data against competitors and world-class standards?

- *Customer Focus and Satisfaction:* Do you know what your customers need? Do you relate well to your customers? Do you have a method to determine customer satisfaction?

they are expected only to obey the rules. But with many rules swept away, what is expected from the empowered?

The answer is *results*. Results measured as the customer would—by better and more efficiently delivered services. If the staff in

> Our bedrock premise is that ineffective government is not the fault of people in it. Our government is full of well-intentioned, hard-working, intelligent people—managers and staff. We intend to let our workers pursue excellence.
>
> **Vice President Al Gore**
> Reinventing Government Summit
> Philadelphia, June 25, 1993

an agency field office are given greater voice over how their workplace and their work are organized, then the customer deserves to spend less time waiting in line, to receive a prompt answer—and everything else we expect from a responsive government.

So how do we change culture? The answer is as broad as the system that now holds us hostage. Part of it, outlined in chapter 1, lies in liberating agencies from the cumbersome burden of over-regulation and central control. Part of it, detailed in chapter 2, hinges on creating new incentives to accomplish more through competition and customer choice. And part of it depends on shifting the locus of control: empowering employees to use their judgment; supporting them with the tools and training they need; and holding them

accountable for producing results. Six steps, described in this chapter, will start us down that road:

First, we must give decisionmaking power to those who do the work, pruning layer upon layer of managerial overgrowth.

Second, we must hold every organization and individual accountable for clearly understood, feasible outcomes. Accountability for results will replace "command and control" as the way we manage government.

Third, we must give federal employees better tools for the job—the training to handle their own work and to make decisions cooperatively, good information, and the skills to take advantage of modern computer and telecommunications technologies.

Fourth, we must make federal offices a better place to work. Flexibility must extend not only to the definition of job tasks but also to those workplace rules and conditions that still convey the message that workers aren't trusted.

Fifth, labor and management must forge a new partnership. Government must learn a lesson from business: Change will never happen unless unions and employers work together.

Sixth, we must offer top-down support for bottom-up decisionmaking. Large private corporations that have answered the call for quality have succeeded only with the full backing of top management. Chief executive officers—from the White House to agency heads—must ensure that everyone understands that power will never flow through the old channels again. That's how GE did it; that's how we must do it as well.

STEP 1: DECENTRALIZING DECISIONMAKING POWER

To people working in any large organization—public or private—"headquarters" can be a dreaded word. It's where cumbersome rules and regulations are created and good ideas are buried. Headquarters never understands problems, never listens to employees. When the Office of Personnel Management (OPM) surveyed federal employees, fewer than half expressed any confidence in supervisors two layers above them—or any confidence at all in their organization's overall structure.[4]

Everyone knows the truth: Management too often is happily unaware of what occurs at the front desk or in the field. In fact, it's the people who work closest to problems who know the most about solving them. As one federal employee asked Vice President Gore, "If *we* can't tell what we're doing right and wrong, who better can?"

The Social Security Administration's Atlanta field office has shown the wisdom of empowering workers to fulfill their mission. Since 1990, disability benefit claims have risen 40 percent, keeping folks in the Atlanta office busy. So workers created a reinvention team. They quickly realized that if they asked customers to bring along medical records when filing claims, workers could reduce the time they spent contacting doctors and requesting the records. That idea alone saved 60 days on the average claim. Even better, it saved taxpayers $351,000 in 1993, and will save half a million dollars in 1994. The same workers also found a better, cheaper way to process disability claims in cases reviewed by administrative law judges. Instead of asking judges to send them written decisions, they created a system for judges to send decisions electronically. It's quicker, and it eliminates paperwork, too.[5]

Now here's the other side of the coin. A *Denver Post* reporter recently uncovered this bureaucracy-shaking news: It takes 43 people to change a light bulb.

An internal memo written by a manager at the U.S. Department of Energy {Rocky Flats} plant recommended a new safety procedure for "the replacement of a light bulb in a criticality beacon." The beacon, similar to the revolving red lamp atop a police car, warns workers of nuclear accidents. The memo said that the job should take at least 43 people over 1,087.1 hours to replace the light. It added that the same job used to take 12 workers 4.15 hours.

The memo called for a planner to meet with six others at a work-control meeting; talk with other workers who have done the job before; meet again; get signatures from five people at that work-control meeting; get the project plans approved by separate officials overseeing safety, logistics, waste management and plant scheduling; wait for a monthly criticality-beacon test; direct electricians to replace the bulb; and then test and verify the repair.[6]

I had seven teams of people each restructure our business... After the third presentation, my executive assistant...said to me, "Bill, this stuff is fabulous. In fact, we never would have thought of these things."

But you've got to trust. People don't come to work with the intent of screwing it up every day. They come here to make it better.

Bill Goins, President
Xerox Integrated Systems Operations,
Reinventing Government Summit,
June 25, 1993

This example drives the point home: Too many rules have created too many layers of supervisors and controllers who, however well-intentioned, wind up "managing" simple *tasks* into complex *processes.* They waste workers' time and squander the taxpayers' money.

Decentralizing the power to make decisions will energize government to do everything smarter, better, faster, and cheaper—if only because there will be more hands and heads on the task at the same time. Vice President Gore likens the effect of decentralization to the advent of "massive parallelism"—the technology used in the world's fastest supercomputers. Standard computers with central processors solve problems in sequence: One by one, each element of information travels back and forth from the machine's central processor. It's like running six errands on Saturday, but going home between each stop. Even at the speed of light, that takes time. In massively parallel computers, hundreds of smaller processors solve different elements of the same problem simultaneously. It's the equivalent of a team of six people each deciding to take on one of the Saturday errands.

America's best-run businesses are realizing enormous cost savings and improving the quality of their products by pushing decisions down as far as possible and eliminating unnecessary management layers. The federal government will adopt this decentralized approach as its new standard operating procedure. This technique can unearth hundreds of good ideas, eliminate employee frustration, and raise the morale and productivity of an entire organization.

If offered greater responsibility, will employees rise to the task? We are confident they will. After all, few people take up federal work for the money. Our interviews with hundreds of federal workers support what survey after survey of public service workers have found: People want challenging jobs.[7] Yet, that's exactly what our rule-bound and over-managed system too often denies them.

Roam on the Range

Ranchers, allowed to graze their cattle in Missouri's Mark Twain National Forest, regularly must move their herds to avoid over-grazing any plot of land. Until recently, ranchers had to apply at the local Forest Service office for permits to move the cattle. Typically, the local office sent them on to the regional office for approval, which, in some cases, sent them on to the national office in Washington. Approval could take up to 60 days—long enough, in a dry season, to hurt the forest, leave the cows hungry, and annoy the rancher.

Thanks to an employee suggestion, the local staffer now can settle the details of moving the herd directly with the rancher. If the rancher comes in by 10 a.m., the cattle can be on the move by noon. Ranchers are happier, cattle are fatter, the environment is better protected—all because local workers now make decisions well within their judgment.

Action: *Over the next five years, the executive branch will decentralize decisionmaking, and increase the average span of a manager's control.*[8]

Currently, the federal government averages one manager or supervisor for every seven employees.[9] Management expert Tom Peters recommends that well-performing organizations should operate in a range of 25 to 75 workers for every one supervisor.[10] One "best company" puts Peters' principle to shame: "Never have so many been managed by so few," Ritz-Carlton Vice President Patrick Mene told Vice President Gore at the Philadelphia Summit. "There's only about 12 of us back in Atlanta for 11,500 employees. And it really starts with passionate leadership."[11]

Working toward a quality government means reducing the power of headquarters vis-à-vis field operations. As our reinvented government begins to liberate agencies from over-regulation, we no longer will need 280,000 separate supervisory staff and 420,000 "systems control" staff to support them.[12] Instead, we will encourage more of our 2.1 million federal employees to become managers of their own work.

Put simply, all federal agencies will delegate, decentralize, and empower employees to make decisions. This will let front-line and front-office workers use their creative judgment as they offer service to customers and solve problems.

As part of their performance agreements with the President, cabinet secretaries and agency CEOs will set goals for increasing the span of control for every manager. (See Step 3.) The federal government should seek to double its managerial span of control in the coming years.

Some employees may view such pruning as threatening—to their jobs or their chances for promotion. It is true that the size of the federal workforce will decrease. But our goal is to make jobs meaningful and challenging. Removing a layer of oversight that adds no value to customers does more than save money: It demonstrates trust in our workers. It offers employees in dead-end or deadly dull jobs a chance to use all their abilities. It makes the federal government a better place to work— which will in turn make federal workers more productive.

As private companies have found, the key to improving service while redeploying staff and resources is thinking about the organization's staffing and operating needs from the perspective of customer needs. What does each person's task add in value to the customer? The Postal Service has developed a single criterion: It asks, "Do they touch the mail?" Where possible, other agencies should develop similar simple, easy-to-understand criteria.

Pioneering federal offices have used the full variety of quality management techniques to decentralize. Many focus on passing decisions on to the work teams that deal directly with the customer. Some have produced impressive results, both in productivity and management delayering.

The Internal Revenue Service's Hartford district office slashed the time required to process a form on "currently non-collectible" taxes from 14.6 days to 1.4 days. Then it replaced time-consuming case reviews with an automated case management system and began using the manager's time to upgrade employees' skills. Delinquent tax dollars collected rose by 22 percent. The office chose not to fill vacant management positions, investing part of its staff savings in new technology to boost productivity further. Eventually, it cut overall case processing time from 40 to 21.6 weeks.[13]

At the Robins Air Force Base, the 1926th Communications-Computer Systems Group cut its supervisory staff in half by organizing into teams.[14] An Agriculture Department personnel office that converted to self-managed work teams beefed up customer satisfaction and now uses only one manager for every 23 employees. At the Defense Logistics Agency, self-managing teams in the Defense Distribution Region Central eliminated an entire level of management, saving more than $2.5 million a year.[15] In 1990, the Airways Facilities Division of the Federal Aviation Administration maintained approximately 16,000 airspace facilities, with roughly 14,000 employees. Today its workforce is organized in self-managed teams instead of units with supervisors. They now maintain more than 26,000 facilities with only 9,000 employees.[16]

Other decentralization and delayering plans are in the works. After a successful pilot program in 11 field service sites, the Department of Veterans Affairs is recommending an agencywide effort.[17] Over the next 5 years, the Department of Housing and Urban Development (HUD) plans to convert HUD's field structure from three to two levels, eliminating the regional offices. HUD will free its five assistant secretaries to organize their own functions in the field. It will transfer many of its application and loan processing functions to private firms. While letting staff attrition dictate staff reductions—HUD promises no layoffs—HUD plans to retrain and redeploy people into more interesting jobs, with better career ladders and better access to managers. HUD believes its restructuring effort will improve customer service while saving $157.4 million in personnel and overhead costs.[18]

STEP 2: HOLDING ALL FEDERAL EMPLOYEES ACCOUNTABLE FOR RESULTS

I t's easy to understand why federal employees—including the hundreds who aired their deep frustrations to the National Performance Review—would care about empowerment. It adds new, positive dimensions to their jobs.

But why should taxpayers or social security recipients care? Taxpayers aren't interested in what rules bureaucracy follows. But they do care, deeply, about how well government serves them. They want education programs to give young people basic skills and teach them how to think, anti-poverty programs that bring the unemployed into the economic mainstream for good, anti-crime programs that keep criminals off the streets, and environmental programs that preserve clean air and water. In other words, they want programs that work.

But management in government does not judge most programs by whether they work or not. Instead, government typically measures program activity—how much it spends on them, or how many people it has assigned to staff them. Because government focuses on these "inputs" instead of real results, it tends to throw good money after bad. It pours more dollars into the old education programs even as student performance sinks. It enrolls jobless people in training programs that teach by the book, but places few graduates in well-paid jobs.

A recent management survey of the largest 103 federal agencies sketches in stark relief this lack of focus on real results. Two-thirds of the agencies reported that they had strategic plans. But only nine said they could link those plans to intended results.[19] In other words, many had planned, but few knew where they were going. That's a bit like trying to steer a ship by looking at its wake. As a result, some of our worst examples of "waste" are not rooted in corruption or incompetence, but rather in the simple lack of knowing what we are actually trying to accomplish. As one despairing federal employee told us, "Process is our most important product."

Recommendations by the National Performance Review aim to revolutionize our method of navigation. "Today," Vice President Gore told one departmental meeting, "all we measure is inputs. We don't measure outputs—and that's one of the things we're going to change throughout the federal government."

Measuring outputs is easy in principle. It means measuring how many unemployed people get jobs, not how many people look for help at local Employment Service offices. Or it means measuring how many people received their social security checks on time, not how many checks were sent out from a local office. "Outputs" are, quite simply, measures of how government

What you do thunders so loudly, I cannot hear what you say to the contrary.

Ralph Waldo Emerson

programs and policies affect their customers. The importance of pursuing the correct measures cannot be underestimated. As Craig Holt, an Oregon Department of Transportation employee who has worked with the ground-breaking Oregon Progress Board—our nation's first statewide experiment in comprehensive performance accountability—cautions: "Our focus has occurred through our *indicators*, not through our strategic plans."[20]

Implementing the Government Performance and Results Act

To its credit, Congress has begun to recognize this need. In July 1993, it passed the Government Performance and Results Act—a pivotal first step toward measuring whether federal programs are meeting their intended objectives. The act requires that at least 10 federal agencies launch 3-year pilot projects, beginning in fiscal 1994, to develop measures of progress. Each agency pilot will develop annual performance plans that specify measurable goals. They then must produce annual reports showing how they are doing on those measures. At least five pilots will also test "managerial flexibility waivers"—which exempt them from some administrative regulations—to help them perform even better. In exchange for greater flexibility, they must set higher performance targets. This is exactly the process of measured deregulation—"we agree to deregulate you if you agree to be held accountable"—that must be the basis of an empowered and accountable government.

At the beginning of fiscal 1998, after learning from the pilot programs, all federal agencies must develop 5-year strategic plans—linked, this time, to measurable outcomes. By the next year, every agency will be crafting detailed annual performance plans—that is, plans that describe what they intend to achieve, not plans that detail how many pencils they will buy or people they will hire. And they will have to report their successes and failures in meeting those

It may seem amazing to say, but like many big organizations, ours is primarily dominated by considerations of input—how much money do we spend on a program, how many people do you have on the staff, what kind of regulations and rules are going to govern it; and much less by output—does this work, is it changing people's lives for the better?

President Bill Clinton
Remarks at the signing of the Government
Performance And Results Act
August 3, 1993

goals. The Office of Management and Budget may exempt very small agencies, and those agencies that cannot easily measure their outcomes will use qualitative rather than quantitative goals and measurements. After all, any agency can, at the very least, survey their customers and report the rating they are given.

Setting goals is not something that agencies do once. It is a continual process in which goals are raised higher and higher to push agency managers and staff harder and harder to improve. As the old business adage states, "If you're standing still, you're falling behind."

That is why we strongly support the act. But agencies should not wait until fiscal 1999 to start integrating performance measurement into their operations. Nor should they limit themselves to the minimum mandates of the new law. The President, through OMB, is encouraging every federal program and agency to begin strategic planning and performance measurement, whether it is selected as a pilot or not.

If government is to become customer-oriented, then managers closest to the citizens must be empowered to act quickly. Why must every decision be signed-off on by so many people? If program managers were instead held accountable for the results they achieve, they could be given more authority to be innovative and responsive.

Senator William V. Roth, Jr.
Congressional Record, July 30, 1993

Action: *All agencies will begin developing and using measurable objectives and reporting results.*[21]

In early 1994—in time to prepare the fiscal 1996 budget—OMB will revise the budget instructions it gives agencies to incorporate performance objectives and results to the greatest extent possible. Agencies will start measuring and reporting on their past goals and performance as part of their 1996 budget requests. The OMB instructions, along with executive office policy guidance, will guide agencies as they develop full-fledged goal-setting and performance-monitoring systems for the first time.

At the outset, managers may feel unprepared to set reasonable performance targets. Some will lack any program data worth its salt on which to base any future goals or performance projections. Others, overwhelmed with "input" indicators about program staffing and spending, will find it difficult to figure out whether—or how—those measures directly relate to achieving desired outcomes. Agencies will start preparing themselves by reallocating enough resources toward performance planning and measurement over the long term.

OMB will help. Its budget analysts will be trained to provide feedback and broad oversight to help craft an effective system, and encourage agencies to improve measures that are clearly ineffective. OMB will negotiate stronger goals for agencies that set their sights too low.

Agencies will gradually build performance information into their own budget guidance and review procedures, into their strategic and operational plans, and into revised position descriptions for their budget, management, and program analysts. Nothing, however, will replace peer pressure as agencies vie for performance awards or seek public recognition for their achievements.

Action: *Clarify the objectives of federal programs.*[22]

Many agencies will be unable to set clear measurable goals until Congress simplifies their responsibilities. Programs are bound by multiple, often conflicting, legislative objectives. The complex politics of passing enabling legislation and then negotiating annual appropriations forces some programs to be all things to all people.

For example, a training program targeted at unemployed steel workers soon is required to serve unemployed farm workers, the disabled, and displaced homemakers. Originally, the program's purpose may have been to refer people to jobs. But congressional maneuvers first force it to offer them training; then to help them find transportation and daycare. All these are important activities. But, by now, the original appropriation is hopelessly inadequate, reporting requirements have multiplied geometrically along with the multiplicity of goals, and the program is not simply unmanaged—it's unmanageable. If agencies are to set measurable goals for their programs, Congress must demand less and clarify priorities more.

In the private sector, leaders do not simply drop goals on their organizations from above. Hewlett-Packard, Microsoft, Xerox, and others involve their full workforces in identifying a few goals that have top priority, and then demand smaller work teams to translate those overall goals into specific team measures. This process enables the people directly responsible for meeting the goals to help set them. It also ensures that every part of an organization aims at the same goals, and that everyone understands where they fit in. It may seem a time consuming process, but boats travel much faster when everyone is pulling their oar in the same direction.

With a new joint spirit of accountability, the executive branch plans to work with Congress to clarify program goals and objectives, and to identify programs where lack of clarity is making it difficult to get results.

Holding Top Management Accountable

When General Eisenhower took command of the Allied Expeditionary Force in World War II, he was given a mission statement that clearly delineated goals for his vast organization of more than a million and a half men and women: "You will enter the continent of Europe and, in conjunction with the other united nations, undertake operations aimed at the heart of Germany and the destruction of her armed forces."

In 1961, President Kennedy gave NASA an even clearer mission: Put a man on the moon and return him safely to earth by the end of the decade. As Vice President Al Gore told his audience at a meeting with Veterans Affairs Department employees: "There has to be a clear, shared sense of mission. There have to be clearly understood goals. There have to be common values according to which decisions are made. There has to be trust placed in the employees who actually do the work."

In Great Britain, Australia, and New Zealand, many department and agency heads are appointed for limited terms and given performance agreements. Their reappointments depend on achieving measurable outcomes. Senior officials from these countries say that these agreements have improved organizational performance more than any other aspect of their reinventing government efforts. In the United States, many local governments do much the same: In Sunnyvale, California, managers can earn bonuses of up to 10 percent if their agencies exceed performance targets.

Action: *The President should develop written performance agreements with department and agency heads.*[23]

Past efforts to institute management by objectives have collapsed under the weight of too many objectives and too much reporting. The President should craft agreements with cabinet secretaries and agency heads to focus on the administration's strategy and policy objectives. These agreements should not "micro-manage" the work of the agency heads. They should not attempt to row the boat. They should set a course.

These agreements will begin with the top 24 agency heads. In fact, Secretaries Mike Espy at the Agriculture Department and Henry Cisneros at the Department of Housing and Urban Development, as well as Roger Johnson at the General Services Administration (GSA) and Administrator J. Brian Atwood of the Agency for International Development, are already working with their top managers on agreements.

Not everyone will welcome outcome measures. People will have trouble developing them. Public employees generally don't focus on the outcomes of their work. For one thing, they've been conditioned to think about process; for another, measures aren't always easy to develop. Consequently, they tend to measure their work volume, not their results. If they are working hard, they believe they are doing all they can. Public organizations will need the several years envisioned under the Government Performance and Results Act to develop useful outcome measures and outcome reporting.

Measuring Outcomes

Outcome-based management is new in the public sector. Some U.S. cities have developed it over the past two decades; some states are beginning to; and foreign countries such as Great Britain, Australia, and New Zealand are on their way.

Sunnyvale, California, a city of 120,000 in the heart of the Silicon Valley, began the experiment 20 years ago. In each policy area, the city defines sets of "goals," "community condition indicators," "objectives," and "performance indicators." "In a normal political process, most decisionmakers never spend much time talking about the results they want from the money they spend," says City Manager Tom Lewcock. "With this system, for the first time they understand what the money is actually buying, and they can say yes or no."[24]

Sunnyvale measures performance to reward successful managers. If a program exceeds its objectives for quality and productivity, its manager can receive a bonus of up to 10 percent. This generates pressure for ever-higher productivity. The result: average annual productivity increases of four percent. From 1985 to 1990, the city's average cost of service dropped 20 percent, in inflation-adjusted dollars. According to a 1990 comparison, Sunnyvale used 35 to 45 percent fewer people to deliver more services than other cities of similar size and type.

At least a half-dozen states hope to follow in Sunnyvale's footsteps. Oregon has gone farthest. In the late 1980s, Governor Neil Goldschmidt developed long term goals, with significant citizen input. He set up the Oregon Progress Board, comprising public and private leaders, to manage the process. The board developed goals and benchmarks through 12 statewide meetings and written materials from over 200 groups and organizations. "Oregon," the board stated, "will have the best chance of achieving an attractive future if Oregonians agree clearly on where we want to go and then join together to accomplish those goals."[25]

The legislature approved the board's recommended 160 benchmarks, measuring how Oregon is faring on three general goals: exceptional individuals; outstanding quality of life; and a diverse, robust economy. Seventeen measures are deemed short-term "lead" benchmarks, related to urgent problems on which the board seeks progress within 5 years. They include reducing the teen pregnancy rates, enrolling people in vocational programs, expanding access to basic health care, and cutting worker compensation costs.

Another 13 benchmarks are listed as "key"— fundamental, enduring measures of Oregon's vitality and health. These include improving basic student skills, reducing the crime rate, and raising Oregon's per capita income as a percentage of the U.S. average.

Barbara Roberts, today's governor, has translated the broad goals and benchmarks into specific objectives for each agency. This year, for the first time, objectives were integrated into the budget—giving Oregon the first performance-based budget among the states.

Great Britain has instituted performance measurement throughout its national government. In addition, the government has begun writing 3-year performance contracts, called "Framework Agreements," with about half its agencies. These agencies are run by chief executive officers, many from the private sector, who are hired in competitive searches and then negotiate agreements specifying objectives and performance measures. If they don't reach their objectives, the CEOs are told, their agencies' services may be competitively bid after the 3 years.

Ultimately, no one can generate results without knowing how the "bottom line" is defined. Without a performance target, managers manage blindly, employees have no guidance, policymakers don't know what's working, and customers have no idea where they may be served best. If, for example, jobless people know how well graduates of local training programs fare when looking for work, they can better choose which new careers and programs offer the best prospects. Informed consumers are the strongest enforcers of accountability in government.

Action: *The administration will issue one set of Baldrige Awards for quality in the federal government.*[26]

For years, the executive branch has taken steps to recognize and support good performance. In typical fashion, however,

we have created three different award systems, each administered by a different organization. The Federal Quality Institute (FQI) administers the Presidential Award for Quality; the President's Council on Management Improvement administers the Award for Management Excellence; and the Office of Personnel Management awards the Presidential Quality and Management Improvement Awards for tangible savings to the government of more than $250,000.

The administration will issue one set of presidential awards for quality. The Baldrige Award Office of the National Institute for Standards and Technology will combine the existing awards into a new set of Baldrige Awards for public service—to go along with its private sector award. The new award will recognize agency and work unit quality initiatives and ideas, based on program performance, cost savings, innovation, and customer satisfaction.

STEP 3: GIVING FEDERAL WORKERS THE TOOLS THEY NEED TO DO THEIR JOBS

Americans today demand a more responsive, more humane government that costs less. Their expectations are neither irrational nor whimsical. Over the past 20 years, the entire way we do things, make things, even contact one another, has changed around us. Businesses have no guarantees, no captive markets. To compete, they must make things and deliver service better and faster, and get their message out sooner. No one benefits more than customers. It's no wonder these same people now turn to government and ask, "Why can't you do things better too?"

Transforming our federal government to do better will mean recasting what people do as they work. They will turn from bosses into coaches, from directors into negotiators, from employees into thinkers and doers. Government has access to the same tools that have helped business make this transformation; it's just been slower to

acquire and use them. We must change that. We must give workers the tools they need to get results—then make sure they use them.

Employee Training

After two decades of organizing for quality, business knows one thing for sure: Empowered people need new skills—to work as teams, use new computer software, interpret financial and statistical information, cooperate with and manage other people, and *adapt.* Indeed, business talks about a new breed of "knowledge worker"—people who understand that, throughout their careers, their most important task is to continue learning and applying new knowledge to the challenge at hand. Knowledgeable workers are our most important source of progress. They are, quite simply, the currency of 21st century commerce.

Business teaches us that ongoing training for every worker is essential for organizations to work well. Not surprisingly, the federal government under-spends on training and education, just as it does on most other productivity-enhancing investments. In 1989, the National Commission on the Public Service, headed by Paul Volcker, estimated that while leading private firms spend 3 to 5 percent of their budgets on training, retraining, and upgrading employee skills, the federal government spends less than one percent.[27]

And the little we do spend is not always allocated wisely. A well-promoted 4-day training seminar packaged to appeal to federal agency managers may seem like a good deal. It is not, however, always what the agency needs. The Volcker Commission concluded:

> *Federal training is suffering from an identity crisis. Agencies are not sure what they should train for (short term or long term), who should get the lion's share of resources (entry level or senior level)...and whether mid-career education is of value...Career paths are poorly designed, executive succession is accidental and unplanned, and real-time training for pressured managers is virtually non-existent. At both the career and presidential level, training is all-too-often ad hoc and self-initiated.[28]*

Perhaps most striking is the paucity of career training for people on the lowest rungs of the civil service ladder, or for people without the leg-up of university degrees. These valued employees may have the most tenure in an office. They may see and know everything. Frequently, they are indispensable, because only they know how the system works—and how to work the system. Unfortunately, their abilities are rarely rewarded, despite their desire to advance.

One staffer in the Justice Department's Civil Division alerted Vice President Gore to her quandary:

> *I'm watching the role of our legal secretaries change. Less and less of the typical secretarial duties are being performed, simply because the attorneys do a lot of their own drafting of documents... However, for a secretary to start to move into a legal assistant position... or into a paralegal role, is frowned upon... As far as training goes it's impossible... That prevents a lot of people from...moving into new jobs that are going to be of more benefit to the department...We've lost a good number of secretaries who have moved elsewhere, because they cannot go any further here.[29]*

Employees at the top rung, too, must keep learning. Managers and executives face the same hurdles in keeping up with technology as do front-line workers. Technicians must stay up to date with system advances and new techniques. The growing band of federal export and trade personnel must learn more than foreign languages—they need to master the language of negotiation as well. Indeed, employees in the Office of the U.S. Trade Representative currently receive no systematic training in negotiation skills or the cross-cultural styles and patterns they are likely to encounter in their work—a situation the office is now planning to correct.[30]

Perhaps most important, training is the key that unlocks the power of bottom-up decisionmaking. At the Reinventing Government Summit, General Electric Executive Vice President Frank Doyle detailed the GE experience: "We had to educate our entire workforce to give them the tools to become meaningfully involved in all aspects of work. Empowerment...is a disorderly and almost meaningless gesture unless people doing the actual work are given the tools and knowledge that self-direction demands."[31]

During the National Performance Review process, almost every one of the agency teams identified a specific learning need critical to their agency's quality improvement and mission. In addition, several common training concerns demand governmentwide action.

Action: *The administration will grant agencies the flexibility to finance training needs.*[32]

Leading corporations view training as a strategic resource, an *investment*. Federal managers tend to view it as a cost. So in government, worker training isn't even included in most budget estimates for new systems or programs. This is puzzling and quite short-sighted, since new workplace innovations, like advanced software, won't transform employee productivity unless those employees know how to use them. Although training may be the best and least costly way to improve worker performance, government executives view it as a "quick fix," unworthy of any planning effort.

Perceptions are changing, however. Today's management literature is full of talk about the value of on-the-job-training, computer-based instruction, expert systems, work exchange, mentors and other tools for learning. Since 1992, OPM has been steering agencies toward more comprehensive training initiatives.

We will grant agencies a substantial portion of the savings they realize from decentralizing staff and reducing operating costs (see chapter 1) to invest in worker training, performance measurement, and benchmarking.

Budget directives further complicate an agency's ability to train workers effectively, particularly when its own budget office, OMB, or Congress cut line items for employee training. Such over-specified reductions deny employees the access to skills they need to be productive, to advance in their careers, and to adapt to new technology.

Action: *The federal government will upgrade information technology training for all employees.*[33]

Every year, more and more federal workers must use computer-based information technology in their jobs. If business is any guide, our government reinvention efforts will only quicken the trend. Pen and paper exercises keep moving to the screen. Lateral files now form database records. Video- and computer-based courses make learning possible anytime, anywhere. Money no longer changes hands; it's transmitted digitally. People not only talk, they "message." A meeting of the minds can take place without the bodies present.

Other chapters discuss how we will speed the procurement process for technology and how we will deploy technology to alter what we do and how well we do it. Here, we want to stress that much of the federal workforce lacks the training and background to use advanced information technologies.

Compared to the private sector, the federal government invests few dollars and scant time in technology training.[34] Federal agencies provide insufficient incentives to motivate their workforce to seek technology training, scarce opportunities to obtain training—even when it's desired and necessary—and rarely incorporate technology training in the strategic planning process. The longer we wait, the farther behind we fall.

This foot-dragging costs the taxpayer dearly. We do things the old way, not the cheaper, more efficient way. Or we start doing things the new way, but we don't go far enough: We buy computers for our workers, but not the training to use them properly, so the software and hardware investments are wasted. We invest in new systems, and our people can't make them work.

Training should begin with top nontechnical managers, to help them focus on uses, management, planning, and acquisition of state-of-the-art information technology. By May 1994, OPM and GSA will jointly develop and administer information technology training for nontechnical managers and presidential appointees. The New York City Department of Personnel, already in the technology training business, offers a useful model of monthly half-day sessions for executives covering ten topics: strategic planning, reengineering, implementing systems, electronic mail, video conferencing, voice-enhanced technologies, geographic information systems, database management, imaging, and multi-agency complaints and inspection systems. Our effort will help every senior manager earn a certificate that signifies his or her level of technology competency. Parallel training and certification efforts will target Senior Executive Service members and information resource managers.

Anyone who has grappled with computers—from the basics of word processing to the complexity of expert systems—knows that we often learn best how to use software by finding a technology "pal": someone who knows the ins and outs of a particular software application and is willing to share that knowledge. To spread information technology training and use in the entire federal workforce, the existing Federal Information Resources Management Policy Council will help motivated agencies set up a program of collegial assistance for a wide range of technology applications. We will tap the cadre of techno-proficient individuals spread across the federal government to provide occasional on-line help or personal assistance on demand to their struggling colleagues.

Finally, starting late in 1993, new contracts for technology acquisition—or those in early stages—must include a provision for training. If agencies work together, they can cut such training costs dramatically. When Texas contracted with four statewide technology training firms to train state employees, it cut the price to $60 to $110 a day per worker for a wide range of skills. An even larger customer, the federal government should be able to land an even better bargain.

Action: *Eliminate narrow restrictions on employee training to help develop a multiskilled workforce.*[35]

The Government Employees Training Act (GETA), which authorizes agencies to manage and determine their training needs, defines training as a tool for "increasing economy and efficiency in government." The rules written behind this 1958 wording severely limit how agencies can use training today. Training too often is ad hoc and seldom linked to strategic or human resource planning. Managers generally are not able to get the information to determine the return on their training investment. Even worse, existing restrictions dictate that any training be related to an employee's official duties—thus ensuring that our Justice Department secretary does not become a paralegal. These rules keep federal employees single-skilled in a multi-skilled world.

By early 1994, OPM will draft legislation to amend GETA on three fronts. OPM will redefine the objective of federal training as the "improvement of individual and organizational performance." It will relate the use of training to achieving an agency's mission and performance goals, not to a worker's official duties. And OPM will seek to end the distinction between government and nongovernment training, giving public employees access to the best training services available, no matter who provides them.

Clarifying the purpose of training in GETA will reinforce the need to use training to improve performance and produce results. Removing the distinction between government and non-government training will deregulate the in-government training monopoly, introducing competition that will improve the quality of learning opportunities for federal employees. And linking training to an agency's mission will ease employees' efforts to become adept at all the skills they need as empowered workers. We urge Congress to join in the quality effort by passing these important amendments early in 1994.

Management Information Systems

Management isn't about guessing, it's about *knowing*. Those in positions of responsibility must have the information they need to make good decisions. Good managers have the right information at their fingertips. Poor managers don't.

Good information comes from good information systems. Management information systems have improved in lockstep with every advance in the telecommunications revolution. New management information systems are transforming government, just as they have business, in two ways. They can make government more productive—the benefit we discuss in this chapter—and let us deliver services to customers in new ways, which we take on in chapter 4. Indeed, today's systems have enabled businesses to slim down data processing staffs, while giving more employees access to more accurate data. This shows up on the bottom line. If federal decisionmakers are given the same type of financial and performance information that private managers use, it too will show up on the bottom line—and cut the cost of government.

Sheer size alone would make the federal government difficult to manage, even under the best of conditions. Unfortunately, federal employees don't work under the best of conditions. Indeed, when it comes to financial information, many are flying blind. It's not for lack of staffing: Some 120,000 workers—almost 6 percent of non-postal service civilian employees—perform budget, accounting, auditing, and financial management tasks.[36] But when OMB surveyed agency financial reporting systems last year, it found that one-third were more than a decade old, and only 6 percent were less than 2 years old. One-third failed to meet Treasury and OMB reporting standards. Two-fifths did not meet their own in-house reporting standards—meaning they did not provide the information managers wanted. And more than half simply lacked the computer power to process the data being entered.[37]

We all know the potential costs of lagging systems: They contributed to the $300 billion savings and loan bailout,[38] $47 billion in nontax delinquent debt, $3.6 billion in student loan defaults, and so on.

Fortunately, the process of updating our management information systems has begun. In 1990, Congress passed the Chief Financial Officers (CFO) Act.[39] It designated an OMB deputy director as the federal government's chief financial management officer. The Office of Federal Financial Management was charged with establishing financial management policies across the government and monitoring agency audits. The act also created chief financial officers in 23 agencies. The OMB deputy chairs a CFO Council to deal with improving financial management across government.

But we need to do more—and quickly.

Action: *The executive branch will create a coherent financial management system, clarify responsibilities, and raise the standards for financial officers.[40]*

Vastly improved financial management is critical to the overall effort to reform government. First, it will save taxpayers money. Trillions of dollars flow through the federal government in any year; even a small improvement in managing those funds could recover billions. Second, we need accurate and timely financial information if managers are to have greater authority to run federal agencies, and decisionmaking moves to the front lines. Greater responsibility requires greater accountability, or the best-intentioned reforms will only create new problems. Finally, better financial management will present a more accurate picture of the federal budget, enabling the President, Congress, and agency leaders to make better policy decisions.

By the end of 1993, OMB and Treasury will sign a formal agreement to clarify their respective policymaking and implementation roles, to eliminate regulatory confusion and overlap for their governmental customers. OMB, working with Treasury and the CFO Council, will charter a governmentwide Budget and Financial Information Steering Group to oversee the stewardship of financial planning and management data for the federal government. By spring 1994, OMB will work with the existing Joint Financial Management Improvement Program and consult with Treasury and the agencies to define exactly what constitutes an integrated budget and financial system. At the same time, working with Treasury and the CFO Council, OMB will develop a long-range strategic plan to link financial information and performance goals to the work of agency managers.

Finally, we will insist on higher qualifications for chief financial officers. After all, many federal agencies are larger than Fortune 500 companies. Americans deserve financial officers with qualifications that match those in our best companies. By March 1994, working with accounting and banking groups, the CFO Council will create a continuing education program for federal financial managers. At the same time, OMB guidelines will clarify the precise financial functions the CFO should oversee, trimming responsibilities like personnel or facilities management that lie outside the CFO's main mission.

Action: *Within 18 months the Federal Accounting Standards Advisory Board will issue a comprehensive set of credible accounting standards for the federal government.*[41]

A recent GAO audit of the Internal Revenue Service unearthed $500,000 of overpayments to vendors in just 280 transactions and a video display terminal that cost only $752 listed at $5.6 million on the IRS books. Other GAO efforts found the Army and Air Force guilty of $200 billion in accounting mistakes, NASA guilty of $500 million, and widespread recordkeeping problems across government.[42] In 1990, Congress concluded that "current financial reporting

standards of the federal government do not accurately disclose the current and probable future cost of operating and investment decisions, including the future needs for cash and other resources." In other words, if a publicly-traded corporation kept its books the way the federal government does, the Securities and Exchange Commission would close it down immediately.

It's not that we have no accounting procedures and standards. It's that we have too many, and too many of them conflict. Even worse, some budget and accounting practices obscure the amount and type of resources managers might leverage to produce savings and increase productivity.

We must agree on stricter accounting standards for the federal books. We require corporations to meet strict standards of financial management before their stocks can be publicly traded. They must fully disclose their financial condition, operating results, cash flows, long-term obligations, and contingent liabilities. Independent certified public accountants audit their accounts. But we exempt the $1.5 trillion federal government from comparable standards.

Currently, the Federal Accounting Standards Advisory Board (FASAB), established in October 1990, develops and recommends federal accounting standards for OMB, Treasury, and GAO—which together must approve them. Although we need almost a dozen sets of standards, only one has been approved using this process in more than two and a half years. We need to quicken the pace.

The administration will give the Federal Accounting Standards Advisory Board an 18-month deadline to release and get approval of all 11 sets of standards. If it fails, the administration will replace it with a new, independent board with greater powers.

Action: *The Administration should issue an Annual Accountability Report to the Citizens.*[43]

The ultimate consumer of information about the performance of federal organizations should be the American public. As agencies develop output and outcome measures, they should publish them. The customer service standards required by the President's directive on improving customer service, outlined in chapter 2, will be a first step.

A second step will be a new report card on the financial condition of the federal government. For the last 20 years, our government has issued "prototype" financial statements, but no one can assure their accuracy. Put simply, they would never pass an audit. We believe Americans deserve numbers they can trust. By 1997, we will require the Department of the Treasury to provide an audited consolidated annual report on federal finances—including tax expenditures, hidden subsidies, and hidden contingent liabilities such as trust funds and government-sponsored enterprises.[44]

The Treasury and OMB will develop a simplified version of the government's financial condition, to be published for public consumption in 1995. Rather than a detailed, unreadable financial account, it will be a straightforward description of the money spent and its effects on achieving goals. We will call this the *Annual Accountability Report to the Citizens.*

Information Technology

A few years ago in Massachusetts, a disabled veterans caseworker who worked to match veterans with available jobs took some initiative. He decided to abandon his sole reliance on the state's central office mainframe computer and take his personal laptop, loaded with readily available software, on the road. Suddenly, he was able to check a database, make a match, and print a resume all during his first contact with an employer. Quickly, he started

beating the mainframe. His state administrator took notice, and managed to squeak through a request to the Department of Labor's Veterans Employment and Training Service for grant funding and permission to reprogram dollars in the fall of 1990. Soon after, 40 Massachusetts caseworkers were working with laptops. In just one year, Massachusetts jumped from 47th in the nation for its veterans job placement rate to 23rd.

Although this story screams success, it is unfortunately the exception, not the rule. Normally, the Labor Department has to approve the purchase of something as small as a $30 modem in the field. Massachusetts got the funding only because it was the end of the fiscal year and money had to be spent.[45]

The point stands: When workers have current and flexible technology to do their jobs, they improve performance. We need to get more computers off the shelf and into the hands of federal employees.

Action: *The administration will develop a strategic plan for using information technology throughout the federal government.*[46]

Transforming the federal government is an enormous, complex undertaking that begins with leadership, not technology. Yet,

> I*n short, it's time our government adjusted to the real world, tightened its belt, managed its affairs in the context of an economy that is information-based, rapidly changing, and puts a premium on speed and function and service, not rules and regulations.*
>
> **President Bill Clinton**
> Remarks announcing the
> National Performance Review
> March 3, 1993

in helping to break down organizational boundaries and speed service delivery, information technology can be a powerful tool for reinvention. To use that tool, government employees must have a clear vision of its benefits and a commitment to its use.

Washington's attempts to integrate information technology into the business of government have produced some successes but many costly failures. Many federal executives continue to overlook information technology's strategic role in reengineering agency practices. Agency information resource management plans aren't integrated, and their managers often aren't brought into the top realm of agency decisionmaking. Modernization programs tend to degenerate into loose collections of independent systems solving unique problems. Or they simply automate, instead of improve, how we do business.

The President should expand the work of the existing Information Infrastructure Task Force to include a Government Information Technology Services Working Group. This working group will develop a strategic vision for using government information services and propose strategies to improve information resource management. Also beginning in October 1993, OMB will convene interagency teams to share information and solve common information technology problems. In addition, OMB will work with each agency to develop strategic plans and performance measures that tie technology use to the agency's mission and budget.

STEP 4: ENHANCING THE QUALITY OF WORK LIFE

When it comes to the quality of work life, as measured by employee pay, benefits, schedule flexibility, and working conditions, the federal government usually gets good marks. Uncle Sam is a family-friendly employer, offering plenty of options that help employees balance their life and work responsibilities. Flextime, part-time, leave-sharing, and unpaid family and medical leave are all available. Pilot projects in telecommuting allow some workers who travel long distances to work at locations closer to home.

The federal government would be smart to keep abreast of workplace trends. Our increasingly diverse workforce struggles to manage child care, elder care, family emergencies, and other personal commitments, while working conditions become ever more important. Recent studies suggest that our ability to recruit and retain the best employees—and motivate them to be productive—depends on our ability to create a satisfying work environment. Johnson & Johnson, for example, reported that its employees who used flextime and family leave were absent 50 percent fewer days than its regular workforce. Moreover, 71 percent of those workers using benefits said that the policies were "very important" to their decision to stay with the company, as compared to 58 percent of the employees overall.[46]

The federal government must maintain its "model employer" status and keep the workplace a humane and healthy place. It must also ensure that, as we move toward improving performance and begin to rely on every worker for valuable ideas, we create a workplace culture in which employees are trusted to do their best.

Action: *The federal government will update and expand family-friendly workplace options.*[47]

Even under current workplace policies, federal workers still encounter some problems. Many agencies do not fully advocate or implement flexible work policies. For example, only 53 percent of our employees with dependent care needs believe their agencies understand and support family issues, according to OPM. Thirty-eight percent indicated that their agencies do not provide the full range of dependent-care services available. As one example, OPM concluded that "...certain agencies may have internal barriers that make supervisors reluctant to approve employee requests to work part-time."[48]

The President should issue a directive requiring that all agencies adopt compressed/flexible time, part-time, and job-sharing work schedules. Agencies will also be asked to implement flexiplace and telecommuting policies, where appropriate. Starting next year, we will allow federal employees to use accrued sick leave to care for sick or elderly dependents or for adoptions.[49] We will also give credit for all sick leave to employees who have been separated from and then rejoin federal employment, no matter how long they were out of government service.

Congress has written into law some barriers to improving the federal workplace. It should lift them. By January 1994, OPM will submit legislation to remove limitations on dependent-care programs and give agencies more authority to craft employee-friendly programs, such as employee benefit packages. By March 1994, OPM and GSA will propose legislation to enable flexiplace and telecommuting arrangements.

Finally, we urge Congress to reauthorize the Federal Employees Leave Sharing Act which expires October 31, 1993 with a few changes to improve program operations and allow interagency transfers of annual leave. Voluntary leave enables employees with family medical emergencies, who have exhausted all their available annual leave, to receive donated annual leave from their fellow federal workers. In just the last two years, voluntary leave served more than 23,000 federal employees with more than 3,742,600 hours of donated annual leave. The dependent-care needs of more than 96 percent of federal employees are met by the leave-sharing program.[50]

One of the things we learned... is that there's a strong correlation between employee satisfaction and customer satisfaction. If your employees are unhappy and worried about the various baseline, basic needs, you know, of the quality of their work life, they won't worry about customers.

Rosetta Riley
Director of Customer Satisfaction
General Motors

Action: *The executive branch will abolish employee time sheets and time cards for the standard work week.*[51]

In a productive workplace, where employees clearly understand their agency's mission, how they fit into it, and what they must accomplish to fulfill it, everyone is a professional. The work culture must send this message in every way possible. One easy way is to put an end—once and for all—to meaningless employee sign-ins and sign-outs on time sheets.

Many may consider this a trivial matter. But consider the salaried Health and Human Services (HHS) employee who must still sign in at a central location in her office every morning—and sign out exactly 8½ hours later. She must do this no matter how many more hours she really works, and every employee in her branch must sign the same list, in order of appearance.

Occasionally, when she gets caught up in a meeting or lost in concentration at her desk, she forgets to sign the book at her appointed hour. Supervisors have "guided" her to avoid this problem. She tells her supervisor, who agrees that the practice is senseless, that it discourages her from working longer hours. "What about us overachievers?" she asks him. "You lose," he answers.

The truth is, we all lose. Yet HHS continues to spend dollars training timekeepers.[52]

The Department of Labor, by contrast, listened to complaints from its employees about the needless paper-pushing and use of administrative time that repetitive timekeeping required. Under the leadership of Secretary Robert Reich, and with full backing of union presidents who represent department employees, Labor has begun to dump the standard time card. After realizing that nearly 14,000 of its 18,000 employees work a standard 40-hour week, department leaders decided to trust their workers to report only exceptions, such as overtime and sick and annual leave. Since only one third of Labor's workforce reports any exception in the average week, the department is already saving paper and time—and money. Standard time records are now submitted electronically, without bothering employees.[56]

The President should encourage all departments and agencies to follow the Department of Labor's lead. The new policy will allow for exceptions—for example, when labor contracts or matters of public safety require them. But if we truly seek the highest productivity from our workers, we must treat them like responsible adults. In today's work environment, time cards are a useless annoyance.

Action: *The President should issue a directive committing the administration to greater equal opportunity and diversity in the federal workforce.*[54]

President Clinton launched his administration by appointing cabinet and senior officials who, in his words, "look like America." In doing so, he sent a clear message: A government that strives for the best must continue to break down stubborn barriers that too often keep us from employing, training, or promoting the best people.

While the President has set the stage, the current federal workforce does not reflect the nation's diverse working population. Overall, the federal government has yet to successfully eliminate some discriminatory barriers to attracting and retaining underrepresented groups at every civil service grade level, or advancing them into senior positions. A glass ceiling still hangs over the employment and career prospects for women, minorities and people with disabilities who work in the federal service. Women account for only 12 percent of the top tier of the federal employment ladder—the Senior Executive Service. Minorities account for nine percent.[55] Serious disparity persists for both groups in promotion rates to professional and administrative levels that serve as the gateway to further advancement. The numbers for Americans with disabilities are even worse.

Much can be done to make equal opportunity an integral part of each agency's mission and strategic plan. The President should issue a directive in 1993 committing the administration to attaining a diverse federal workforce and increasing the representation of qualified minorities, women, and people with disabilities at all career levels. The order should instruct agency heads to build equal employment opportunity and affirmative employment elements into their agency strategic plans and performance agreements. In turn, agency leaders should require managers and teams throughout their agencies to build the same goals into their own performance plans—and should publicly recognize those who succeed.

STEP 5: FORMING A LABOR-MANAGEMENT PARTNERSHIP

The federal workforce is changing. While the number of employees has remained constant for a decade, the workforce is much more diverse, with more minorities and women. It is better educated and more mobile. And more employees work in professional, scientific, and highly technical jobs than ever before.

Today, more than 125 federal unions represent about 60 percent of the federal workforce. That's 1.3 million civilian, non-postal employees, or 80 percent of the workforce eligible to participate in federal unions. The three largest federal employee unions are the American Federation of Government Employees (AFGE), the National Treasury Employees Union (NTEU), and the National Federation of Federal Employees (NFFE).

Federal employees and their unions are as aware of the quality revolution as are federal managers. Consistent with the quality push, federal employees want to participate in decisions that affect their work. Indeed, GAO estimates that 13 percent of federal workers already are involved in formal quality management processes.[56] At the IRS, for example, a Joint Quality Improvement Process with the NTEU has spread throughout the agency—saving money, producing better service, and improving labor-management relations.

Corporate executives from unionized firms declare this truth from experience: No move to reorganize for quality can succeed without the full and equal participation of workers and their unions. Indeed, a unionized workplace can provide a leg up because forums already exist for labor and management exchange. The primary barrier that unions and employers must surmount is the adversarial relationship that binds them to noncooperation. Based on mistrust, traditional union-employer relations are not well-suited to handle a culture change that asks workers and managers to think first about the customer

We want to be full partners. We want to work. We want government to work better.

We want to be there in partnership to help identify the problems. We want to be there in partnership to help craft the solution. We want to be there in partnership to help implement together the solution that this government needs.

And we're prepared to work in partnership to make some bold leaps to turn this government around and make it work the way it should work.

John Sturdivant, President
American Federation of Government Employees
Reinventing Government Summit,
Philadelphia June 25, 1993

and to work hand-in-hand to improve quality.

The current context for federal labor-management relations, title VII of the 1978 Civil Service Reform Act, presents such a barrier. In 1991, the GAO concluded after an exhaustive survey of union leaders, government managers, federal employees and neutral experts, that the federal labor-management relations program embodied in title VII "is not working well." GAO characterized the existing bargaining processes as too adversarial, bogged down by litigation over minute details, plagued by slow and lengthy dispute resolution, and weakened by poor management. One expert interviewed by GAO summed up the prevailing view: "We have never had so many people and agencies spend so much time, blood, sweat, and tears on so little. In other words, I am saying I think it is an awful waste of time and money on very little results." Indeed, the cost of handling unfair labor practice disputes using this system runs into tens of millions of dollars every year.[57]

We can only transform government if we transform the adversarial relationship that dominates federal union-management interaction into a partnership for reinvention and change.

Action: *The President should issue a directive that establishes labor-management partnership as an executive branch goal and establishes a National Partnership Council to help implement it.*[58]

The President's executive order will articulate a new vision of labor-management relations. It will outline the roles of managers and unions in creating a high-performance, high-quality government. It will call for systematic training in alternative dispute resolution and other joint problem-solving approaches for managers, supervisors and union officials. And it will call for agencies to form their own internal councils.

By October, 1993, the President should appoint the National Partnership Council

and charge it with the task of championing these efforts and developing the next steps. The council will include appropriate federal cabinet secretaries, deputy secretaries, and agency directors; the presidents of AFGE, NTEU, and NFFE; and a representative of the Public Employee Department of the AFL-CIO. Federal agencies and unions will assign existing personnel to staff the council.

Action: *The National Partnership Council will propose the statutory changes needed to make labor-management partnership a reality.*[59]

GAO cited the need for a new labor-management relations framework that "motivates labor and management to form productive relationships to improve the public service."[60] The Federal Labor Relations Authority, The Federal Mediation and Conciliation Service, and several agencies have been encouraging and facilitating new labor-management cooperation efforts. However, their efforts are being hampered by legal restrictions that focus on the traditional adversarial models. The council will recommend legislation to the President to create a better framework.

STEP 6: EXERTING LEADERSHIP

Despite the federal government's solid core of capable employees, it lacks effective leadership and management strategies. In 1992, GAO delivered a stark diagnosis of the situation. Our government, GAO reported, lacks the "processes and systems fundamental to a well-run organization. Most agencies have not created a vision of their futures, most lack good systems to collect and use financial information or to gauge operational success and accountability, and many people do not have the skills to accomplish their missions." This situation, GAO concluded in a burst of understatement, was "not good."[61]

The sweeping change in work culture that quality government promises won't happen by itself. Power won't decentralize of its own accord. It must be pushed and pulled out of the hands of the people who have wielded it for so long. It will be a struggle.

We must look to the nation's top leaders and managers to break new ground. The President, the Vice President, cabinet secretaries, and agency heads are pivotal to bringing about governmentwide change. It is they who must lead the charge. Under President Clinton's leadership they are determined to make it happen.

If we want to make the federal government a better place, our current leadership must make it clear by *what we do* that, when we offer change, we mean business. That is a promise we must make to the entire community of hardworking, committed federal workers. It is a promise we must keep.

Action: *The President should issue a directive detailing his vision, plan, and commitment to creating quality government.*[62]

Graham Scott, who as Secretary of Treasury for New Zealand helped shepherd reinvention of that country's government, cautioned Vice President Gore, "Our experience is that government won't change unless the chief executive is absolutely 100 percent committed to making it change."[63] CEOs of corporations the world over echo Scott's call.

The first directive issued along with this report will clarify the President's vision of a quality federal government. It will commit the administration to the principles of reinventing government, quality management, and perpetual reengineering, as well as the National Performance Review's other recommendations. In addition, it will detail the strategic leadership roles of the cabinet and agencies in implementing them.

Action: *Every federal department and agency will designate a chief operating officer.*[64]

Transforming federal management systems and spreading the culture of quality throughout the federal government is no small task. To accomplish it, at least one senior official with agencywide management authority from every agency will be needed to make it happen.

Every cabinet-level department and federal agency will designate a chief operating officer (COO). In addition to ensuring that the President's and agency heads' priorities are implemented, COOs will be responsible for applying quality principles in transforming the agencies' day-to-day management cultures, for improving performance to achieve agencies' goals, for reengineering administrative processes, and for implementing other National Performance Review recommendations.

The COO will not add an additional position in the secretary's or director's staff. Secretaries and agency directors should designate a deputy secretary or under secretary with agencywide authority as the COO. The COO will report directly to the agency's top official.

Action: *The President should appoint a President's Management Council to lead the quality revolution and ensure the implementation of National Performance Review plans.*[65]

A new President's Management Council (PMC) will be the President's chief instrument to retool management systems throughout the executive branch. It will act as the institutional lever to drive management and cultural changes throughout the bureaucracy. The PMC will ensure that quality management principles are adopted, processes are reengineered, performance is assessed, and other National Performance Review recommendations are implemented.

> U*nless everyone understands what a work process is, how to map it, how to analyze and quantify its essential elements, no organization will be able to reap the enormous gains in performance that come with an involved and empowered workforce.*
>
> **Frank Doyle**
> Executive Vice President, General Electric
> Reinventing Government Summit, Philadelphia
> June 25, 1993

The President should appoint the Deputy Director for Management of OMB to chair the PMC, and its progress will be overseen by the Vice President. The council will include the COOs from 15 major agencies and three other agencies designated by the chairperson, the heads of GSA and OPM, and the President's Director of Cabinet Affairs (ex officio). Its agenda will include setting priorities; identifying and resolving cross-agency management issues; establishing interagency task forces to transform governmentwide systems such as personnel, budget, procurement, and information technology; and soliciting feedback from the public and government employees. It will secure assistance from the CEOs, officials and consultants who have helped transform major American corporations, state and local governments, and non-profit organizations. In addition, the PMC will conduct future performance reviews of the federal government and report to the public on its findings.

Working together, the President, Vice President, PMC and every agency head will carry the quality message into the sleepiest corners of the bureaucracy. Successful and innovative agencies will be cheered; slower moving organizations will be prodded and encouraged until change occurs.

Action: *The President's Management Council will launch quality management "basic training" for all employees, starting with top officials and cascading through the entire executive branch.[66]*

However pressing the need, we cannot expect leaders, managers and employees caught up in old ways to change overnight. To nurture a quality culture within government, we must help the entire workforce understand the President's vision. Unless we train everyone in the new skills they need—and help them understand the new roles they are expected to play—they can, through passive or active resistance,

frustrate well-intentioned attempts to progress. So first and foremost, everyone will need to learn what working and managing for quality is all about.

The President and agency heads must send a clear message about their commitment by becoming directly involved in the design and delivery of quality training in their agencies. Therefore, the PMC, working with the Federal Quality Institute, will begin quality training with the cabinet secretaries and agency heads. Training sessions will focus on defining a shared vision, developing a strategy to embed that vision in the each department, committing participants to lead and be responsible for change, and establishing a process for training the next level of management.

Even as agencies reorganize around quality and customers, their staff may need training to fulfill expanded job responsibilities. Line staff may need to learn budget and procurement processes. Managers may need help in becoming coaches rather than commanders. We will pursue the goal of reaching the entire federal workforce with quality training.

It is worth noting that some cabinet secretaries already are up on the quality learning curve. During the past few months, more than 60 top field managers, contract lab directors, and assistant secretaries have joined Energy Secretary Hazel O'Leary for 6 days of total quality management training at Motorola University in Chicago. They've agreed on a mission statement, set the department's core values, and put strategic planning in motion. In the process, skeptics have become energized, egos have been subsumed, hidden agendas unearthed and dispensed. In the words of one participant, "Everyone is working as a team. We're incredibly excited about doing better. In just 6 days of quality training, we have moved from 'I' to 'we'."[67]

Other departments are hot on Energy's heels. Such agency leadership is pivotal to moving quality forward. As leading quality innovator Dr. Joseph Juran told Vice President Gore, "As we go at it energetically in the federal government... we're still going to see some of the agencies step out in front and everybody else is going to watch. And as they get results and nobody's hurt in the process, others will be stimulated to do the same thing."[68]

Conclusion

To change the employee culture in government, to bring about a democracy of leadership within our bureaucracies, we need more than a leap of faith. We need a leap of *practice*. We must move from control to collaboration, from headquarters to every quarter. We must allow the people who face decisions to make decisions. We must do everything we can to make sure that when our federal workers exercise their judgment, they are prepared with the best information, the best analysis, and the best tools we have to offer. We must then trust that they will do their best—and measure the results.

Indeed, we must let our managers and workers fail, rather than hold them up to public ridicule when they do. Only if they fail from time to time on their way to success will we be sure they are even trying to succeed. Someone once asked an old man known for his wisdom why he was so smart. "Good judgment comes from experience," he said. And experience? "Well, that comes from *bad* judgment."

To transform the culture of our government, we must learn to let go. When we do, we will release the same kind of creativity, energy, productivity, and performance in government service that was unleashed 200 years ago, and that continues to guide us today.

Chapter 4

CUTTING BACK TO BASICS

I feel like that person in the old movie who writes in lipstick on bathroom mirrors, "Stop me before I kill again." However, in my case, the legend should be, "Stop me before I steal some more."

Letter from Bruce Bair of Schoenchen, Kansas,
to Vice President Al Gore, May 24, 1993

Bruce Bair admitted to "stealing" from the federal government—at a rate of about $11 an hour. His job was checking the weather in Russell, Kansas, every hour, and reporting to the Federal Aviation Administration. The FAA used his information to warn planes in the area about bad weather. But Russell isn't a busy flight station any more. Bair saw just two landings in more than a year during his night shift. Days were only slightly busier. Before the advent of automated weather gathering devices, human weather watchers at Russell and at other small stations throughout the Midwest were vital for aircraft safety. Today, they could be replaced with machines. "From my experience with the machine," wrote Bair, "it is very adequate to protect the air space over Russell." In fact, Russell has had a machine for some time, but the FAA had not yet eliminated the human staff.

Bair concluded his letter to Vice President Gore with these words: "I feel there is very little doubt among professionals that we are basically useless here." A few months later, he quit. Now he says, "I'm no longer stealing from the government."[1]

Bruce Bair's story tells us much about our federal government: its entrenchment in old ways, its reluctance to question procedures, and its resistance to change. Its inflexibility has preserved scores of obsolete programs. This is not news to most of us—obsolescence is part of our stereotype of government.

Why is it so difficult to close unneeded programs? Because those who benefit from them fight to keep them alive. While the savings from killing a program may be large, they are spread over many taxpayers. In contrast, the benefits of keeping the program are concentrated in a few hands. So special interests often prevail over the general interest.

That's why we can't eliminate unnecessary programs simply by making lists. Politicians, task forces, commissions, and newspaper articles have been ridiculing wasteful programs for as long as we have enjoyed democratic government. But most programs survive attack. After a decade of tight budget talk, for example, federal budget expert Allen Schick says he can identify just three major nondefense programs eliminated since 1980: general revenue sharing, urban development action grants, and the fast breeder reactor program.[2]

To shut down programs, therefore, we must change the underlying culture of government. As we described in the preceding chapters, we will do this by introducing market dynamics, sharing savings from cuts with agencies, exposing unnecessary programs to the spotlight of annual performance measures, and giving customers the power to reject what they do not need. As government begins operating under these new rules, we are confident that agencies will request the consolidation and elimination of programs. Billions of dollars will be returned to taxpayers or passed on to customers.

We will begin this process today.

First, we will eliminate programs we do not need—the obsolete, the duplicative, and those that serve special, not national interests.

Second, we will collect more—through imposing or increasing user fees where pricing makes economic sense, and by collecting what the government is owed in delinquent debt or fraudulent overpayment of benefits.

Third, we will reengineer government activities, making full use of computer systems and telecommunications to revolutionize how we deliver services.

The actions and recommendations described in this Chapter are the first dividend on what we can earn from streamlining government. They won't be the last—or even the largest. The strategy of the National Performance Review differs from that of previous budget cutting efforts. Our recommendations have been discussed thoroughly with agency heads to determine which cuts are warranted, feasible, and can be done quickly. We are ready to act with the full force of the cabinet.

STEP 1: ELIMINATE WHAT WE DON'T NEED

After World War II, a British commission on modernizing government discovered that the civil service was paying a full-time worker to light bonfires along the Dover cliffs if a Spanish Armada was sighted. The last Spanish Armada had been defeated some years before—in 1588, to be precise.

This story may be apocryphal. But not all such stories are. In Brooklyn, New York, there is a Federal Tea Room where a federal employee sips imported tea to test its quality.[3] For one hundred years, taxpayers paid for the position. It was not until press coverage angered enough members of Congress that things were changed: now, tea importers pay to have their tea tested— although the taster remains a government employee.

These stories capture an essential truth about governments; they rarely abandon anything. Like the FAA that employed Bruce Bair to check the weather, federal agencies do many things not because they make sense, but because they have always been done that way. They become like the furniture: They are simply there.

Other programs are not so much obsolete as duplicative. When confronted with new problems, we instinctively create new programs. But we seldom eliminate the old programs that have failed us in the first place. Still other programs were never needed in the first place. They were created to benefit influential industries or interest groups. The National Performance Review has targeted several programs in each of these categories for immediate elimination.

Although we make specific recommendations in the pages that follow, we believe the government must tackle the problem systematically. The single best method would be to give the President greater power to eliminate pork that creeps into federal budgets.

Action: *Give the President greater power to cut items from spending bills*[4]

Today, the President's powers to cut spending are limited—more limited than most of the nation's fifty governors. He can either sign or veto appropriations bills; he can't veto individual items—a power most governors have. For the President to cut wasteful spending, he needs the power of what is called, in Washington, "expedited rescission." Under current law, the President can submit proposed rescissions to Congress, which then has 45 legislative days to act. If Congress does not act, proposals are rejected. The President should have greater authority to reject individual items.

Broader rescission powers were envisioned in HR 1578, which the House passed in late April 1993. This bill would force Congress to vote on the President's proposals to cancel funding, rather than let it kill those requests by ignoring them, as under current procedures. If enacted, the new procedure would, as President Clinton wrote in a letter to House Speaker Thomas S. Foley, "provide an effective means for curbing unnecessary or inappropriate expenditures without blocking enactment of critical appropriations bills."

Eliminate the Obsolete

Not all employees of useless programs act with Bruce Bair's forthrightness. But that doesn't mean their offices or programs are any more useful. The vast nationwide network of 30,000 federal government offices, for example, reflects an era when America was a rural country and the word "telecommunications" was not yet in the dictionary. While circumstances have changed, the government hasn't. As a result, workloads are unevenly distributed—some field offices are underworked, others are overworked, some are located too far from their customers to serve them well, and few are connected to customers through modern communications systems.

Action: *Within 18 months, the President's Management Council will review and submit to Congress a report on closing and consolidating federal civilian facilities[5]*

All agencies will develop strategies to cut back or consolidate their field office systems

This is a precious opportunity to make fundamental change in government. I look forward to working together on areas of mutual agreement.

U.S. Rep. William F. Clinger (R. Penn.)

in ways that are compatible with our principle of better services to customers. The President's Management Council will submit the report to Congress within 18 months showing which offices may be closed, which can be consolidated and which can be slimmed. We urge Congress to act quickly on this package.

We are confident that the savings will be large because several agencies are already committed to far-reaching reforms in their field office systems. Their efforts will be models for those that haven't moved as quickly as they prepare their plans for the President's Management Council.

Action: *The Department of Agriculture will close or consolidate 1,200 field offices.[6]*

The Department of Agriculture (USDA) operates the most elaborate and extensive set of field offices—more than 12,000 across the country. Under Secretary Mike Espy's leadership, the department is planning dramatic reforms. USDA runs 250 programs in such vital but diverse areas as farm productivity, nutrition, food safety, and conservation. Its focus has shifted dramatically since the 1930s, when its present structure evolved: 60 percent of its budget now deals with nutrition; less than 30 percent with agriculture.

As the basis for reorganization, USDA will concentrate its activities on six key functions: commodity programs, rural development, nutrition, conservation, food quality, and research. This focus will allow it to consolidate from 42 to 30 agencies and from 14 to six support staffs, cutting administrative costs by more than $200 million over five years.

As part of this process, USDA will consolidate or close about 1,200 field offices within the Agricultural Stabilization and Conservation Service, the Soil Conservation Service, the Farmers Home Administration, the Cooperative Extension System, and the Federal Crop Insurance Corporation. Some of these offices now serve suburban counties, others have few rural customers left. In 1991, the General Accounting Office reported that in Gregg County, Texas, the Agricultural Stabilization and Conservation Service office served only 15 farmers; in Douglass County, Georgia, two USDA programs served a total of 17 farmers.[7]

Field office closings will be determined by a six-part scoring system developed to evaluate each office. Once in place, this restructuring will save more than $1.6 billion over five years and eliminate the equivalent of 7,500 full time employees. Customers will be better served because operations will be combined in multi-purpose USDA field service offices.

Action: *The Department of Housing and Urban Development will streamline its regional office system.*[8]

The Department of Housing and Urban Development (HUD) has also developed a strategy to close offices without cutting customer services. Roughly 10,000 of HUD's 13,500 employees work in field offices, but their workloads vary: the New York regional office monitors 238,000 federal public housing units, the Seattle office only 30,000 units. Management restructuring, described in the previous chapter, will streamline HUD's field operations.[9] Under a five-year plan, HUD will eliminate all regional offices, pare down its 80-field office system, and cut its field staff by 1,500 people.

Action: *The Department of Energy will consolidate and redirect the mission of its laboratory, production, and testing facilities to meet post-Cold War national priorities.*[10]

For the first time in 50 years, the United States is not engaged in producing or testing nuclear weapons. Significant reductions in funding for these programs are already underway—$1.25 billion in fiscal year 1994 alone. Yet, the Department of Energy's weapons laboratories and production plants represent an irreplaceable investment in world-class research and development, intellectual, and computing capabilities, carefully cultivated over five decades. As the department redirects its facilities, the challenge is to eliminate unnecessary activities, while shifting appropriate resources to meet non-defense objectives.

Under Secretary of Energy Hazel O'Leary's leadership, DOE will review its labs, weapons production facilities, and testing sites in the context of its mission—and will recommend the phased consolidation or closure of obsolete or redundant facilities. The secretary will also identify facilities that other government agencies may find useful, encourage laboratory managers to bid on contracts with other agencies, and increase cooperation with the private sector.

Action: *The U.S. Army Corps of Engineers will reduce the number of regional offices.*[11]

The U.S. Army Corps of Engineers, too, has a plan: it will cut its divisional offices from 11 to 6. It cannot, however, close district offices because Congress prevented such actions by law—an example of costly congressional micro-managing. The Corps has carried out the nation's largest civil works projects. Its role is changing: it builds fewer large projects and faces more complex environmental projects.

Action: *The Small Business Administration will reduce the number of field offices and consolidate services.*[12]

The Small Business Administration is developing criteria for consolidating field offices based on the customer load. It has already demonstrated in pilot programs how to cut local office staff by providing routine loan servicing for several local SBA offices and by adopting automated procedures for processing applications for the agency's many different loan programs.

Action: *The U.S. Agency for International Development will reduce the number of its overseas missions.*[13]

With the dramatic changes in U.S. foreign policy, agencies with overseas operations are rethinking their responsibilities. J. Brian Atwood, administrator for the U.S. Agency for International Development (AID), believes the number of countries in which his agency operates missions can be cut from 105 to perhaps 50. Cuts will be made in the number of missions in developing countries so that the agency's efforts can focus on those nations that can absorb and manage assistance.

Action: *The United States Information Agency will cut the number of libraries and reference centers it pays for overseas.*[14]

Savings are also possible in overseas facilities maintained by the United States Information Agency. USIA maintains libraries and other facilities in many developed countries, as well as in emerging countries. While facilities in the latter are often crowded, those in developed countries attract few customers: In Canada, for example, a USIA library attracted only 568 walk-in visitors in a year. Eliminating some of these facilities or turning them over to their host countries could save an estimated $51.5 million through 1999.[15]

> W*e'll challenge the basic assumptions of every program, asking does it work, does it provide quality service, does it encourage innovation and reward hard work. If the answer is no, or it there's a better way to do it or if there's something that the federal government is doing, it should simply stop doing, we'll try to make the changes needed."*
>
> **President Bill Clinton**
> Announcement of initiative to streamline government
> March 3, 1993

Action: *The Department of State will reduce by 11 the number of Marine Guard detachments it employs.*[16]

By consolidating the storage of top secret documents in overseas missions, the Department of State can reduce the need for Marine Guard detachments. The Bureau of Diplomatic Security has identified 11 posts where the Marine Security Guard program could be eliminated simply by moving documents to other places.

Action: *Pass legislation to allow the sale of the Alaska Power Administration.*[17]

The federal government once played a crucial role in financing, developing and operating the Alaska Power Administration (APA). No longer. APA was created to encourage economic development in Alaska by making low-cost hydro-power available to industry and to residential customers. The project has succeeded and can now be turned over to local ownership.

The federal government retains four other Power Marketing Administrations (PMAs), which own hydropower facilities and sell the power they generate to public, private, and cooperative utilities at cost. These PMAs serve customers spread throughout many states, so the facilities cannot easily be sold to a local entity. APA, on the other hand, is unique: Its facilities and customers are located in a single state. Various public agencies have already urged the federal government to sell the APA facilities. APA signed purchase agreements to do so before 1993.

The sale is supported by state and local officials, Alaska's congressional delegation, the Energy Department, the Office of Management and Budget, and the House Appropriations Committee. But Congress has yet to pass the necessary authorizing legislation. We urge it to do so. The sale would bring $52.5 million into the U.S. Treasury and save millions more in yearly operating costs.

Action: *Terminate federal grant funding for Federal Aviation Administration higher education programs.*[18]

Success has rendered two FAA federal subsidies obsolete. They have met the objectives for which they were established and can now be terminated. For example, in 1982, the Federal Aviation Administration (FAA) launched a program to improve the development and teaching of aviation curricula at universities and other post-secondary schools. The goal was to produce graduates better prepared for jobs in the industry.

So far, the FAA has spent about $4 million on consultants to upgrade schools' programs Another $100 million was appropriated—most at Congress' insistence, rather than FAA's request—to be given out in grants so that the schools could buy better facilities and equipment. Many schools now offer high quality aviation training programs without support from the FAA. Since $45 million of the appropriation remains unspent, stopping the program now can save this money.

Another program we no longer need is the Collegiate Training Initiative for Air Traffic Controllers. It was set up to determine whether other institutions could offer the same quality training for

controllers as the FAA Academy does. If they could, it would save the government the $20,000 it costs to train each new controller at the academy. The answer is clearly yes. Five schools participating in the program are producing well-qualified controllers, although only two are receiving government subsidies. It is now time to phase out these remaining subsidies.

Action: *Close the Uniformed Services University of the Health Sciences.*[19]

The Department of Defense (DOD) once faced shortages of medical personnel, particularly of physicians. So, in 1972, Congress created the Uniformed Services University of the Health Sciences. Today, the University provides less than 10 percent of the services' physicians at a cost much higher than other programs: University physicians cost the federal government $562,000 each, while subsidies under the Health Professionals Scholarship Program cost only $111,000 per physician. Closing the facility and relying on the scholarship program and volunteers would save DOD $300 million over five years.

Action: *Suspend the acquisition of new federal office space.*[20]

Over the next 5 years, the federal government is slated to spend more than $800 million a year acquiring new federal office space and courthouses. Under current conditions, however, those acquisitions don't make sense.

The federal workforce is being reduced, the Resolution Trust Corporation is disposing of real estate once held by failed savings and loans at 10 to 50 cents on the dollar, commercial office vacancy rates are running in the 10 to 25 percent range, and U.S. military bases are being closed. All of these factors suggest that the government has many potential sources for office space without buying any more buildings.

The GSA administrator will place an immediate hold on GSA's acquisition—through construction, purchase, or lease—

of net new office space. The administrator
will begin aggressive negotiations for
existing and new leases to further reduce
costs. And GSA will reevaluate and reduce
the costs of new courthouse construction.
These actions should save at least $2 billion
over the next 5 years.

Eliminate Duplication

Government programs accumulate like
coral reefs—the slow and unplanned
accretion of tens of thousands of ideas,
legislative actions, and administrative
initiatives. But, as a participant at the Vice
President's HUD meeting told us, "There
isn't always a rational basis for the way we
are set up in this organization. Over the
years, branches have developed; they have
been taken over by divisions; and we don't
look at the organization as a whole." Now
we must clear our way through these reefs.

The National Performance Review has
looked at government as a whole. We have
identified many areas of duplication. What
follow are recommendations for the first
round of cuts and consolidations.

Action: *Eliminate the President's Intelligence Oversight Board.[21]*

No branch of government—including
the Executive Office of the President
(EOP)—is free of duplication. We will
begin the streamlining process in the EOP,
where two groups oversee intelligence—at
times tripping over each other and allowing
some issues to fall through jurisdictional
cracks. The President, by directive, should
terminate the President's Intelligence
Oversight Board and assign its functions to
a standing committee of the President's
Foreign Intelligence Advisory Board.

Action: *Consolidate training programs for unemployed people.[22]*

Government's response to changing
circumstance often creates duplication. As
the economy has evolved, for example, we
have created at least four major programs to
help laid-off workers: the Economic
Dislocation and Worker Adjustment
Assistance Act (EDWAA) program, which
spends $517 million annually for those who
lose their jobs through plant closings or
major layoffs; the Trade Adjustment
Assistance program (TAA), which
distributes $170 million for those who lose
jobs due to increased imports; the Defense
Conversion Adjustment program, which
dispenses $150 million for those
unemployed because of defense cuts; and a
program that allocates $50 million for those
unemployed due to the enforcement of new
clean air standards. Even more programs are
in the pipeline.

But multiple programs aimed at
common goals don't work well.
Administrative overhead is doubled and
services suffer. Because each training
program is intended to help people
rendered jobless for different reasons, people
seeking work must wait for help until the
government determines which program
they are eligible for. The process is slow.
The General Accounting Office estimates
that less than one-tenth of TAA-eligible
workers receive any benefits within 15
weeks of losing their jobs, for example.[23]

The unemployed care less about why
they lost their jobs than about enrolling in
training programs or finding other jobs.
Labor Secretary Robert Reich is proposing
legislative changes to consolidate programs
for workers who lose their jobs, regardless of
the cause. His bill would also allow more
funds to be used before workers lose
their jobs. In Chapter 1, we recommend
the consolidation of 20 education,
employment, and training programs. We
urge Congress to support both initiatives.

Action: *Consolidate the Veterans' Employment and Training Service and the Food Stamp Training Program into the Employment and Training Administration.*[24]

Several training programs offer similar services through the same offices—sometimes even using the same employees—but requiring separate management and reporting systems. We can cut bureaucracy and paperwork while improving services to the customer by merging these programs.

Consider the case of the Veterans' Employment and Training Service (VETS) in the Department of Labor (DOL). Another operation in DOL, the Employment and Training Administration (ETA), funds local Employment Services, which, in turn, house staff dedicated to providing veterans with advice on training programs. But these staff are legally prohibited from serving non-veterans. So, if a local office is crowded with non-veterans, these specialists cannot help out—even if they have no veterans to serve. Moving VETS into the ETA will generate much greater efficiency in the use of staff, leading to shorter lines and better service.

We also recommend moving the Food Stamp Training Program into the ETA. Most training under the program is already performed under contract by ETA staff, by the Employment Service, or by local education institutions. Overall, ETA can offer poor people a much more comprehensive range of job-search and training services than can the Food Stamp Training Program.

Action: *Reduce the number of Department of Education programs from 230 to 189.*[25]

The nation's concern with education has led to an explosion of programs at all levels of government. The Education Department now funds 230 programs, many of which overlap. Since many are grants to state and local governments, we face duplication in triplicate—multiple administrative systems at all levels of government.

Of these 230 programs, 160 will award money through 245 different national competitions this year. The cumbersome administrative systems divert money from activities more central to the department's mission. These programs should be reduced in number and their procedures streamlined.

The department has begun reforming and streamlining programs, particularly those under the Elementary and Secondary Education Act. This will make it easier for schools to get the money without jumping through so many bureaucratic hoops. We propose to eliminate and consolidate more programs that have served their original purpose or would be more appropriately funded through non-federal sources. The savings, as much as $515 million over 6 years, can be better used for other departmental priorities. For example:

- The department administers two programs—the National Academy of Space, Science, and Technology program and the National Science Scholars program—that give scholarships to post-secondary math, science, and engineering students. These two should be combined.

- State Student Incentives Grants were created to encourage states to develop needs-based student aid programs. Since all states now have their own programs, the federal program is no longer needed.

- The Research Libraries' program funds research libraries to build their collections. University endowments could and should support these efforts, without federal subsidy.

Action: *Eliminate the Food Safety and Inspection Service as a separate agency by consolidating all food safety responsibilities under the Food and Drug Administration.*[26]

Sometimes duplication among federal programs can make us ill—even kill us. Take the way we inspect food for contamination. Several agencies are involved, each operating under separate legislation, with different standards, and with staff trained in different procedures. In 1992, the Food and Drug Administration (FDA)—part of the Department of Health and Human Services—devoted about 255 staff years to inspecting 53,000 food stores, while the Food Safety and Inspection Service (FSIS)—part of the Department of Agriculture—devoted 9,000 staff years to inspecting 6,100 food processing plants.

But this duplication doesn't mean that we cover all sources of contamination thoroughly. Meat and poultry products must be inspected daily, while shellfish, which have the same risk of causing food borne illness, are not required by law to be federally inspected. Too many items fall through the bureaucratic cracks. Not only that, enforcement powers vary among the different agencies. If the FDA finds unsanitary plant conditions or contaminated products, compliance is usually voluntary because the agency lacks FSIS's powers to close plants or seize or detain suspect or known contaminated products. And if one agency refers a problem to another, follow up is at best slow and at worst ignored.[27]

With no fewer than 21 agencies engaged in research on food safety, often duplicating each other's efforts, we aren't progressing fast enough in understanding and overcoming life-threatening illness. As recent and fatal outbreaks of food-borne illness attest, multiple agencies aren't adequately protecting Americans.

Under our recommended streamlining, the FDA would handle all food safety regulations and inspection, spanning the work of the many different agencies now involved. The new FDA would have the power to require all food processing plants to identify the danger points in their processes on which safety inspections would focus. Where and how inspections are carried out, not the number or frequency of inspections, determines the efficiency of the system.

The FDA would also develop rigorous, scientifically based systems for conducting inspections. Today, we rely, primarily, on inspection by touch, sight, and smell. Modern technology allows more reliable methods. We should employ the full power of modern technology to detect the presence of microbes, giving Americans the best possible protection. Wherever possible, reporting should be automated so that high-risk foods and high-risk food processors can be found quickly. Enforcement powers should be uniform for all types of foods, with incentives built in to reward businesses with strong safety records.

Action: *Consolidate non-military international broadcasting.*[28]

The U.S. government funds several overseas broadcasting services—including those operated by the United States Information Agency's Bureau of Broadcasting, which accounts for one-third of the agency's $1.2 billion budget, and services such as Radio Free Europe and Radio Liberty, which have budgets totalling $220 million a year. All non-military international broadcasting services should be consolidated under the USIA. Part of this was propsed in the President's budget request for fiscal year 1994.

Action: *Create a single civilian polar satellite system.*[29]

Collecting temperature, moisture, and other weather and environmental information from polar satellites is a vital task, both for weather forecasting and for global climate studies. But we have two different systems, one run by the Department of Defense and the other by the National Oceanic and Atmospheric Administration. On top of this, the National Aeronautics and Space Administration is planning a third. Over the next ten years these three systems will cost taxpayers about $6 billion. Congress should enact legislation requiring these agencies to consolidate their efforts into a single system, saving as much as $1.3 billion over the same period.

Action: *Transfer the functions of the Railroad Retirement Benefits Board to other agencies*[30]

The government can operate with fewer pension management systems. In 1934, Congress set up the Railroad Retirement Board to protect railroad workers in the face of financial problems, to allow workers to transfer among railroads, and to encourage early retirement to create jobs for the millions of younger workers. In those days, the huge national public pension system, Social Security, was not yet in place; neither were the state-federal unemployment insurance systems nor Medicare.

Today, it makes no sense for a separate agency to administer benefits for a single industry. Social Security Administration can administer social security benefits for railroad workers as it administers them for everyone else; unemployment insurance systems can serve unemployed railroad workers as well as it serves other unemployed people; and the Health Care Financing Administration can incorporate railroad workers' health care benefits into the Medicare system.[31]

Action: *Transfer law enforcement functions of the Drug Enforcement Administration and the Bureau of Alcohol, Tobacco, and Firearms to the Federal Bureau of Investigation.*[32]

More than 140 federal agencies are responsible for enforcing 4,100 federal criminal laws. Most federal crimes involve violations of several laws and fall under the jurisdiction of several agencies; a drug case may involve violations of financial, firearms, immigration and customs laws, as well as drug statutes. Unfortunately, too many cooks spoil the broth. Agencies squabble over turf, fail to cooperate, or delay matters while attempting to agree on common policies.

The first step in consolidating law enforcement efforts will be major structural changes to integrate drug enforcement efforts of the DEA and FBI. This will create savings in administrative and support functions such as laboratories, legal services, training facilities, and administration. Most important, the federal government will get a much more powerful weapon in its fight against crime.

When this has been successfully accomplished, we will move toward combining the enforcement functions of the Bureau of Alcohol, Tobacco and Firearms (BATF) into the FBI and merge BATF's regulatory and revenue functions into the IRS. BATF was originally created as a revenue collection agency but, as the war on drugs escalated, it was drafted into the law enforcement business. We believe that war would be waged most successfully under the auspices of a single federal agency.

Eliminate Special Interest Privileges

Some programs were never needed. They exist only because powerful special interest groups succeeded in pushing them through Congress. Claiming to pursue national objectives, Congress, at times, funds programs that guarantee profits to specific industries by restricting imports, raising prices, or paying direct and unnecessary subsidies.

Special interest groups come in all shapes and sizes and their privileges are as diverse. Producers of crops, residents of certain areas, and holders of some occupations have all succeeded in persuading Congress that their needs are special and their claim on special treatment is deserving.

Action: *Eliminate federal support payments for wool and mohair.*[33]

During World War II and the Korean conflict, the U.S. was forced to import about half the wool needed for military uniforms. To cut dependence on foreign suppliers, Congress in 1954 passed the National Wool Act, providing direct payments to American wool producers. The more wool a producer sold, the greater the government subsidy. In 1960, the Pentagon removed wool from its list of strategic materials. But the Wool Act remained in effect—a tribute to adept lobbying.

Between 1994 and 1999, wool subsidies will cost an estimated $923 million. About half the payments will go to ranchers who raise Angora goats for mohair—a product that is 80 percent exported. So American taxpayers will subsidize the price of mohair sweaters overseas! In some years, subsidies provide more income than sales. The 1990 mohair checks, for example, totalled $3.87 for every dollar's worth of mohair sold.

Today, about half the beneficiaries receive only $44 a year each. But the top one percent of sheep raisers capture a quarter of the money—nearly $100,000 each. The national interest does not require this program. It provides an unnecessary subsidy for the wealthy.

Action: *Eliminate federal price supports for honey.*[34]

World War II also brought us federal subsidies for honey production. During the war, honey was declared essential because the military used bees' wax to wrap ammunition, and citizens replaced rationed sugar with honey. When honey prices dropped after the war, the federal government began subsidizing honey production.

The program was intended to be temporary—to last until there were enough honeybees available for pollination. But more than 40 years later, every bee keeper in the U.S. is eligible for federal loans. In 1992, the federal government paid 7 cents a

pound more to borrow money than it charged bee keepers. Taxpayers paid the difference. If it were to scrap the program, Congress would save taxpayers $15 million over the next six years.

Action: *Rescind all unobligated contract authority and appropriations for existing highway demonstration projects.*[35]

The practice of directing federal highway funds toward spending on specific demonstration projects—and away from regular state-level allocations—is increasing. This is not, for several reasons, a good trend.

In 1991, the General Accounting Office (GAO) examined the contributions of demonstration projects—which range from paving a gravel road to building a multi-lane highway—to the nation's overall highway needs. Looking specifically at the $1.3 billion authorized to fund 152 projects under the 1987 Surface Transportation and Uniform Relocation and Assistance Act, GAO found that "most of the projects...did not respond to states' and regions' most critical federal-aid needs." Indeed, in more than half the cases, the projects weren't even included in regional and state plan— typically because officials believed the projects would provide only limited benefits. GAO also discovered that 10 projects—worth $31 million in demonstration funds—were for local roads not even entitled to receive federal highway funding. In other words, many highway demonstration projects are little more than federal pork.

Perhaps even worse, there's no guarantee that all these highway demonstration projects, once started, will ever be finished. GAO noted that project completion costs will greatly exceed authorized federal and state contributions, and that state officials are uncertain where they will find more funding. Further, only 36 percent of the project funds GAO reviewed had even been obligated by the beginning of fiscal year 1991, even though they were authorized in 1987. Some projects with no activity since

1987 may never use their funds. Finally, no federal provisions allow for canceling or redirecting funds, nor can states redirect demonstration funds to other transportation projects.[36]

We urge Congress to rescind all unobligated authority and appropriations for highway demonstration projects. Some of the savings would go to the taxpayers. We recommend that all highway projects be forced to compete for any remaining savings through the normal allocation and planning processes set up in more recent legislation.

Action: *Cut Essential Air Service subsidies.*[37]

Sometimes, to push through controversial changes, Congress grants affected groups special privileges. This was the case when airlines were deregulated in 1978. Because people living in small towns feared the loss of air service, Congress created the Essential Air Service program. The program guaranteed continue services for a decade—with federal subsidies if necessary. The purpose was to allow these communities to learn to live in a deregulated environment.

But the program didn't end in 1988 as scheduled. Quite the opposite. Congress extended it for another ten years and its budget has grown—from $30.6 million in 1988 to $38.6 million in 1993.

The program is unneeded: 25 subsidized communities are less than 75 miles from hub airports. It is also costly: nine locations, receiving $3 million in subsidies in 1992, carried five or fewer passengers a day—one community, only 60 miles from a hub airport, received subsidies averaging $433 per passenger.

Opposition to the program is rising. The Transportation Department's Inspector General has concluded that the program's costs outweigh its benefits. And after many years of resistance, a Congressional subcommittee agreed this year that the program lacks merit-based criteria. It's time to prune these subsidies. We recommend eliminating subsidies to locations in the 48 contiguous states within 70 miles of a hub airport; limiting subsidies to no more than $200 a passenger, and giving the Transportation Department authority to establish more restrictive criteria over time. This would save $13 million a year.

STEP 2: COLLECTING MORE

Given the size of the federal deficit, government must find better, more efficient, and more effective ways to pay for its activities. In Chapter 2, we showed how government could become more businesslike. In this section, we propose three ways to increase federal revenues: introducing or increasing market-based user fees, collecting what is due the government in delinquent loans and in accidental or fraudulent overpayment of benefits, and refinancing debt at lower interest rates.

Some people take advantage of government's largesse. They default on loans, or they double claim for health insurance benefits. Government has made it far too easy for people to get away with such actions. As a result, honest people are

subsidizing their less scrupulous neighbors. Their actions raise the costs of federal programs, divert money from where it was intended, and discredit our system of governance. Here are the first steps we will take to end these practices.

Raising User Fees

Congress and federal agencies have shied away from charging for federal services. But government surely produces many goods and services for which consumers could, and should, pay." User fees can serve exactly the same function as prices do—providing federal managers with invaluable information about their customers. If customers like the services they are paying for—if they find the experience of visiting a particular national park enjoyable, for example—revenues will increase. If the agency can keep some of its additional revenues, it will be able to pay the increased operating costs associated with its rising number of customers. It will, as a result, learn to care about satisfying those customers.

Paying for the services you receive also is an issue of fairness. Why should taxpayers subsidize concessionaires or visitors to National Parks, or pay the cost of determining whether a business should dump sludge into the nation's waterways? Many services government provides because they are in the national interest or because we do not expect people to pay for them. But the customers of some government activities could and should pay. Many agencies, including the Food and Drug Administration, The Patent and Trademark Office, the National Technical Information Service, and the Securities and Exchange Commission already charge their customers fees. In some cases, these fees cover the full cost of operations. Taxpayers are not called upon to pay for the services that others receive. But, most agencies aren't allowed to keep the fees—the revenues are sent to the Treasury. Under these circumstances, agencies have no incentive to increase fees if market conditions merit it.

Where fees are allowed, Congress often limits them—removing any discretion from local managers. The National Park Service, for example, cannot charge more than $5 per car or $3 a visitor at many parks. At busy Yellowstone, Grand Teton, and the Grand Canyon, fees are limited to $10 a vehicle and $5 a visitor. Ending subsidies to concessionaires and moderately increasing fees would let the National Park Service invest more in its crumbling infrastructure, and spend more to protect America's priceless natural heritage.

Two-thirds of all the National Park Services facilities charge no admission fee at all. Yet the Park Service suffers from a multi-billion dollar backlog in infrastructure repair and rehabilitation projects for the National Park System. One-third of NPS primary paved roads are in poor or failing condition; a tenth of employee housing is obsolete or deteriorated; and 4,700 planned natural and cultural resource projects are on the waiting list for funding. Meanwhile, demands on the parks are rising sharply as the number of visitors—both American and foreign—grows each year.[38]

Action: *Allow all agencies greater freedom in setting fees for services and in how the revenues from these fees may be used.[39]*

Even with a modest increase in fees, a family of four will pay less to spend a week in Yellowstone National Park than they would to see a first-run movie. The National Park Service should be allowed to keep 50 percent of revenues from fees to pay for vital services and projects.

The natural fear is that federal facilities are monopolies and, unless their pricing policies were regulated, they would become price-gauging profiteers. The concern is appropriate, but the policies it has led to are not. We would not recommend that national parks or documents repositories, for example, become federal profit centers—but they could, certainly, cover a larger part of their costs. They cannot charge exorbitant prices—after all, parks are in competition with each other, and with many privately owned recreation areas. The market will control the revenues they can realistically collect.

Pricing policy is an important management tool, and we recommend that Congress place it in the hands of many more federal managers. The National Performance Review recommends increasing the use of user fees for many activities. For example:

• The FDA must ensure that 1.5 million food products imported each year meet the same safety and labeling standards as domestic products. It also certifies the safety of exported foods. Taxpayers, not manufacturers, pay for these inspections. User fees could save taxpayers as much as $1.4 billion over 5 years.[40] The agency should also have the power to collect fees for conducting inspections and reviews, processing petitions and applications, analyzing samples and issuing device reports for food, drugs, devices, and radiological products.

- The Department of Veterans Affairs runs a program to guarantee home loans for veterans. It lets them borrow at lower costs and make smaller down payments than would be possible without assistance, because the guarantee protects lenders in the event of foreclosure by reducing their potential loss. The department collects fees for this service, yet they are set very low. A modest increase in fees costing an extra $6 per month, for example, would still provide homebuyers with better-than-market terms. Yet it would generate an additional $811.4 million over 6 years.[41]

- Under the Clean Water Act, the Army Corps of Engineers issues permits for discharges of dredged or filled materials into rivers, lakes and streams. The Corps has processed 15,000 applications at a total cost of $86 million. Yet it has charged only token fees for its services, collecting only $400,000 annually. This amounts to a $12 million annual subsidy for commercial customers, according to Defense Department estimates. Higher fees would help not only taxpayers but Corps customers, because additional revenues could pay for faster processing of applications.[42]

- The Small Business Administration should have the power to establish user fees for the services they provide through the nationwide Small Business Development Center (SBDC) program. SBDC customers like the services they get, so the revenues from fees will enable the centers to expand successful programs.

Action: *Increase revenues by refinancing debt or raising federal hydropower rates to cover full operating costs.*[43]

The Power Marketing Administrations (PMAs), such as Alaska Power, were mandated in 1944 to sell their power at low rates to help promote development in sparsely populated areas. Rates are still low today; in fact, the PMAs sell power to their public, private and cooperative utility customers at below market rates. Thus, the low electricity rates enjoyed by customers in some areas are subsidized by American taxpayers in others. Taxpayers subsidize PMA utility customers through low-interest loans. The interest rates most PMAs pay the government are artifically low. As the interest on the Treasury's long-term debt climbed in the 1960s, 1970s, and 1980s, the differential between those rates and rates on PMA loans created federal subsidies for these projects.

The Energy Department will take immediate steps to increase revenues from hydropower operations. The department will set a new rate policy for specified PMAs to seek recovery of full operating costs. As an alternative, the Energy Department may attempt to restructure the financing of the Bonneville Power Administration's debt, allowing Bonneville to issue bonds at market rates and repay its low-interest Treasury loans. The department will attempt to achieve such a refinancing with minimal effects on the near-term rates paid by its customers by seeking favorable bond interest rates and lengthening terms of repayment.

Collecting Debt

At the end of last year the federal government was owed $241 billion by former students, small businesses, farmers, companies developing alternative energy sources—even foreign companies and governments. This makes the federal government the nation's largest lender. Of this total, a shocking $47 billion—20 percent of the total—was delinquent.[44]

To some extent, the federal government's unpaid debts reflect the fact that some of its loan programs operate more like grant programs. They are designed to meet national policy goals such as increasing the number of physicians in rural areas and supporting democratic governments overseas. But in other cases agencies have done a poor job in collecting what they are owed. After all, agencies are rarely held accountable for unpaid loans. All too frequently, neither are delinquent borrowers.

If agencies were to put a higher priority on pursuing delinquent debt and if Congress were to grant them greater flexibility in their debt collection operations, the federal government could collect more of what it is owed. The Office of Management and Budget will work with each agency to develop debt collecting strategies that employ the following expanded powers.

Action: *Give agencies the flexibility to use some of the money they collect from delinquent debts to pay for further debt collection efforts, and to keep a portion of the increased collections.*[45]

Small investments in debt collecting can yield high returns. In 1989, the GAO discovered that the Veterans Administration had not recovered $223 million in health payments from third parties, such as insurers. Congress then changed the rules, allowing the VA to keep a portion of recovered third-party payments for administrative costs. With this incentive, the VA increased its recovery effort. The result: a four-fold increase in collections since 1989.

The VA, now called the Department of Veterans Affairs, wants to go even further by expanding its cost recovery efforts into its loan programs and establishing cost-sharing, performance incentives. Local hospitals, for example, might be allowed to keep some of the revenues they generate to buy new medical equipment. Overall, VA believes it could pull in another $500 million through 1999.

Opportunities like this occur throughout the federal government. The Education Department, for example, wants to use the additional repayments it would collect to pay for further collections of Higher Education Act debts. Budget offices tend to oppose the idea of sharing new earnings with the agency in question, because they want 100 percent of the earnings to meet deficit reduction targets. But unless the agencies have incentives to generate the earnings, they rarely produce them in the first place.

The solution is twofold. First, Congress should allow agencies to use some of the money they now collect from delinquent debts to pay for further debt collection efforts. Second, it should increase the incentives agencies have to pursue debt collections, by letting them use a small portion of their increased collections to invest in improving their overall operations.

Action: *Eliminate restrictions that prevent federal agencies from using private collection agencies to collect debt.*[46]

In addition to sharing in their earnings, agencies would benefit from being able to use private debt collectors, as the Department of Education has done. While we know how cost-effective private collection agencies are, many agencies—including the Farmers Home Administration, Social Security, the IRS, and the Customs Service—are statutorily prohibited from using private agencies for the job, even on a contingency-fee basis. Congress should lift those restrictions.

Action: *Authorize the Department of Justice to retain up to one percent of amounts collected through civil debt collections to cover costs.*[47]

When borrowers default on their federal loans, the first step is for the lending agency to try to collect—or, if permissible, to use a private debt collection agency. If these measures fail, agencies refer claims to the Department of Justice. While the Department handles the larger claims itself, it refers those under $500,000—which constitute 90 percent of all claims—to local U.S. attorneys' offices. In overworked U.S. attorney's offices, debt collection is often a low priority.

To encourage the Department of Justice to collect debts, Congress should allow the department to retain 1 percent of everything it collects through litigating civil debt cases under $500,000. These retained funds should be used for paying staff working on debt collection, for paying case-related costs, and for paying for training and other investments to improve local debt collection programs.

Action: *The Royalty Management Program will increase the royalty payments it collects by developing new computer programs to analyze and cross-verify data.*[48]

The federal government collects royalty payments from mining companies recovering minerals from federal land. The Interior Department's Minerals Management Service (MMS), the agency charged with the job, collects $4.7 billion annually. But its auditing system is limited and focuses heavily on the companies paying the largest royalties—so smaller companies don't always pay their share. The Department of the Interior will increase its collections—by as much as $28 million over five years—by developing better accounting and auditing systems. To make sure MMS can collect its dues, the Interior Department will ask Congress for permission to assess penalties on substantial

underpayments and to impose fees on a broader range of administrative costs.

Action: *HUD should offer incentive contracts to private companies to help federally subsidized home owners refinance their mortgages at lower rates.*[49]

HUD has succeeded in extending the dream of home ownership to many people. But the HUD section 235 program does not take advantage of lower interest rates because the assisted owners do not have enough incentive to go through the work and bother of refinancing.

We recommend that HUD offer incentive contracts to private companies to let them share a percentage of the savings to the government of refinancing the mortgages. They could work with the home owners to arrange refinancing, doing the necessary leg work and make cost effective payments to home owners to induce them to refinance. Projected savings from this program could exceed $210 million over five years. Yet program beneficiaries would continue to receive exactly the same benefits.

Eliminating Fraud

While many think government steals from people, the reverse is also true: People steal from government. And, unlike private companies, some government agencies aren't very good at finding and prosecuting thieves. Moreover, the bureaucracy does too little to deter dishonest people.

Action: *Make it a felony to knowingly lie on an application for benefits under the federal Employees' Compensation Act and amend Federal law so individuals convicted of fraud are ineligible for continued benefits.*[50]

The federal government manages many programs that provide benefits to people injured or taken sick. Not all the recipients are legitimate. When agencies discover fraud, however, they are often hamstrung in their ability to terminate benefits—so they keep paying fraudulent claims. For example, under the Federal Employees' Compensation Act (FECA), the Office of Workers' Compensation Programs cannot terminate benefits even after finding that someone made false statements about a disability or an illness.

In one case, a former federal employee collected almost $200,000 in benefits under the FECA disability program while working. When a witness told the government about the fraud, the employee hired someone to kill him. The employee was convicted of falsifying his application for FECA benefits, but the government could not cut off his compensation on the basis of his original false statements alone.[51]

Action: *Improve processes for removing people who are no longer disabled from disability insurance rolls.*[52]

The Social Security Administration serves more than 10 million people through two disability programs, Disability Insurance and Supplemental Security Income. But the General Accounting Office has estimated that 30,000 of these recipients are no longer eligible. Overpayments from the trust funds to ineligible people are projected to reach $1.4 billion by 1997.[53] The Social Security Administration faces a dual problem: overpayment to unlawful claimants and lengthy delays in providing benefits to legitimate claimants. Using present management practices, the agency lacks the staff to review its rapidly escalating caseload. The backlog of 700,000 pending claims is taking priority over reviewing continuing cases.

The agency is working to create a single disability claims processing system, but it needs greater budget flexibility to invest in hardware and software and to redeploy staff to meet growing demands.[54]

Action: *Create a clearinghouse for the reporting and disclosure of death data.*[55]

Obviously, no federal agency should continue paying benefits after recipients have died. But stopping payments is not easy because sharing death information among different levels of government is restricted and not always reliable. The Social Security Administration regularly obtains death information from states under agreements with each of them (except Virginia). But most agreements restrict SSA's disclosure of death data, so the information the SSA collects cannot always be shared with those running other federally- and state-administered benefits programs. The result is millions of dollars in overpayments. For Americans living overseas, the problem is even worse. SSA gives benefit checks to overseas embassies to deliver. The State Department claims that SSA must check that the recipients are still alive; SSA says that it's the State Department's job.

We need not serve customers who are no longer alive. Congress should amend the Social Security Act to allow SSA to share death information with other programs.[56]

STEP 3: INVESTING IN GREATER PRODUCTIVITY

One of the greatest obstacles to innovation in government is the absence of investment capital. The appropriations for most federal agencies last only one year: anything left over at the end of the year disappears. So it's difficult for organizations to scrape together enough money to make even small investments in training, technology, new work processes, or program innovations. We have recommended that agencies be allowed to keep half of any savings they can generate. In addition, we propose a series of innovation funds from which they can borrow. When managers and their employees are allowed to borrow for long-term investments, they have a real incentive to implement creative new ideas.

The IRS and Interior Department already have innovation funds.[57] Treasury and Justice operate working capital funds that finance specific innovations, such as modernizing information technology and computer systems. And the Commerce Department has a Pioneer Fund that gives employees cash grants (rather than loans) of up to $50,000 to finance quality and productivity improvements. The money can be used for supplies, equipment, or expert services. Some funds have financed projects related to advanced technology, such as the development of public information on CD-ROMs.

State and local governments use this approach quite often. Many cities have long had some form of innovation fund. In Florida, Governor Lawton Chiles cut departmental budgets by five percent across the board, then gave half back to agencies that developed plans to invest in higher

The Productivity Bank: Paying Big Interest in Philadelphia

Mayor Ed Rendell says it's not hard to change incentives so that public employees save money.

"We tell a department, 'You go out there and do good work,' " Rendell told the National Performance Review's Reinventing Government Summit in his city. "'You produce more revenue. You cut waste. And we'll let you keep some of the savings of the increased revenue.'"

Traditionally, the mayor said, "every nickel that they would have saved would have gone right back to the general fund… They would have gotten a pat on the back, but nothing else." Now, city employees save because their departments can keep some of the savings for projects to help them perform better.

When the Department of License and Inspection beefed up collection and enforcement efforts and generated $2.8 million more than expected in 1992, Rendell said, the city let the department keep $1 million of the savings to hire more inspectors and, in turn, exceed the $2.8 million in 1993.

The city also opened a Productivity Bank, from which departments can borrow for investment-type projects—that is, capital equipment—to produce either savings or enough revenues to repay the loan in five years. To ensure that departments don't apply frivolously, the city subtracts loan payments from annual departmental budgets.

Successes already abound. The Public Property Department repaid a $350,000 loan to buy energy efficient lamps in one year—after saving $700,000 in energy costs.

productivity and effectiveness.

At the federal level, one important use for such funds would be technology investments. These are often considered too expensive for agencies' operating budgets, even though they save money in the future. The Agency for International Development, for instance, needs a centralized information management system to coordinate its central office with its international field offices. Because its information systems lack essential data and are not coordinated, they provide inconsistent, inaccurate, and incomplete reporting that managers frequently do not trust. Agencies such as AID should have authority to create innovation funds for capital investment loans to reduce future operating costs.

Action: *Allow all agencies and departments to create innovation funds*[58]

Congress should authorize a two tier system of innovation funds: small loan funds within agencies; larger funds at the departmental level. These would be capitalized through retained savings from operational appropriations. For the new system to work well, Congress should allow all new and existing innovation funds to invest in joint projects with other agency funds, with state or local governments, or with industry.

If managed according to market principles, innovation funds would produce measurable improvements in agency efficiency and significant taxpayers savings. Strict repayment schedules, with interest, would discourage careless borrowing.

Action: *The government should ensure that there is no budget bias against long-term investments.*[59]

Part of straightening out the government's books will involve adopting some financial distinctions that business uses. Federal bookkeeping rules discourage government investments in productive fixed assets, like computer systems. Right now, we count a $5 million investment to purchase a Local Area Network computer system in exactly the same way as we count $5 million spent on staff salaries. American businesses do it differently. Business depreciates fixed assets over time: If the $5 million computer system has a useful life of five years, then its $5 million acquisition costs will be spread out over five years. Poor choices of capital investment and the acquisition methods are currently costing the taxpayer millions of dollars each year.

Listen to Eleanor Travers, the director of Pathology and Laboratory Medicine for the Veterans Hospital Administration. She told the National Performance Review meeting at the Department of Veterans Affairs in August 1993:

> *Procurement of equipment is held up because capital dollars to purchase equipment are frozen. And you asked what dumb rules there were we could change. Allow our hospital directors and our top managers to use operating dollars when they find it's necessary to do leasing rather than purchasing . . . Please help us loosen up the capital fund so that we don't have to go to Congress and wait two and a half years for this line item to change.*

The budget should recognize the special nature and long-term benefits of investments in fixed assets through a separate capital budget, operating budget, and cash budget. The separate capital budget will explicitly show expenditures on fixed assets, and will help to steer our scarce resources toward the most economical means of acquisition of the most needed assets. The cash budget reflects the effect of both the capital and the operating budget on the economy. Therefore, the discipline of the cash outlay caps in the Budget Enforcement Act must be maintained.

STEP 4: REENGINEERING PROGRAMS TO CUT COSTS

In the past turbulent decade, many companies have been forced to recognize that they weren't organized in the right way to do what they were doing. Their organization structure reflected history, not current needs. Reform wasn't easy—too many people had vested interests in preserving their particular part of the organization. As a result, most attempts at reorganization were reduced to shifting things among different boxes on organizational charts. Businesses found that

> *We are determined to move from an industrial age government to information age government, from a government pre-occupied with sustaining itself to a government clearly focused on serving the people.*
>
> **Vice President Al Gore**
> May 24, 1993

the only way to break the mold was to reengineer—to forget how they were organized, decide what they needed to do, and design the best structure to do it. An obvious insight? Perhaps. But the best ideas are always the ones that seem obvious—after their discovery.

We will reengineer the work of government agencies in two ways. First, we will expand the use of new technologies. With computers and telecommunications, we need not do things as we have in the past. We can design a customer-driven electronic government that operates in ways that, 10 years ago, the most visionary planner could not have imagined.

Second, we will speed up the adoption of new ways to improve federal operations. Most of this work will be done by the federal agencies themselves. An outside

performance review could never learn enough about internal agency work processes to redesign them intelligently. But we can begin to redesign several broad government-wide processes: The way we design programs, develop regulations, and resolve disputes.

Electronic Government

The history of the closing decade of this century is being written on computer. You wouldn't know it if you worked for many federal agencies, however. While private businesses have spent the past two decades either getting rich by developing new computer technologies or frantically trying to keep up with them, government is still doing things our parents—perhaps even our grandparents—would recognize.

Offshoots of the unexpected and fertile marriage between computers and telephones have changed just about everything we do—how we work, where we work, the design of the workplace, and the skills we need to continue working.

Organizations don't need as many people collecting information because computers can do much of it automatically. They don't need as many people processing that information because clever software programs can give managers what they need at the press of a button.

Factories don't need to stockpile large inventories because smart machines on the assembly lines order components from equally smart machines working for suppliers. Yet government agencies stand guard over warehouses of unused office furniture. Retailers ship the right size of clothing to customers as soon as they receive a telephone order and a credit card number. Yet we can't pay our taxes that way.

Computer companies give technical advice for our computers and software over the telephone 24 hours a day by fax, modem, or voice. Yet, the Social Security Administration can't do the same.

Failure to adapt to the information age threatens many aspects of government. Take the State Department, a globe-spanning organization dependent on fast and accurate communications. Its equipment is so old-fashioned that the Office of Management and Budget says "worldwide systems could suffer from significant downtime and even failure."[60] According to OMB, its systems are so obsolete and incompatible that employees often have to re-enter data several times. These problems jeopardize our ability to meet our foreign policy objectives.

Or think about the way our government sends out checks. For 15 years, electronic funds transfers have been widely used. They cost only 6 cents per transfer, compared with 36 cents per check. Yet each year, Treasury's Financial Management Service still disburses some 100 million more checks than electronic funds transfers.

We still pay about one federal employee in six by check and reimburse about half of travel expenses by check. Only one-half of Social Security payments—which account for 60 percent of all federal payments—are made electronically, making SSA the world's largest issuer of checks. Only 48 percent of the Veterans Affairs Department's payments are made electronically. Fewer than one in five Supplemental Security Income payments and one in ten tax refunds are transferred electronically.[61] We have only begun to think about combining electronic funds transfers for welfare, food stamps, subsidies for training programs, and many other government activities.

Private financial transactions have become a lot easier in the past decade: bank cash machines are open 24 hours a day, credit cards let us avoid carrying cash, and we can buy goods over the telephone. This saves many of us a lot of time and money. It could save the Government a lot of time and money, too. Consider the paper chase involved in running the welfare system. The Food Stamp Program, alone, involves billions of bits of paper that absorb thousands of administrative staff years. More than 3 billion food stamps will be printed this year and distributed to more than 10 million households. Each month, 210,000 authorized food retailers receive these coupons in exchange for food. These retailers carry stacks of coupons to 10,000 participating financial institutions, which then exchange them with Federal Reserve Banks for currency. The Federal Reserve Banks count the coupons—although they already have been counted more than a dozen times—and destroy them. The administrative cost of this system—shared equally by federal and state governments—is almost $400 million a year.

We will support Agriculture's commitment to the goal of issuing food stamps electronically by 1996. Electronic benefits transfer could eliminate the paper chase, improve services to customers, and reduce fraud. At the same time, it could be used to authorize Medicaid payments, distribute welfare payments, infant nutrition support, state general assistance, and housing assistance. It could eliminate billions of checks, coupons, and all the other paperwork, record keeping and eligibility forms that clutter the welfare system.

Why has business moved faster than government into the electronic marketplace? In the first place, government is a monopoly. Public organizations don't go out of business if they don't have the latest and smartest machines or the best approach to managing resources. In the second, employees who do want to modernize management have their hands tied with red tape—detailed budgets and cumbersome procurement procedures—that deter investment. Finally, there is a natural inclination, familiar to private and public managers alike, to do things as they've always been done.

What can we do to help our federal bureaucracy catch up?

Action: *Support the rapid development of a nationwide system to deliver government benefits electronically.*[62]

OMB has already begun the process. The electronic benefits transfer steering committee, which OMB oversees, will develop an implementation plan for electronic benefits transfer by March 1994.

The system is workable with today's technology. For cash programs such as federal retirement, social security, unemployment insurance, or AFDC, benefits would be electronically deposited directly into recipient bank accounts electronically. If people didn't have bank accounts, these could be created once the individual enrolled in a program. For "non-cash" programs such as food stamps, participants would have accounts through which they could make purchases at approved food stores—analogous to credit cards with credit limits. Stores would debit accounts as eligible items were purchased. The entire system could operate on or be compatible with the existing commercial infrastructure through which private funds are transferred electronically.

Agencies have begun experiments with electronic benefits transfers. Welfare checks, food stamps, and state-collected child support, for example, are distributed electronically in Maryland. There are test sites in Iowa, Minnesota, New Mexico, Ohio, Pennsylvania, Texas, and Wyoming. We know that a joint federal-state effort to transfer welfare benefits electronically works—and works well. The system is strongly supported by recipients, the state welfare agencies, food retailers, banks, and participating commercial networks. We also know that direct federal delivery of funds by electronics is cost-effective. We can't yet project with certainty what the savings might be, but preliminary estimates suggest $1 billion over five years once electronic benefits transfer of food stamps is fully implemented.

In the future, the concept of electronic government can go beyond transferring money and other benefits by issuing plastic, "smart" benefit cards. With a computer chip in the card, participants could receive public assistance benefits, enroll in training programs, receive veterans services, or pay for day care. The card would contain information about participants' financial positions and would separately track their benefit accounts—thus minimizing fraud. Electronic government will be fairer, more secure, more responsive to the customer, and more efficient than our present paper based systems.

Barriers still stand in the way. Agencies will have to work together to develop a comprehensive nationwide strategy for implementation; it will do no good for each agency to develop its own process. We will need to strengthen the partnership between state and federal governments in developing and operating the system. We will have to eliminate some regulations that would prevent this radical change in how government operates. And the National Institute of Standards and Technology will have to issue final standards and protocols for electronic signatures to facilitate electronic funds transfers and the electronic approval of budget and financial documents.

Action: *Federal agencies will expand their use of electronic government.*[63]

Opportunities abound for cutting operating costs by using telecommunications technologies. The National Performance Review has identified several projects that would improve government's productivity and reduce the burden of reporting on individuals and businesses.

The IRS is introducing an efficient computer system, automating tax returns, and creating a wholly new work environment for its 115,000 full-time personnel. The agency currently operates a computer system put together in the 1960s—not the tool our principal revenue collector should be using. To make the new system work, the agency will need to figure out how to train its staff to operate in a reengineered agency. We will support the agency's investments in new hardware and training, as discussed in Chapter 3.

The IRS will also manage the creation of an integrated electronic system for financial filing, reporting, and tax payment by 1996. The system will serve federal, state, and local taxpayers. It will allow the electronic filing of tax returns by individuals and companies, the electronic reporting of wages and withholding information, and other data required by all levels of government. In addition, the inter-agency Wage Reporting Simplification Project (WRSP) will be in place quickly—allowing businesses to file information once to serve many different purposes. The savings from fully implementing this program over the life of the system have been projected at $1.7 billion for government agencies and $13.5 billion for private employers. Individuals will be able to file federal and state income taxes simultaneously through an Electronic Data Interchange, with their privacy protected and fraud prevented through digital signature standards. Electronic filing alone will save the IRS and state agencies from having to mail out the equivalent of 75 boxcars of forms.

Working together, the Labor Department and IRS will develop an automated system all employers can use to file electronically the pension plan forms employers required by the Employee Retirement Income Security Act.[64] At present, it costs the Internal Revenue Service more than $10 million a year to enter all these forms into its data base.

The Labor Department will develop computer programs to determine quickly the appropriate wages on federal service contracts.[65] Currently, all federal agencies contracting for services—from cleaning services to building management—must apply to the department for a determination of appropriate wages. The process is supposed to ensure that federal contracts don't undermine local prevailing wages. The process takes an average of 57 days and, with a growing number of service contracts, more and more are subject to delays.

We will continue investing in the Social Security Administration's massive project to create a single nationwide disability processing system.[66] This will require considerable investments in new telecommunications and computer systems as well as in staff retraining. It will also mean that the SSA will have to work cooperatively with state-run disability determination offices, set performance standards, and take over those that don't meet standards. Many of the system's worst processing bottlenecks are in the state offices that approve individual claims.

Money for Numbers

The National Technical Information Service runs a large and complex information collection and marketing operation. It is the nation's largest clearinghouse for scientific and technical information. Yet it covers the costs of its operations without receiving a penny in federal appropriations. Its customers pay — and their numbers are growing every year.

NTIS's archives contain about 2 million documents (from research reports to patents), more than 2,000 data files on tape, diskette, or CD-ROM, and 3,000 software programs. This resource is growing at the rate of about 70,000 items each year. NTIS's press releases, on-line services, and CD-ROMs serve 70,000 customers, three-quarters of whom are from business and industry.

In 1991, NTIS collected $30.7 million in revenues — 77 percent from its clearinghouse activities, the rest from other government agencies that reimburse NTIS for patent licensing services, and from billing other agencies for producing and distributing documents. NTIS is required by law to be self-sufficient.

Some of these investments will require Congressional appropriations. But some can be financed through the innovation funds, described above, and some will become possible to pay for as soon as rigid budget regulations are relaxed.

Action: *Federal agencies will develop and market data bases to business.*[67]

Federal agencies must treat the data they compile and process as potentially valuable resources. Congress alerted the bureaucracy to the value of information in 1991 by passing the American Technology Preeminence Act. The act required federal agencies to transfer to the National Technical Information Service copies of federally funded research. At NTIS, the information is organized and made available to research scientists in academia and in industry. NTIS has developed an aggressive marketing strategy and pricing policy that have greatly increased its revenues.

The Census Bureau has pioneered the use of computer technology such as CD-ROM technology to make federal data available. By 1992, the Bureau sold census data to 380,000 customers on tape or disc directly, and served another 1.1 million customers indirectly.

Unfortunately, some federal agencies lag behind private data retailers in the services they offer their customers. People buying Census data must order it through paper order forms or by telephone during business hours—only 9 hours a day, 5 days a week. If private software companies offer 24-hour a day technical support, so should the Census Bureau.

Other agencies will begin to exploit the potential of the information they collect. The Commerce Department, for example, will develop a manufacturing technology data bank that brings together information residing in the National Institute of Standards and Technology, the Defense Department, federal research laboratories, and other organizations. Commerce will also use its climate data as the basis for developing a National Environmental Data

Index. Good data will be vital in solving the problems associated with global climate changes. The U.S. must be a leader in developing these information resources.

Action: *In partnership with state and local governments and private companies, we will create a National Spatial Data Infrastructure.*[68]

Dozens of agencies collect spatial data— for example, geophysical, environmental, land use, and transportation data. They spend $1 to 3 billion a year on these efforts. The administration will develop a National Spatial Data Infrastructure, (NSDI) to integrate all of these data sources into a single digital resource accessible to anyone with a personal computer. This resource will help land developers and conservationists, transportation planners and those concerned with mineral resources, and farmers and city water departments.

Because of the value of the data, it will be possible to attract private sector funding for its collection, processing, and distribution. The Federal Geographic Data Committee, which operates under the auspices of OMB, plans to raise enough non-federal funding to pay for at least 50 percent of the project's cost. It will set the standards for data collection and processing by all agencies to ensure that NSDI can be developed as economically as possible.

Action: *The Internal Revenue Service will develop a system that lets people pay taxes by credit card.*[69]

The Customs Service lets people pay duties on imported goods by credit card. Americans should have the same convenient way to pay taxes. It will save time and cut the IRS's collection costs.[70] There is one hitch: Those who pay by credit card could avoid paying back taxes simply by filing for personal bankruptcy. This escape mechanism can't be employed today because back taxes are, under bankruptcy law, a "non-dischargeable" debt—that is, they are a debt that remains even after someone becomes insolvent. Therefore, the use of credit cards for tax payments should be delayed until Congress has amended the bankruptcy statute to prevent taxes paid by credit card from becoming a dischargeable debt. Our goal is to increase customer convenience, not to open up another loophole through which people can dodge paying delinquent taxes.

Reengineering to Use Cost-Cutting Tools

Our reinvented government will be able to cut further costs by using new ways to carry out traditional duties. To begin with, we will have to get a lot smarter about how we design government programs. The President's Management Council will play a lead role in helping government learn from its past failures and successes to design better programs. In addition, new approaches to regulation—such as negotiated rule making—can reduce conflict and produce better results. Finally, alternative techniques for resolving disputes can avoid many of the costs of traditional litigation.

Action: *The President's Management Council will help agencies design and redesign better programs.*[70]

As taxpayers and customers we have been, time and time again, victims of the thoughtless expansion of government. When new programs were introduced or old ones retargeted, little thought was given to what economists blandly label "second order effects"—the unintended and unwanted consequences of actions. These unintended consequences are the collateral damage responsible for so much of the waste documented in this report. When we placed limits on crop deficiency payments, we didn't realize how easy it would be to establish eligible shell-corporations. When we added new procurement standards, we didn't anticipate the difficulties caused by centralized decision making. When we tried

to target training programs on dislocated workers, we didn't anticipate the bureaucratic hassles involved in establishing eligibility.

But the fact that we *did not* anticipate consequences does not mean that we *could not* have done so. Many different programs have been tried—by federal agencies, by state and local agencies, and by governments overseas. We have built up what lawyers would call "case law": lots of useful precedents about what works and what doesn't. The trouble is that, unlike case law, these precedents aren't easy to find. Congressional staff or agency employees designing new programs have no systematic way to find out what has been tried before and how well it has worked. The result? Endless reinvention of third rate or failed programs.

In 1981, for example, the chairman of the House Banking Committee asked the Congressional Budget Office if it knew of any studies evaluating government loans as an effective policy tool. CBO did not. Yet the federal government had lent hundreds of billions of dollars—and it continues to do so today. The price we pay for this ignorance is a mountain of delinquent debt and a raft of discredited government initiatives. Too many policies and programs are built on equally feeble foundations.

In 1988, Congress recognized this dilemma and provided for the establishment of a National Commission on Executive Organization, patterned after the first Hoover Commission. Its charter would have included a requirement to "establish criteria for use by the President and Congress in evaluating proposals for government corporations and government-sponsored enterprises and subsequently overseeing their performance."[71] The new commission could have been activated by Presidential directive. It was not.

To begin our attack on ignorance, the President should direct the President's Management Council to make program design a formal discipline throughout the federal government. The PMC will commission the preparation and publication of a program design handbook and establish pilot efforts within agencies to strengthen their ability to design programs. These pilot programs will help senior management design new programs, evaluate current programs, and create models for many different types of programs (research contracts, loan programs, tax preferences, and insurance programs to name just a few.)

Since many programs originate in Congress, the Legislative branch should also work to improve staff capacity. We urge the Offices of the Legislative Counsel, the Congressional Research Service, and the General Accounting Office to fill this role. As both the legislative and executive branches elevate the discipline of program design, we will get better programs and less contentious relations between the two branches of government.

But we need more than good programs. We need better rules and more efficient rulemaking. Federal agencies administer tens of thousands of laws, rules, and regulations—and the number is growing quickly. For better or worse, government's rulemaking, even more than its appropriations, shapes our lives.

Costs, for the most part, are offset by benefits. Our system of laws and rules is the foundation for our economic success. It defines and protects personal and property rights and provides the framework for the orderly conduct of social and business affairs.

But some aspects of rulemaking don't work well. As rules extend into increasingly complex areas of our environment, workplace safety, health, and social rights, their consequences—both deliberate and unintended—also grow. As this happens, we introduce more and more safeguards into the rulemaking process. The result is not always what we want. Hearings, reviews, revisions, more reviews, more hearings, and even more reviews are cumbersome, costly, and time consuming. For example, because the Department of Health and Human Services has been slow to issue regulations on such vital areas as the allocation of funds for the elderly and for

children, states have had to introduce their own regulations without the benefit of federal guidance. Some of these state regulations have later been overturned after federal regulations were eventually issued, leaving states financially liable.

New rules and regulations can also generate costly litigation—a bonanza for lawyers. Agencies writing the rules to implement environmental laws, according to one expert, often find "too frequently that their proceedings become a battleground for interest groups and other affected parties—in effect little more than the first round of the expected litigation."[72]

There are better ways to make rules. A small group of federal agencies has pioneered a process called negotiated rulemaking. In 1990, Congress recognized and encouraged the process with passage of the Negotiated Rulemaking Act. We believe negotiated rulemaking—colloquially referred to as "reg neg"—is a process every rulemaking agency should use more frequently.[73]

Action: *Agencies will make greater use of negotiated rule making.[74]*

The "reg neg" process brings together representatives of the agencies and affected groups before draft regulations are issued and before all sides have formally declared war. The group meets with a mediator or "facilitator." The negotiators reach consensus on the regulation by evaluating their own priorities and making trade-offs. The negotiating process allows informal give and take that can never happen in court or in a public hearing. If agreement is reached, the agency can publish the proposed rule, accompanied by a discussion of the issues raised during negotiations. Even if both sides are too far apart to reach consensus, agency staff learn a lot during the process that helps them improve the regulations. When the parties do reach consensus, regulations are issued faster and costly litigation is avoided.

When EPA applied reg neg techniques to the issue of emission standards for wood burning stoves, it was able to put standards into effect two years faster, and with much better factual input, than it could have without negotiations. Manufacturers of stoves, in turn, were able to begin retooling to meet standards without another two years of uncertainty.

Action: *Agencies will expand their use of alternative dispute resolution techniques.*[75]

Federal agencies also need better and cheaper ways to resolve disputes. Enforcing thousands of difficult and sometimes controversial rules—however carefully they are designed—leads to disagreements. State and local governments, businesses, and citizens challenge Washington's right to regulate certain issues, or they challenge the the enforcement of specific regulations.

Solving these disputes can be expensive. It involves high-priced lawyers, it clogs the courts, and it delays action. Each year, 24,000 litigation matters reach the 530 full-time attorneys and 220 support staffers employed by the Labor Department alone. It often takes years to resolve these disputes, postponing the implementation of important programs and preventing a lot of people from doing what they are paid to do.

In some cases, litigation is important: It interprets the law, sets important precedents, and serves as a deterrent to future wrongdoing. But in many cases, no one really wins—and the taxpayer loses. It is often cheaper to resolve conflicts through new techniques known collectively as Alternative Dispute Resolution (ADR).

Alternative Dispute Resolution (ADR) includes mediation (a neutral third party helps the disputants negotiate), early neutral evaluation (a neutral, often expert, person evaluates the merits of both sides), factfinding (a neutral expert resolves disputes that arise over matters of fact, not interpretation), settlement judges (a mediator settles disputes coming before tribunals), mini-trials (a structured settlement process), and arbitration (an arbitrator issues a decision on the dispute).

Overcrowded courts are already encouraging private litigants to use ADR. Private contracts often specify the use of ADR to resolve disagreements among signatories. In 1990, Congress passed the Administrative Dispute Resolution Act, authorizing every federal agency to develop its own ADR policy. Some have, but some have dragged their feet.

Those that have used ADR have saved time and money and avoided generating ill will. The Labor Department started a pilot program last year for OSHA and Wage and Hour cases and found it much quicker and cheaper. The Federal Deposit Insurance Corporation saved more than $400,000 with a single, small pilot program. The Farmers' Home Administration has used ADR on foreclosure cases—not only saving money but actually avoiding foreclosure on several families. This type of innovation should spread faster and further across the federal government.

Conclusion

If we follow these steps, we will move much closer to a government that costs less and works better for all of us. It will be leaner, more effective, fairer, and more up-to-date. It will be a government worth what we pay for it.

We do not deny that many groups will oppose the actions we propose to take. We all want to see cuts made, but we want them elsewhere. Eliminating or cutting programs hurts. But it hurts less, at least in the long run, than the practice of government as usual. Writing about Britain's monarchy in the eighteenth century, Samuel Pepys once observed that it was difficult for the king to spend a million pounds and get his money's worth. Fawning courtiers, belligerent Lords and hundreds of other claimants each demanded their share. The same is true today. The money spigot in Washington is much easier to turn on than to turn off—and too little of the funds that gush from it irrigate where water is scarce. That is why we have not simply offered a list of cuts in this report. Instead, we have offered a new process—a process of incentives that will imbue government with a new accountability to customers and a new respect for the public's money.

CONCLUSION

Though I do not believe that a plant will spring up where no seed has been, I have great faith in a seed. Convince me that you have a seed there, and I am prepared to expect wonders.

Henry David Thoreau

Unlike many past efforts to change the government, the National Performance Review will not end with the publication of a report. We have identified what we must do to make government work better and cost less: We must serve our customers, cut red tape, empower employees to get results, and cut back to basics. Now, we will take action.

The task is immense. The federal government has 2.1 million civilian employees, 800,000 postal workers, 1.8 million military personnel, and a $1.5 trillion budget—more than the entire gross domestic product of Germany, the world's third largest economy.

The National Performance Review has identified the problems and defined solutions. The President will issue directives, cabinet secretaries will change administrative practices, and Office of Management and Budget will issue guidance. We will work with Congress for legislation where it's needed. Senseless regulations will be repealed; mechanisms to enhance customer service will be created; change will begin.

But we do not pretend to have solved every problem. We will transform the federal government only if our actions—

This performance review will not produce another report just to gather dust in some warehouse. We have enough of them already.

President Bill Clinton
Remarks announcing the National Performance Review,
March 3, 1993

and the Reinvention Teams and Labs now in place in every department—succeed in planting a seed. That seed will sprout only if we create a process of ongoing change that branches outward from the work we have already done.

How we proceed will be as important as what we have done to date. We must avoid the pull of implementation models that are familiar and comfortable but poorly suited to today's world. We must avoid creating new bureaucracies to reform the old. We must actively involve government leaders at all levels. We must seek the guidance of those who have successfully transformed large organizations in both the private and public sectors.

The nature of our strategies will no doubt cause discomfort. They will be unfamiliar. They will not look like business as usual. They will challenge the current federal culture. And they will demand risk-taking.

If we are to bring about true change, however, some discomfort is inevitable. Our strategies are not untested; they have been used successfully by both public and private organizations throughout the country.

To succeed where others have failed, the President and Vice President have committed to specific initiatives that will create a culture capable of sustaining fundamental change. This shift in culture will not occur overnight. To bring it about, we will continue:

- a cascading process of education, participation, and ownership at the highest levels of the executive branch;

What we're trying to do is to create a large number of changes, simultaneously, in the federal government. Because if you just change one thing without changing some of the other things that need to be changed, we won't get anywhere.

We can bring the quality revolution, for example, into the federal workforce as well as it could possibly be done, and if we didn't fix some of the other problems, it wouldn't amount to much. We could fix the personnel system, but if we didn't fix the budgetary system and the procurement system, then we would still be mired in a lot of the difficulties that we encounter today. We are trying to do a lot of things at the same time.

Vice President Al Gore
Town Hall Meeting,
Department of Veterans Affairs
August 4, 1993

- two-way communication with federal employees and their organizations;

- bi-partisan partnership with Congress;

- processes to listen to and use feedback from customers and citizens; and

- government-wide mechanisms to monitor, coordinate, and facilitate plans for reinvention.

The administration has already taken a number of steps to bring about the changes we are recommending.

First, we have launched Reinvention Teams and Reinvention Labs in every department to continue seeking ways to improve the government and put these ideas in practice.

Second, we have begun to work—and will continue to expand relationships—with leaders and representatives of federal employees from throughout the government. Indeed, the National Performance Review is the first government-wide change initiative to be run and staffed by federal employees. Our actions will make employees' jobs better, and their participation will make our actions better.

Third, the President and Vice President have begun to work with the cabinet to develop performance agreements that will institutionalize a commitment to and establish accountability for change.

Fourth, we have developed a mechanism to spread our basic principles throughout the government. The President will meet with the cabinet to develop strategies reflecting these principles and ideas, committing all involved to take responsibility for changing the way we do business. Cabinet members will then go through the same process with their senior managers, who will go through it with their senior managers, and so on.

Fifth, the President is establishing a management council to monitor change and provide guidance and resources to those working to bring it about. The President's Management Council will be charged with responsibility for changing the culture and management of the federal government.

Sixth, the Federal Quality Institute will help agencies with access to information, education, research, and consultation on quality management. Like our other initiatives, this models a basic tenet of the behavior we recommend—encouraging managers to define their own missions and tasks, but providing the support they need to do a good job.

Seventh, we will launch future reviews of the federal government, targeted at specific problems. The National Performance Review was a learning experience; we learned what we could do in six months, and what we still need to do. We focused heavily on the basic systems that drive federal agencies: the budget, personnel, procurement, financial management, accountability, and management systems. In subsequent reviews, we will narrow our focus. For example, we plan a review of the antiquated federal field office structure, which dates from the 1930s and contains some 30,000 field offices. (See Chapter 4.) Other targets might include the abandonment of obsolete programs; the elimination of unproductive subsidies; the redesign of failed programs; the redefinition of relationships between the federal government and state and local governments; and the reinvigoration of relationships between the executive and legislative branches.

Finally, the National Performance Review will continue to rely on its greatest asset: the federal employees who made it happen. They have all worked hard for change, and many will continue to work on reinvention in their own agencies. They constitute a network that will reach out to other employees, sharing their enthusiasm, energy, and ideas.

During this process, a vision of change will emerge beyond that which is contained in this report. Leadership and management

> *Our task is not to fix the blame for the past, but to fix the course for the future.*
>
> **President John F. Kennedy**

values will, over time, change—not in response to a mandate, but because people are working together to change their government. If we have done our job well, the next generation of changes will be built on the foundation we have laid with this report. We are merely initial planners; the President, the Vice President, the cabinet, federal managers and employees will be the architects and builders.

Despite all the horror stories and years of scorn heaped on federal employees, our government is staffed by people committed to their jobs, qualified to do them better, and hungry for the opportunity to try. The environment and culture of government have discouraged many of these people; the system has undermined itself. But we can—and will—change that environment and culture.

Over time, it will become increasingly obvious that people are not the problem. As old ways of thinking and acting are replaced by a culture that promotes reinvention and quality, a new face of government will appear—the face of employees newly empowered and newly motivated, and of customers newly satisfied.

What Reinventing Government Means for You

We have talked enough of what we will do and how we will change. The more important question is how life will change for *you*, the American people.

If we succeed—if the administration can implement our recommended actions and Congress can pass our legislative package— you will begin to see a different government. Your mail will be delivered more rapidly. When you call a Social Security office, you'll get through. When you call the Internal Revenue Service, you'll get accurate answers—and if you don't, you will no longer be penalized.

If you lose your job, a local career center will help you find a new one. If you want retraining, or you want to go back to school, you'll find counselors who can help you sort out your options, pick the best program, and pay for it. If you run a

> *Make no little plans; they have no magic to stir men's blood, and probably themselves will not be realized. Make big plans; aim high in hope and work, remembering that a noble logical diagram, once recorded, will never die, but long after we are gone will be a living thing, asserting itself with ever-growing insistency.*
>
> **Daniel Burnham**
> **1907**

small business, you will have fewer forms to fill out.

If you live in public housing, your apartment complex might get cleaner and safer. Perhaps you'll even be able to move your family to a safer, quieter, more stable neighborhood.

Our workplaces will get safer because they are inspected more often. Our water will get cleaner. Your local government will work better because it is no longer hamstrung by silly federal regulations.

And perhaps the federal debt—that $4 trillion albatross around the necks of our children and grandchildren—will slow its rampage. Our federal agencies will begin to figure out, bit by bit by bit, how to cut spending, eliminate the obsolete, and provide better service for less money.

You will begin to feel, when you walk into a post office or social security office or employment service or veterans' hospital, like a valued customer. We will begin to spend more money on things you want and need—health care, training, education, environmental protection—and less on bureaucracy. One day you will be able to conclude that you are getting a dollar of value for every dollar of taxes you pay.

This is our vision of a government that works better and costs less. We know it will not come to be overnight, but we believe it is a vision we *can* bring to life. We believe this because we have already seen this vision come to life—in local governments, in state agencies, even in a few federal agencies. We believe it is the *right* vision for government as we approach the 21st century.

It will take more than a dedicated President and Vice President to make this vision a reality, however. It will take more than dedicated employees. It will take dedicated citizens, willing to work long and hard to improve their government.

It will take citizens willing to push their social security offices and unemployment offices to treat them like customers—and to demand that their voices be heard when they don't get satisfaction. It will take citizens willing to demand information about the performance of their federal organizations. And it will take citizens willing to act on the basis of that information.

As our President has said so often, the future is ours—if we have the courage to create it.

ENDNOTES

PREFACE

1. Bill Clinton and Al Gore, *Putting People First,* (New York, Times Books, 1992) pp. 23-24.

INTRODUCTION

1. Data taken from the following sources: "The average American...," Senator William Roth, vol. 138 no. 51, Cong. Rec. (April 7, 1992), p. S1; "Five out of every six Americans...," CBS News Poll, unpublished, May 27-30, 1992, released June 1, 1992; "Only 20 percent...," an ABC News-Washington Post poll, taken April 23-26, 1993, asked: "How much of the time do you trust the government in Washington to do what is right: Just about always, most of the time, or only some of the time?" Four percent said "just about always," 16 percent said "most of the time," 74 percent said "only some of the time," and 6 percent volunteered "none of the time;" 1963 figure, University of Michigan poll, cited in "From Camelot to Clinton: A Statistical Portrait of the United States," *Washington Post* (August 23, 1993), p. A15.

2. U.S. General Accounting Office (GAO), *High-Risk Series: Defense Inventory Management,* GAO/HR-93-12 (December 1992).

3. U.S. Office of Management and Budget (OMB), *Budget of the U.S. Government FY 93* (Washington, D.C., 1992) and *Budget of the U.S. Government FY 94* (Washington, D.C., 1993); and interview with Department of Housing and Urban Development Budget Officer Herbert Purcell, August 26, 1993.

4. U.S. Congress, Senate, Committee on Appropriations, Subcommittee on Education, Labor and Health and Human Services, testimony of Clarence C. Crawford, U.S. GAO, "Multiple Employment Programs: National Employment Training Strategy Needed," June 18, 1993.

5. Democratic Leadership Council, *The Road to Realignment: The Democrats and the Perot Voters* (Washington, D.C.: Democratic Leadership Council, July 1993), p. III-12. Pollster Stanley Greenberg asked people if they agreed that "government always manages to mess things up." Seventy-two percent of Perot voters agreed, 64 percent of Clinton voters agreed, and 66 percent of Bush voters agreed.

6. Dilulio, John J., Jr., Gerald Garvey, and Donald F. Kettl, *Improving Government Performance: An Owner's Manual* (Washington, D.C.: Brookings Institution, 1993), p. 79.

7. Yankelovich, Daniel, *American Values and Public Policy* (Washington, D.C.: Democratic Leadership Council, 1992), p. 7.

8. National Performance Review Accompanying Report, *Transforming Organizational Structures* (Washington, D.C.: U.S. Government Printing Office [GPO], September 1993).

9. Finegan, Jay, "Four-Star Management," *Inc.* (January 1987), pp. 42-51; Osborne, David, and Ted Gaebler, *Reinventing Government: How the Entrepreneurial Spirit is Transforming the Public Sector* (Reading, MA: Addison-Wesley Publishing Company, Inc., 1992), pp. 255-259; and Creech, General W. L., "Leadership and Management — The Present and the Future," address presented at the Armed Services Leadership and Management Symposium (October 11-14, 1983) (available from the Office of the Assistant Secretary of Defense for Installations, Pentagon, Washington, D.C.).

10. National Performance Review Accompanying Report, *Improving Customer Service* (Washington, D.C.: U.S. GPO, September 1993).

11. U.S. Department of Agriculture, Forest Service, Regional Office, *Profile of a Reinvented Government Organization* (Milwaukee, WI, May 24, 1993); "The U.S. Forest Service: Decentralizing Authority," *Government Executive* (March 1993), pp. 23-4; and interviews with Forest Service officials.

12. The President's Fiscal 1994 budget (page 40) estimates 2.1 million Federal non-postal workers and 1.8 million military for 1994. Manpower, Inc. employs 560,000. General Motors employs 362,000.

CHAPTER 1—CUTTING RED TAPE

1. U.S. Department of Agriculture, *Starting Over* (Washington, D.C., undated), p. 1.

2. Estimate by Office of Management and Budget.

3. National Performance Review Accompanying Report, *Mission-Driven, Results-Oriented Budgeting* (Washington, D.C.: U.S. GPO, September 1993).

4. Letter to Vice President Gore from Bob Peterson, Jackson, NJ (undated).

5. Department of Energy town meeting of the National Performance Review, July 13, 1993.

6. Peter, Dr. Lawrence J., *Peter's Quotations: Ideas for Our Time* (New York: Quill/William Morrow, 1977), p. 124.

7. Osborne, David, and Ted Gaebler, *Reinventing Government: How the Entrepreneurial Spirit is Transforming the Public Sector* (Reading, MA: Addison-Wesley Publishing Company, Inc., 1992), p. 118.

8. *Mission-Driven, Results-Oriented Budgeting.*

9. 3. National Performance Review Accompanying Report, *Agency for International Development* (Washington, D.C.: U.S. GPO, September 1993).

10. This estimate is derived from federal employment statistics as of September 30, 1991, provided in Office of Personnel Management publication MW 56-22.

11. $35 billion = 700,000 central staff x $50,000 in salary and benefits per person year.

12. *The Budget of the United States Government* (Washington, D.C.: U.S. Government Printing Office): for 1966 total full-time permanent employment in the executive branch was 1,876,419 (excluding Post Office); for 1967 the numbaer increased to 2,043,797.

13. Haas, Lawrence J., *Running on Empty: Bush, Congress, and the Politics of a Bankrupt Government* (Homewood, IL: Business One Irwin 1990), p. xxiii.

14. *Mission-Driven Results-Oriented Budgeting.*

15. Ibid.

16. Ibid.

17. Unpublished case study by Pamela Varley, John F. Kennedy School of Government, Harvard University, Cambridge, MA, July 1993.

18. *Mission-Driven, Results-Oriented Budgeting.*

19. Ibid.

20. Broder, David S. and Stephen Barr, "Hill's Micromanagement of Cabinet Blurs Separation of Powers," *Washington Post* (July 25, 1993), p. A1.

21. *Mission-Driven, Results-Oriented Budgeting,* "BGT04: Eliminate Employment Ceilings and Floors by Managing Within Budget."

22. *Mission-Driven, Results-Oriented Budgeting.*

23. U.S. Congress, House, Democratic Caucus, Task Force on Government Waste, *The Challenge of Sound Management* (Washington, D.C., June 1992).

24. Office of Personnel Management, Central Personnel Data File, unpublished analysis, March 1993. Calculations by Robert Knisely, National Performance Review.

25. National Performance Review Accompanying Report, *Reinventing Human Resource Management* (Washington, D.C.: U.S. GPO, September 1993).

26. Ibid.

27. National Academy of Public Administration, *Modernizing Federal Classification: An Opportunity for Excellence* (Washington, D.C.: July 1991).

28. *Reinventing Human Resource Management.*

29. Ibid.

30. Ibid.

31. National Performance Review Accompanying Report, *Reinventing Federal Procurement* (Washington, D.C.: U.S. GPO, September 1993).

32. Ibid.

33. U.S. Merit Systems Protection Board, *Work Force Quality and Federal Procurement: An Assessment* (Washington, D.C.: U.S. GPO, July 1992), p. 21.

34. National Performance Review Accompanying Report, *Reinventing Federal Procurement,* "PROC08: Reform Information Technology Procurements" (Washington, D.C.: U.S. GPO, September 1993).

35. Ibid.

36. Ibid.

37. Ibid.

38. Ibid.

39. Ibid.

40. National Performance Review Accompanying Report, *Streamlining Management Control* (Washington, D.C.: U.S. GPO, September 1993).

41. National Performance Review Accompanying Report, *Improving Regulatory Systems* (Washington, D.C.: U.S. GPO, September 1993).

42. *Streamlining Management Controls.*

43. Department of Veterans Affairs, Management Efficiency Pilot Program, *Innovative Test is Meeting All Expectations* (Washington, D.C.: U.S. GPO, March 1990).

44. *Improving Regulatory Systems.*

45. *Streamlining Management Control.*

46. *Streamlining Management Control* and National Performance Review Accompanying Report, *Improving Financial Management* (Washington, D.C.: U.S. GPO, September 1993).

47. *Streamlining Management Control* and *Improving Financial Management*.

48. Interview with Stephen Cleghorn, Director, Jobs for Homeless People, Washington, D.C., August 1993.

49. National Performance Review Accompanying Report, *Strengthening the Partnership in Intergovernmental Service Delivery* (Washington, D.C.: U.S. GPO, September 1993).

50. Ibid.

51. Ibid.

52. Ibid.

53. Ibid.

54. National Performance Review Accompanying Report, *Housing and Urban Development,* (Washington, D.C.: U.S. GPO, September 1993)

55. Peters, Tom, *Thriving on Chaos: Handbook for a Management Revolution,* (New York: Harper & Row, 1989).

CHAPTERS 2—PUTTING CUSTOMERS FIRST

1. National Performance Review Accompanying Report, *Reengineering Through Information Technology* (Washington, D.C.: Government Printing Office [GPO], September 1993).

2. National Performance Review Accompanying Report, *Improving Customer Service* (Washington, D.C.: U.S. GPO, September 1993).

3. General Accounting Office (GAO), *Tax and Administration 1989 Test Call Survey,* GAO/GGD-90-36 (January 4, 1990) and *Tax and Administration IRS Budget Request of FY94,* GAO/T-GGD-93-23 (April 28, 1993).

4. *Improving Customer Service.*

5. Department of Health and Human Services, *Report of the Inspector General,* on the Social Security Administration's services, 1993.

6. *Improving Customer Service.*

7. Ibid.

8. National Performance Review Accompanying Report, *Streamlining Management Control* (Washington, D.C.: U.S. GPO, September 1993).

9. National Performance Review Accompanying Report, *Department of Transportation* (Washington, D.C.: U.S. GPO, September 1993).

10. National Performance Review Accompanying Report, *Department of Labor* (Washington, D.C.: U.S. GPO, September 1993).

11. Ibid

12. U.S. General Accounting Office, testimony of Franklin Frazier, *Tax Administration: U.S. and Foreign Strategies for Preparing Noncollege Youth for Employment,* GAO/T-HRD-90-31 (June 14, 1990).

13. National Performance Accompanying Reports, *Health and Human Services,* and *Strengthening the Partnership in Intergovernmental Service Delivery* (Washington, D.C.: U.S. GPO, September 1993).

14. National Commission on Children, *Beyond Rhetoric, A New American Agenda for Children and Families* (Washington D.C., 1991), p. 314.

15. *Health and Human Services.*

16. Sylvester, Kathleen, "New Strategies to Save Children in Trouble," *Governing* (May 1990), pp. 32-37.

17. National Performance Review Accompanying Report, *Office of Science and Technology Policy and the National Science Foundation* (Washington, D.C.: U.S. GPO, September 1993).

18. Executive Office of the President, Office of Management and Budget, *A Vision of Change for America* (Washington D.C.: U.S. GPO, February 1993), p. 52.

19. National Performance Review Accompanying Report, *Department of Commerce* (Washington, D.C.: U.S. GPO, September 1993).

20. Nothdurft, William, *It's Time the U.S. Got Serious About Exporting* (St. Paul, MN: The Northwest Area Foundation), pp. 28-31.

21. National Performance Review Accompanying Report, *Reinventing Environmental Management* (Washington, D.C.: U.S. GPO, September 1993).

22. Ibid.

23. *Department of Commerce.*

24. *Transforming Organizational Structures.*

25. National Performance Review Accompanying Report, *Reinventing Support Services* (Washington, D.C.: U.S. GPO, September 1993).

26. Ibid.

27. National Performance Review Accompanying Report, *Improving Financial Management* (Washington, D.C.: U.S. GPO, September 1993).

28. *Department of Commerce.*

29. National Performance Review Accompanying Report, *Department of Defense* (Washington, D.C.: U.S. GPO, September 1993).

30. *Department of Labor.*

31. *Improving Financial Management.*

32. Cummins, Keren Ware, National Technical Information Service, *Reinventing Government's Role: The Turnaround of the National Technical Information Service* (Washington, D.C.: U.S. GPO, January 27, 1993).

33. *Department of Transportation.*

34. Competitiveness Policy Council, *A Competitiveness Strategy for America* (March 1993), p. 274. The Competitiveness Policy Council is an independent advisory committee established by Congress in 1988.

35. *Reinventing Support Services.*

36. National Performance Review Accompanying Report, *Housing and Urban Development* (Washington, D.C.: U.S. GPO, September 1993).

37. *Department of Labor.*

38. National Performance Review Accompanying Report, *Environmental Protection Agency* (Washington, D.C.: U.S. GPO, September 1993).

39. Osborne, David, and Ted Gaebler, *Reinventing Government: How the Entrepreneurial Spirit is Transforming the Public Sector* (Reading, MA: Addison-Wesley Publishing Company, Inc., 1992), pp. 304-5.

40. *Housing and Urban Development.*

CHAPTER 3— EMPOWERING EMPLOYEES TO GET RESULTS

1. *Budget of the U.S. Government FY 1994* (Washington, D.C., 1993), p. 40.

2. National Academy of Public Administration (NAPA), *Revitalizing Federal Management: Managers and Their Overburdened Systems* (Washington, D.C.: NAPA 1983).

3. "Department of Transportation Town Hall Meeting with Vice President Al Gore," unpublished transcript, May 11, 1993, pp. 11-12.

4. Office of Personnel Management (OPM), Office of Systems Innovation and Simplification, *Survey of Federal Employees*, publication OS-92-06. (Washington, D.C.: OPM, May 1992).

5. Telephone interview with the Social Security Administration, Atlanta office, on April 1, 1993.

6. Obmascik, Mark, "Light-Bulb Change a 43-Person Task," *Denver Post* (November 1, 1992), p. A1.

7. U.S. General Accounting Office (GAO), *Program Performance Measures: Federal Collection and Use of Performance Data*, GAO/GGD-92-65 (Washington D.C.: U.S. Government Printing Office [GPO], May 1992).

8. National Performance Review Accompanying Report, *Transforming Organizational Structures* (Washington, D.C.: U.S. GPO, September 1993).

9. Office of Personnel Management (OPM), Central Personnel Data File, unpublished analysis, March 1993.

10. Peters, Tom, *Thriving on Chaos: Handbook for a Management Revolution* (New York: Harper & Row, 1989).

11. National Performance Review, *Reinventing Government Summit* Proceedings (Washington, D.C.: U.S. GPO, June 25, 1993), p. 87.

12. OPM, Central Personnel Data File, unpublished analysis, March 1993. Calculations by Robert Knisely, National Performance Review.

13. *Transforming Organizational Structures.*

14. Ibid.

15. Ibid.

16. National Performance Review, Town Hall Meeting Department of Transportation, unpublished transcript (Washington, D.C., May 11, 1993).

17. National Performance Review Accompanying Report, *Department of Veterans Affairs* (Washington, D.C.: U.S. GPO, September 1993).

18. National Performance Review Accompanying Report, *Housing and Urban Development* (Washington, D.C.: U.S. GPO, September 1993).

19. GAO, *Program Performance Measures.*

20. 1992 Commission on the Future of the South, *Heading Home: New Directions Toward Southern Progress* (Research Triangle Park, NC: Southern Growth Policies Board, September 1993).

21. National Performance Review Accompanying Report, *Mission Driven, Results-Oriented Budgeting* (Washington, D.C.: U.S. GPO, September 1993).

22. Ibid.

23. National Performance Review Accompanying Report, *Creating Quality Leadership and Management* (Washington, D.C.: U.S. GPO, September 1993).

24. Osborne, David, and Ted Gaebler, *Reinventing Government: How the Entrepreneurial Spirit is Transforming the Public Sector* (Reading, MA: Addison-Wesley Publishing Company, Inc., 1992), p. 144.

25. Ibid., p. 145.

26. *Creating Quality Leadership and Management.*

27. National Commission on the Public Service (Volcker Commission), *Leadership for America: Rebuilding the Public Service* (Washington D.C., 1989).

28. Ibid.

29. National Performance Review, Department of Justice Town Hall Meeting, unpublished transcript, Washington, D.C., July 14, 1993.

30. National Performance Review, *Executive Office of the President* (Washington, D.C.: U.S. GPO, September 1993).

31. National Performance Review, *Reinventing Government Summit*.

32. National Performance Review Accompanying Report, *Reinventing Human Resource Management* (Washington, D.C.: U.S. GPO, September 1993).

33. National Performance Review Accompanying Report, *Reengineering Through Information Technology* (Washington, D.C.: U.S. GPO, September 1993).

34. Kendrick, James E., "IT Management Focus Must Extend Beyond Tip of the Iceberg," *Federal Computer Week* (September 21, 1992), p. 17.

35. *Reinventing Human Resource Management*.

36. OPM, *1969-1991 Trends of the Federal Civilian Workforce in Accounting and Budget Occupations*, Special Report. Figures represent 1991 employment in occupation series 501, 503, 505, 510-11, 525, 530, 540, 544-45, 560-61, 593, 599, and half the total number in 343.

37. National Performance Review Accompanying Report, *Improving Financial Management* (Washington, D.C.: Government Printing Office, September 1993).

38. To date, Congress has appropriated $130 billion to cover the savings and loan bailout. General Accounting Office estimates project the cost will reach $500 billion over the next few decades, including interest costs.

39. *Improving Financial Management*.

40. Ibid.

41. Ibid.

42. Barr, Stephen, "See IRS's Books. Color Them Red," *Washington Post* (August 18, 1993), p. A19.

43. *Improving Financial Management*.

44. Not all federal agencies will have audited financial statements completed by 1997, but the 1997 consolidated financial statements will footnote any discrepancies. See *Improving Financial Management*.

45. Telephone interview with Rick Weidman, Administrator, New York State Veterans Program (New York Department of Labor), August 20, 1993.

46. *Reengineering Through Information Technology*.

47. Galen, Michele, Ann Therese Palmer, Alice Cuneo, and Mark Maremont, "Work & Family," *Business Week*, (June 28, 1993), p. 82.

48. *Reinventing Human Resource Management*.

49. OPM, *A Study of the Work and Family Needs of the Federal Workforce* (Washington, D.C., April 1992), pp. 5, 6, 20, 26.

50. OPM, *Report to Congress on the Federal Employees Leave Sharing Act of 1988* (Washington, D.C., April 30, 1993), p. 30; and *A Study of the Work and Family Needs*, p. 96.

51. *Improving Financial Management*.

52. Interview with Lani Horowitz, Administration for Children and Families, Department of Health and Human Services, August 20, 1993.

53. Interview with Tom Komarek, Assistant Secretary for Administration and Management, Department of Labor, August 20, 1993.

54. *Reinventing Human Resource Management*.

55. U.S. Merit Systems Protection Board, *A Question of Equity: Women and the Glass Ceiling in Federal Government* (Washington D.C., October 1992), p. 37.

56. GAO, *Quality Management in Government*, GAO/GGD-93-9-BR (Washington D.C.: GAO, October, 1992).

57. GAO, *Federal Labor Relations: A Program in Need of Reform*, GGD-91-101 (Washington, D.C.: GAO, July 1991), p. 2.

58. *Reinventing Human Resource Management*.

59. Ibid.

60. GAO, *Federal Labor Relations*, p. 76.

61. GAO, *Government Management Issues*, GAO/TR-93-3 (Washington, D.C.: GAO, December 1992).

62. *Creating Quality Leadership and Management*.

63. *Reinventing Government Summit*.

64. *Creating Quality Leadership and Management*.

65. Ibid.

66. Ibid and *Reinventing Human Resource Management*.

67. Interview with Robert DeGrasse, Special Assistant to Hazel O'Leary, Secretary of Energy, August 22, 1993.

68. *Reinventing Government Summit*.

CHAPTER 4—CUTTING BACK TO BASICS

1. Letter and personal communications with Bruce Bair, Schoenchen, KS, May 24, 1993.

2. La Franiere, Sharon, "Hair That Defies Cutting; Subsidy Program Seems a Lock in Budget," *Washington Post*, April 6, 1993, p. A1.

3. Gladwell, Malcolm, "Epicurean Niche Barely Survives a Boiling Dispute," *Washington Post*, August 20, 1993, p. A21.

4. National Performance Review Accompanying Report, *Mission-Driven, Results-Oriented Budgeting* (Washington, D.C.: U.S. Government Printing Office [GPO], September 1993).

5. National Performance Review Accompanying Report, *Transforming Organizational Structures* (Washington, D.C.: U.S. GPO, September 1993).

6. National Performance Review Accompanying Report, *Department of Agriculture* (Washington, D.C.: U.S. GPO, September 1993).

7. U.S. General Accounting Office (GAO), *U.S. Department of Agriculture: Farm Agencies' Field Structure Needs Major Overhaul*, RCED-91-09 (Washington, D.C.: January 1991), p. 10.

8. National Performance Review Accompanying Report, *Housing and Urban Development* (Washington, D.C.: U.S. GPO, September 1993).

9. Ibid.

10. National Performance Review Accompanying Report, *Department of Energy* (Washington, D.C.: September 1993).

11. National Performance Review Accompanying Report, *Department of Defense* (Washington, D.C.: U.S. GPO, September 1993).

12. National Performance Review Accompanying Report, *Small Business Administration* (Washington, D.C.: U.S. GPO, September 1993).

13. National Performance Review Accompanying Report, *U.S. Agency for International Development,* (Washington, D.C.: U.S. GPO, September 1993).

14. National Performance Review Accompanying Report, *Department of State* (Washington, D.C.: U.S. GPO, September 1993).

15. Ibid.

16. Ibid.

17. National Performance Review Accompanying Report, *Department of Energy* (Washington, D.C.: U.S. GPO, September 1993).

18. National Performance Review Accompanying Report, *Department of Transportation* (Washington, D.C.: U.S. GPO, September 1993).

19. *Department of Defense.*

20. National Performance Review, Accompanying Report, *Reinventing Federal Procurement* (Washington, D.C.: U.S. GPO, September 1993).

21. National Performance Review Accompanying Report, *Intelligence Community* (Washington, D.C.: U.S. GPO, September 1993).

22. National Performance Review Accompanying Report, *Department of Labor* (Washington, D.C.: U.S. GPO, September 1993).

23. GAO, *Dislocated Workers: Comparison of Assistance Programs,* Briefing Report to Congressional Requesters, GAO/HRD-92-153BR (Washington D.C., September 1992), p. 2.

24. *Department of Agriculture* and *Department of Labor.*

25. National Performance Review Accompanying Report, *Department of Education* (Washington, D.C.: U.S. GPO, September 1993).

26. National Performance Review Accompanying Report, *Health and Human Services* (Washington, D.C.: U.S. GPO, September 1993).

27. Ibid.

28. *Department of State.*

29. National Performance Review Accompanying Report, *Department of Commerce* (Washington, D.C.: U.S. GPO, September 1993).

30. *Health and Human Services.*

31. Ibid.

32. National Performance Review Accompanying Report, *Department of Justice* (Washington, D.C.: U.S. GPO, September 1993).

33. *Department of Agriculture.*

34. U.S. Department of Agriculture, Office of the Inspector General, International Affairs, Commodity Programs, and Science and Education Division, *Report on Agricultural Stabilization and Conservation Service* (Washington D.C.: Department of Agriculture, May 1993), p. 11.

35. *Department of Transportation.*

36. U.S. General Accounting Office, Highway Demonstration Projects: Improved Selection and Funding Controls Are Needed (Washington, DC: GAO, 1991), pp. 1-6.

37. *Department of Transportation.*

38. National Performance Review Accompanying Report, *Department of the Interior* (Washington, D.C.: U.S. GPO, September 1993).

39. Ibid.

40. *Health and Human Services.*

41. National Performance Review Accompanying Report, *Department of Veterans Affairs* (Washington, D.C.: U.S. GPO, September 1993).

42. *Department of Defense.*

43. *Department of Energy.*

44. Office of Management and Budget (OMB), *Fact Sheet on Reform of Federal Power Marketing Administration Debt Repayment Practices* (Washington D.C., 1990), p. 3.

45. OMB, *Status Report on Credit Management and Debt Collection,* Report to Congress (Washington D.C., 1993), p. 1.

46. National Performance Review Accompanying Report, *Improving Financial Management* (Washington, D.C.: U.S. GPO, September 1993).

47. *Department of Justice.*

48. *Department of the Interior.*

49. *Housing and Urban Development.*

50. *Department of Labor.*

51. Ibid.

52. *Health and Human Services.*

53. GAO, *SSA's Processing of Continuing Disability Reviews,* testimony of Jane L. Ross before the House Select Committee on Aging, GAO/T-HRD-93-3 (March 9, 1993), p. 3.

54. *Health and Human Services.*

55. Ibid.

56. GAO, *Federal Benefit Payments: Agencies Need Death Information from Social Security to Avoid Erroneous Payments,* GAO/HRD-9-3 (Washington D.C., February 1991).

57. National Performance Review Accompanying Reports: *Department of the Treasury and the Resolution Trust Corporation; Department of the Interior; Improving Financial Management;* and, *Department of Defense* (Washington, D.C.: U.S. GPO, September 1993).

58. *Improving Financial Management.*

59. Ibid.

60. *Department of State.*

61. *Department of the Treasury.*

62. National Performance Review Accompanying Report, *Reengineering Through Information Technology* (Washington, D.C.: U.S. GPO, September 1993).

63. Ibid.

64. *Department of Labor.*

65. Ibid.

66. *Health and Human Services.*

67. *Department of the Interior.*

68. *Department of the Treasury.*

69. Ibid.

70. National Performance Review Accompanying Report, *Rethinking Program Design* (Washington, D.C.: Government Printing Office, September 1993).

71. Moe, Ronald C., "Reorganizing the Executive Branch," in *The Twentieth Century: Landmark Commissions,* 92-293 GOV (Washington, D.C.: Library of Congress, Congressional Research Service, March 19, 1992), p. 50.

72. Pritzker, David M., "Working Together for Better Regulations," vol. 5, no. 2, *Natural Resources and the Environment* (Fall 1990).

73. *Department of Labor* and *Health and Human Services,* and National Performance Review Accompanying Report, *Improving Regulatory Systems* (Washington, D.C.: U.S. GPO, September 1993).

74. *Department of Labor* and *Improving Regulatory Systems.*

75. *Improving Regulatory Systems.*

APPENDIX A

NATIONAL PERFORMANCE REVIEW
MAJOR RECOMMENDATIONS
BY AGENCY

Recommendation	Fiscal Impact, 1994-99* (Millions of Dollars)	
	Change in Spending	Change in Revenues

AGENCY FOR INTERNATIONAL DEVELOPMENT

AID01	**Redefine and Focus AID's Mission and Priorities** With the end of the Cold War, AID must rethink how it will operate. NPR recommends steps to plan for this new mission and proposes new authorizing legislation to define its post-Cold War mission and priorities.	cbe	cbe
AID02	**Reduce Funding, Spending and Reporting Micromanagement** Eliminate AID's outdated or unduly burdensome reporting requirements and reduce legislative earmarks to provide greater operating flexibility.	cbe	cbe
AID03	**Overhaul the AID Personnel System** Recommendations include changes in AID's personnel system to integrate its multiple systems and review benefits.	na	na
AID04	**Manage AID Employees and Consultants as a Unified Work Force** Lift some current personnel restrictions and give managers authority to manage staff resources more efficiently and effectively.	cbe	cbe
AID05	**Establish an AID Innovation Capital Fund** Create a capital investment fund to improve information and financial management systems and customer service.	na	na
AID06	**Reengineer Management of AID Projects and Programs** AID should use pilot programs and new approaches to emphasize flexibility, innovation, customer service and program results.	cbe	cbe
AID07	**Consolidate or Close AID Overseas Missions** AID should regionalize missions and staff services overseas and close nonessential missions. It should establish "graduation" criteria for countries receiving U.S. assistance.	cbe	cbe

DEPARTMENT OF AGRICULTURE

USDA01	**End the Wool and Mohair Subsidy** The subsidy is no longer needed since wool is no longer a strategic commodity.	-$923.0	$0.0
USDA02	**Eliminate Federal Support for Honey** Eliminate the honey subsidy because the program does not serve the intended purpose of ensuring the availability of honeybees for crop pollination.	-15.0	0.0
USDA03	**Reorganize the Department of Agriculture to Better Accomplish Its Mission, Streamline Its Field Structure and Improve Service to Its Customers** USDA should streamline its field operations to eliminate unnecessary offices, reduce costs and better serve farmers.	-1,673.6	0.0
USDA04	**Implement a Consolidated Farm Management Plan** The farm management plan proposed by Secretary Espy provides an opportunity to simplify regulations for farm management and is a good way to consolidate competing requirements into a single plan for each farm.	cbe	cbe
USDA05	**Administer the Employment and Training Requirements for Food Stamp Recipients More Effectively and Efficiently** Redirect funds from an ineffective training program for food stamp recipients and allow them to participate in programs with proven results.	-1,041.1**	0.0
USDA06	**Encourage Better Food Package Management Practices and Facilitate Multi-State Contracts for Infant Food and Formula Cost Containment in the WIC Program** The recommendation encourages increased competition among infant formula vendors and manufacturers of other items in the UDSDA's Special Supplemental Food Program for Women, Infants and Children (WIC). Savings accrue to program.	-500.0**	0.0

* Fiscal estimates were made for 1994 only where action could impact spending in that year. Most estimates cover 1995-99. Estimates shown are for cumulative budget authority changes. Negative numbers indicate reduced spending.

** The NPR recommends that these savings be redirected to alternative uses. Savings totals exclude these amounts.

*** Savings will be invested in the program to serve additional customers.

cbe = cannot be estimated (due to data limitations or uncertainties about implementation time lines).

na= not applicable—recommendation improves efficiency or redirects resources but does not directly reduce budget authority.

Recommendation	Fiscal Impact, 1994-99 (Millions of Dollars)	
	Change in Spending	Change in Receipts
USDA07 Deliver Food Stamp Benefits Via Electronic Benefits Transfer to Improve Service to Customers While Remaining Cost Effective Use electronic technology to distribute food stamp benefits, thereby improving service and reducing the need for current paper stamps.	cbe	cbe

DEPARTMENT OF COMMERCE

Recommendation	Change in Spending	Change in Receipts
DOC01 Reinvent Federal Economic and Regional Development Efforts Improve coordination of federal economic development efforts with the goals of eliminating duplication and better directing federal resources to improve business conditions.	na	na
DOC02 Provide Better Coordination to Refocus and Leverage Federal Export Promotion This recommendation is designed to improve federal services to U.S. businesses competing in the world export markets.	na	na
DOC03 Reform the Federal Export Control System for Commercial Goods To help ensure leading U.S. industries are competitive in the global marketplace, changes should be made in the export control system.	na	na
DOC04 Strengthen the Tourism Policy Council Revitalize the Tourism Policy Council and give it greater authority to coordinate federal tourism promotion efforts.	na	na
DOC05 Create Public / Private Competition for the NOAA Fleet A pilot program is recommended to open the National Oceanic and Atmospheric Administration fleet to public and private competition to bolster the aging fleet.	cbe	cbe
DOC06 Improve Marine Fisheries Management To help protect fishing resources and provide new income to the government, NOAA should collaborate with Congress and fishing industry representatives to establish appropriate user fees to help offset management costs for national fishery zones.	0.0	375.0
DOC07 Provide EDA Public Works Loan Guarantees for Infrastructure Assistance This recommendation would provide the Economic Development Administration with authority to use part of its funding as a reserve for loan guarantees for various public economic development projects.	na	na
DOC08 Establish a Manufacturing Technology Data Bank To help U.S. manufacturing firms increase their technical capabilities, Commerce should create a new database to provide technical information and contacts.	na	na
DOC09 Expand the Electronic Availability of Census Data To increase access to and use of census data, the Census Bureau should create a computerized census information center.	na	na
DOC10 Amend the Omnibus Trade and Competitiveness Act to Increase the Data Quality of the National Trade Data Bank This recommendation outlines improvements needed in the quality and quantity of data in this business-oriented data bank.	na	na
DOC11 Eliminate Legislative Barriers to the Exchange of Business Data Among Federal Statistical Agencies Eliminate legislative barriers to the exchange of business data among federal agencies (the Census Bureau, Bureau of Labor Statistics, and Bureau of Economic Analysis) to reduce the reporting burden on American business.	na	na
DOC12 Establish a Single Civilian Operational Environmental Polar Satellite Program To reduce duplication and save taxpayers a billion dollars over the next decade, various current and proposed polar satellite programs should be consolidated under NOAA.	-300.0	0.0
DOC13 Use Sampling to Minimize Cost of the Decennial Census Use sampling rather than more costly methods of counting nonrespondents to next deciennial census. (Savings will occur but are beyond the time frame of this analysis.)	cbe	cbe

cbe = cannot be estimated (due to data limitations or uncertainties about implementation time lines).

na= not applicable—recommendation improves efficiency or redirects resources but does not directly reduce budget authority.

Recommendation	Fiscal Impact, 1994-99 (Millions of Dollars)	
	Change in Spending	Change in Receipts
DOC14 Build a Business and Economic Information Node for the Information Highway To assist in the distribution of government information to private citizens, Commerce should build a business and economic information node to the "information highway."	cbe	cbe
DOC15 Increase Access to Capital for Minority Businesses Commerce and SBA should provide the President with recommendations to improve SBA and Minority Business Development Administration programs.	na	na

DEPARTMENT OF DEFENSE

—— **The Bottom-Up Review** This is a general summary of the Bottom-Up Review of DOD's force structure and requirements and its part in the National Performance Review effort. A total of $79 billion in savings through 1997 are already incorporated into the President's 1994 budget. These savings are not included in the NPR analysis.	—	—
—— **Acquisition Reform** The DOD acquisition system is large and extraordinarily complex. It needs to enable DOD to take advantage of the technological advances and efficient procurement practices of the commercial marketplace.	—	—
DOD01 Rewrite Policy Directives to Include Better Guidance and Fewer Procedures DOD should clarify policy directives and procedures to reduce administrative burden and unnecessary regulatory controls.	cbe	cbe
DOD02 Establish a Unified Budget for the Department of Defense Give commanders greater flexibility to set priorities, solve funding problems, and resolve unplanned requirements at the lowest appropriate operating level.	cbe	cbe
DOD03 Purchase Best Value Common Supplies and Services Allow managers and commanders to purchase the best value common supplies and services from public, private, or nonprofit sources.	cbe	cbe
DOD04 Outsource Non-core Department of Defense Functions By contracting out non-core functions (from towing services to certain information technology functions), DOD will be better able to focus on its core responsibilities.	cbe	cbe
DOD05 Create Incentives for the Department of Defense to Generate Revenues This recommendation proposes giving managers and commanders the ability to generate income at the installation level by allowing the Corps of Engineers to recover its costs for processing certain commerical applications and by establishing goals for solid waste reduction and recycling.	-500.0	60.0
DOD06 Establish and Promote a Productivity-Enhancing Capital Investment Fund DOD should be authorized to expand its capital investment fund and manage its operations in a more business-like manner.	-110.3	0.0
DOD07 Create a Healthy and Safe Environment for Department of Defense Activities To create a safe environment, DOD must take action in the areas of clean-up of hazardous wastes, use of environmental technology, and pollution prevention.	na	na
DOD08 Establish a Defense Quality Workplace This is an internal department recommendation to encourage the use of quality management concepts at all levels of DOD.	cbe	cbe
DOD09 Maximize the Efficiency of DOD Health Care Operations Use emerging technology to upgrade care at DOD health care facilities and reduce costs to train health care professionals.	-350.0	0.0
DOD10 Give Department of Defense Installation Commanders More Authority and Responsibility Over Installation Management By giving DOD installation commanders more authority over installation management, DOD will be better able to manage its resources, provide services to its employees and move toward more entrepreneurial management.	cbe	cbe

cbe = cannot be estimated (due to data limitations or uncertainties about implementation time lines).

na= not applicable—recommendation improves efficiency or redirects resources but does not directly reduce budget authority.

Recommendation	Fiscal Impact, 1994-99 (Millions of Dollars)	
	Change in Spending	Change in Receipts

DOD11 Reduce National Guard and Reserve Costs — -900.0 / 0.0
This recommendation makes two changes in the current costs for reservists: (1) to limit compensation of federal employees on reserve duty to the greater of civilian or reserve compensation or to allow the reservist to take annual leave; and (2) to limit the basic allowance for quarters only to reservists who actually bring their dependents on short-term duty assignments when quarters are not provided to dependents.

DOD12 Streamline and Reorganize the U.S. Army Corps of Engineers — -68.0 / 0.0
NPR recommends implementing a 1992 reorganization proposal that would reduce the number of division offices from 11 to six and would allow the Corps to work with OMB and other agencies to make maximum use of Corps' engineering and technical capabilities.

DEPARTMENT OF EDUCATION

ED01 Redesign Chapter 1 of Elementary and Secondary Education Act — -$3,000.0* / $0.0
Recommendations focus education funds on the neediest students and simplify requirements on schools receiving federal education aid. Existing funds are redirected.

ED02 Reduce the Number of Programs the Department of Education Administers — -515.0* / 0.0
Eliminate or consolidate more than 40 existing education grant programs and free up funds for use in other educational programs.

ED03 Consolidate the Eisenhower Math and Science Education Program with Chapter 2 — na / na
NPR proposes combining this teacher training program, which is largely consumed with short-term training, with other ED programs to create a new program with a more coherent national focus on teacher training and professional development.

ED04 Consolidate National Security Education Act Programs — na / na
The NSEA trust fund, administered by the Department of Defense, should be consolidated with the Center for International Education in ED to strengthen foreign language study and eliminate duplication of effort.

ED05 Streamline and Improve the Department of Education's Grants Process — cbe / cbe
Statutory restrictions on the department's rulemaking process should be removed, flexibility added to certain procedures, and unnecessary requirements eliminated to shorten the grant award process.

ED06 Provide Incentives for the Department of Education's Debt Collection Service — na / na
This recommendation would allow ED to use a portion of revenues collected from defaulted student loans to pay for collections costs, thereby providing an incentive for increased collections.

ED07 Simplify and Strengthen Institutional Eligibility and Certification for Participation in Federal Student Aid — -175.0 / 0.0
NPR recommends developing ways of measuring default indicators, creating profiles of high-risk institutions, and removing elgibility of institutions to participate in federal financial aid programs once the schools have become ineligible to receive federal student loan funds.

ED08 Create a Single Point of Contact for Program and Grant Information — 1.8 / 0.0
ED should create an electronic system that can be used by students, parents, researchers and administrators to learn about department programs, funding opportunities, best practices and other information.

ED09 Improve Employee Development Opportunities in Department of Education — na / na
ED should create a full spectrum of activities which can contribute to career development, including conducting a departmentwide assessment of training and development needs.

---

* The NPR recommends that these savings be redirected to alternative uses. Savings totals exclude these amounts.

cbe = cannot be estimated (due to data limitations or uncertainties about implementation time lines).

na= not applicable—recommendation improves efficiency or redirects resources but does not directly reduce budget authority.

Recommendation	Fiscal Impact, 1994-99 (Millions of Dollars)	
	Change in Spending	Change in Receipts
ED10 Eliminate the Grantback Statutory Provision of the General Education Provisions Act NPR recommends repealing this provision which permits the department to return to a grantee a percentage of funds recovered from the grantee as a result of an audit.	0.0*	0.0
ED11 Build a Professional, Mission-Driven Structure for Research NPR recommends establishing a research advisory board, consolidating and targeting research and development efforts, and establishing an office to translate research findings into education reform assistance.	na	na
ED12 Develop a Strategy for Technical Assistance and Information Dissemination ED should develop a strategy for its $290 million technical assistance efforts designed to promote the National Goals 2000 themes.	na	na

DEPARTMENT OF ENERGY

Recommendation		
DOE01 Improve Environmental Contract Management NPR proposes improvements in DOE environmental clean-up contracts to achieve efficiency.	cbe	cbe
DOE02 Incorporate Land Use Planning in Cleanup NPR recommends that DOE incorporate land use planning into the nuclear facilities clean-up process.	cbe	cbe
DOE03 Make Field Facility Contracts Outcome-Oriented This recommendation would modify the current DOE contract process at field facilities to make the contracts more outcome-oriented to improve efficiency and contractor performance.	-570.0	0.0
DOE04 Increase Electrical Power Revenues and Study Rates NPR proposes increasing federal income by allowing the Power Marketing Administrations to recover a larger portion of their operating costs through rate increases or by changing the financing of Bonneville Power Administration.	0.0	3,601.0
DOE05 Strengthen the Federal Energy Management Program NPR recommends a number of improvements to this program, designed to better management of federal energy use.	na	na
DOE06 Redirect Energy Laboratories to Post-Cold War Priorities This recommendation provides guidance for use of the DOE energy labs, focusing on defining new missions, consolidating or eliminating unneeded facilities, and making their services of greater benefit in the post-Cold War era.	-2,150.0	0.0
DOE07 Save Costs Through Private Power Cogeneration This would allow the private sector to cogenerate power at DOE labs as a means of saving money. DOD has similar authority at this time.	-112.0	0.0
DOE08 Support the Sale of the Alaska Power Administration The federal government should divest its interests in the Alaska Power Administration.	-20.5	-52.5

ENVIRONMENTAL PROTECTION AGENCY

Recommendation		
EPA01 Improve Environmental Protection Through Increased Flexibility for Local Government EPA should amend the regulations it determines are most troublesome for local governments pursuant to the Regulatory Flexibility Act of 1980. The goal is to provide alternative, flexible approaches to meeting environmental mandates.	na	na
EPA02 Streamline EPA's Permit Program Streamlining efforts include establishing a permit clearinghouse to serve as a single point of contact and piloting a cross-program permit tracking system.	-22.5	0.0

*This recommendation saves an estimated $18.5 million in expenditures but makes no change in budget authority.

cbe = cannot be estimated (due to data limitations or uncertainties about implementation time lines).

na= not applicable—recommendation improves efficiency or redirects resources but does not directly reduce budget authority.

Recommendation	Fiscal Impact, 1994-99 (Millions of Dollars)	
	Change in Spending	Change in Receipts

EPA03 **Shift EPA's Emphasis Toward Pollution Prevention and Away from Pollution Control** EPA needs to emphasize pollution prevention by implementing an effective pollution prevention strategy that includes amending regulations and motivating the private sector to invest in cleaner, less polluting technologies and practices.	cbe	cbe
EPA04 **Promote the Use of Economic and Market-Based Approaches to Reduce Water Pollution** EPA should work with Congress to propose language amending the Clean Water Act to explicitly encourage market-based approaches to reduce water pollution. EPA should also identify wastewater discharge fees that could be included in the Clean Water Act reauthorization.	cbe	cbe
EPA05 **Increase Private Sector Partnerships to Accelerate Development of Innovative Technologies** NPR recommends that EPA develop an action plan with specific milestones for improving the regulatory and statutory climate for innovative technologies.	na	na
EPA06 **Stop the Export of Banned Pesticides** EPA should work with Congress to develop legislation to stop the exportation of banned pesticides from the U.S. by June 1994.	na	na
EPA07 **Establish Measurable Goals, Performance Standards and Strategic Planning within EPA** EPA should draft measurable environmental goals for the range of environmental problems the U.S. faces. The agency should also draft internal goals to provide direction for assessing and redirecting existing EPA strategies.	na	na
EPA08 **Reform EPA's Contract Management Process** NPR recommends reforms in EPA's contract management process by implementing performance standards and by maximizing competition in the contracting process.	cbe	cbe
EPA09 **Establish a Blueprint for Environmental Justice Through EPA's Operations** EPA should develop a blueprint of actions that will incorporate environmental justice consideration into all aspects of EPA operations.	na	na
EPA10 **Promote Quality Science for Quality Decisions** Improvements include establishing guidelines for professional development of EPA's scientific and technical staff and expanding the use of peer-review and quality assurance procedures.	na	na
EPA11 **Reorganize EPA's Office of Enforcement** EPA should initiate a reorganization of its headquarter's enforcement organization by October 1, 1993.	-10.5	0.0

EXECUTIVE OFFICE OF THE PRESIDENT

NOTE: **White House Office and Office of the Vice President** The White House Office and the Office of the Vice President are regularly "reinvented" with each change of administration. This analysis focuses on the other portions of the Executive Office of the President.	—	—
EOP01 **Delegate Routine Paperwork Review to the Agencies and Redeploy OMB' Resources More Effectively** These recommendations outline improvements to streamline the government's paperwork review process and reduce unnecessary burdens on agencies.	cbe	cbe
EOP02 **Modify the OMB Circular System** OMB should reinvigorate the process for the review, updating, and consolidation of management circulars. It should also develop uniform processes for developing circulars and for obtaining input during their development.	na	na
EOP03 **Strengthen the Office of U.S. Trade Representative's Coordination with State and Local Governments** The Trade Representative's Office should examine the trade policy needs of state and local governments and work with them on relevant issues.	0.5	0.0

cbe = cannot be estimated (due to data limitations or uncertainties about implementation time lines).

na= not applicable—recommendation improves efficiency or redirects resources but does not directly reduce budget authority.

Recommendation	Fiscal Impact, 1994-99 (Millions of Dollars)	
	Change in Spending	Change in Receipts
EOP04 Improve Federal Advisory Committee Management Discontinuing the "anti pass the hat" language annually inserted into appropriations acts would allow appropriate pooling of executive resources for certain multi-agency projects.	-1.4	0.0
EOP05 Reinvent OMB's Management Mission NPR recommends a series of actions by OMB to redirect resources to provide better management information for Presidential decision making.	0.1	0.0
EOP06 Improve OMB's Relationship with Other Agencies This recommendation outlines methods by which OMB can work more effectively with agencies and with states.	na	na
EOP07 Strengthen the Office of the U.S. Trade Representative's Trade Policy Coordination Process These recommendations outline ways to improve the interagency trade policy coordination process.	na	na
EOP08 Strengthen the Office of the U.S. Trade Representative's Negotiation Process The Office of the USTR should implement various techniques for upgrading the negotiating skills of its employees and the analysis of the negotiation process itself.	cbe	cbe
EOP09 Establish a Customer Service Bureau in the EOP Using available resources, EOP management should establish a small, one-stop customer service bureau within the EOP.	na	na
EOP10 Conduct Qualitative Self-Reviews of Critical Administrative Processes The Assistant to the President for Management and Administration should establish a formal program of ongoing, internal quality reviews of administrative processes in the EOP to save money and improve service.	cbe	cbe
EOP11 Improve the Presidential Transition Process Past difficulties with the Presidential transition should be corrected by amendment of the Presidential Transition Act and related actions.	cbe	cbe
EOP12 Improve Administrative Processes This recommendation outlines a series of steps to improve internal administrative processes within the EOP, including mail processing, paperwork flow, and supply management.	na	na
FEDERAL EMERGENCY MANAGEMENT AGENCY		
FEMA01 Shift Emphasis to Preparing for and Responding to the Consequences of All Disasters FEMA's early focus was on preparedness for nuclear war. The current world situation and recent natural disasters highlight the need for FEMA to continue to shift its resources to respond to all hazards.	na	na
FEMA02 Develop a More Anticipatory and Customer-Driven Response to Catastrophic Disasters These recommendations should make FEMA respond faster and more effectively to catastrophic disasters.	na	na
FEMA03 Create Results-Oriented Incentives to Reduce the Costs of a Disaster The Midwest floods, Hurricanes Hugo and Andrew and the Loma Prieta Earthquake all illustrate the enormous costs of disaster to society. These recommendations will move toward reducing that cost.	cbe	cbe
FEMA04 Develop A Skilled Management Team Among Political Appointees and Career Staff Leadership has been the weak link in FEMA's mission as the federal government's emergency management coordinator. These recommendations strive to improve FEMA leadership to successfully implement its new, all-hazards mission.	na	na

cbe = cannot be estimated (due to data limitations or uncertainties about implementation time lines).

na= not applicable—recommendation improves efficiency or redirects resources but does not directly reduce budget authority.

Recommendation	Fiscal Impact, 1994-99 (Millions of Dollars)	
	Change in Spending	Change in Receipts

DEPARTMENT OF HEALTH AND HUMAN SERVICES

NOTE: **Treatment of Health Care and Welfare Reform Issues by the NPR** — —
Two primary concerns of the Department of Health and Human Services are the delivery of health and welfare services to individuals. Since the Administration has special, ongoing efforts dealing with these areas, they are not covered by the National Performance Review.

HHS01 **Promote Effective, Integrated Service Delivery for Customers by Increasing Collaborative Efforts** cbe cbe
These recommendations outline a number of steps needed to better integrate and deliver social services to communities and families.

HHS02 **Reengineer the HHS Process for Issuing Regulations** cbe cbe
HHS should improve the timeliness and quality of regulations issued and should involve stakeholders in the development of regulations.

HHS03 **Develop a National, Uniform Inspection System to Ensure a Safe Food Supply** cbe cbe
Responsibility for food safety should be consolidated into a single agency, and policies and inspection systems should be implemented on an objective, scientific basis.

HHS04 **Reconfigure Support for Health Professions Education** na na
Existing programs should be consolidated and/or eliminated.

HHS05 **Restructure the Management of Railroad Industry Benefit Programs** cbe cbe
Railroad Retirement Board functions should be integrated into existing programs administered by federal, state, and private sector service providers.

HHS06 **Improve Social Security Administration Disability Claims Processing to Better Serve People with Disabilities and Safeguard Trust Fund Assets** -4,010.0* 0.0
SSA should apply resources and management tools needed to reduce backlogs and to avoid paying benefits to individuals who are no longer disabled.

HHS07 **Protect Social Security, Disability and Medicare Trust Fund Assets by Removing Barriers to Funding Productive Oversight Activities** na na
HHS should aggressively pursue options to assure that adequate investments are made to avoid unnecessary payments from trust funds.

HHS08 **Coordinate Collection and Dissemination of Social Security Administration Death Information to Protect Federal Program Assets** cbe cbe
SSA's clearinghouse for death information and "best practices" can be used by dozens of federal and state agencies to reduce federal program outlays.

HHS09 **Take More Aggressive Actions to Collect Outstanding Debts Owed to the Social Security Trust Fund** -335.0* 0.0
SSA should be given the authority to use a full range of debt collection tools available under the Debt Collection Act of 1982 to collect debts owed by individuals who are no longer on benefit rolls.

HHS10 **Institute and Collect User Fees on FDA's Inspection and Approval Processes** -1,439.8 0.0
Food, drug and medical device manufacturers, processors and suppliers should be required to pay for FDA services.

HHS11 **Redesign SSA Service Delivery and Make Better Use of Technology to Provide Improved Access and Services to Customers** na na
SSA's organizational structure needs to be updated to reflect changing customer needs and to take full advantage of emerging technologies.

HHS12 **Strengthen Departmentwide Management** na na
The department should conduct a review of its organizational structure and management systems to determine an appropriate balance between centralized and decentralized functions.

HHS13 **Review the Field and Regional Office Structure of the HHS and Develop a Plan for Shifting Resources to Match Workload Demands** cbe cbe
The review should emphasize customer service, results and increased accountability.

*These savings, included in the Grand Total, will be realized in the Social Security Trust Funds and will not affect discretionary spending levels.
cbe = cannot be estimated (due to data limitations or uncertainties about implementation time lines).
na = not applicable—recommendation improves efficiency or redirects resources but does not directly reduce budget authority.

Recommendation	Fiscal Impact, 1994-99 (Millions of Dollars)	
	Change in Spending	Change in Receipts
HHS14 Amend the Health Care Financing Administration's Contracting Authority to Allow for Competitive Contracting HCFA should be authorized to fully and openly compete Medicare claims processing contracts to reduce costs and eliminate inefficiencies and conflicts of interest.	-985.0	0.0

DEPARTMENT OF HOUSING AND URBAN DEVELOPMENT

Recommendation	Change in Spending	Change in Receipts
HUD01 Reinvent Public Housing HUD should create pilot programs to devolve greater authority over housing funds to sound local agencies. It should create demonstrations of mixed-income public housing with portable subsidies. HUD should also streamline public housing rules and take other steps to improve public housing management.	cbe	cbe
HUD02 Improve Multi-Family Asset Management and Disposition HUD should use public-private partnerships to manage and sell HUD-held loans and real estate for non-subsidized housing projects. Congress should reduce restrictions on HUD sale of multi-family properties, including use of portable subsidies for tenants when the Secretary determines that to be best for tenant needs.	na	na
HUD03 Improve Single-Family Asset Management and Disposition HUD should use a combination of early assistance to borrowers having financial difficulties, contract loan servicing, contract mortgage assistance programs and public-private partnerships to streamline and improve management of HUD-assigned single-family mortgages.	na	na
HUD04 Create an Assisted-Housing/Rent Subsidy Demonstration Project HUD should be authorized to experiment in negotiated restructuring of privately owned assisted-housing projects to improve management, promote mixed-income housing and save taxpayer funds.	na	na
HUD05 Establish a New Housing Production Program HUD should stimulate housing production through FHA risk-sharing arrangements with housing finance agencies, stimulate a secondary market for multi-family properties, improve access to FHA insurance for first-time home buyers, provide special FHA programs to revitalize neighborhoods and improve FHA management.	na	na
HUD06 Streamline HUD Field Operations HUD should streamline its Washington, regional and field office structure and consolidate and reduce its size over time.	-167.0	0.0
HUD07 Refinance Section 235 Mortgages HUD should use incentive contracts to speed savings from refinancing expensive old mortgages subsidized by HUD.	-210.0	0.0
HUD08 Reduce Section 8 Contract Rent Payments HUD should modify its process to reduce unjustified increases in annual payments to Section 8 projects.	-225.0	0.0
HUD09 Consolidate Section 8 Certificates and Vouchers This recommendation would consolidate two overlapping projects to eliminate duplication.	cbe	cbe
HUD10 Reduce Operating Subsidies for Vacancies This recommendation would encourage public housing agencies to make better use of their assets by reducing subsidies paid for unjustifiably vacant units.	cbe	cbe

INTELLIGENCE COMMUNITY

Recommendation	Change in Spending	Change in Receipts
INTEL01 Enhance Intelligence Community Integration The end of the Cold War and the constrained fiscal environment in the U.S. create an imperative for the 13 components of the Intelligence Community to act more effectively and more efficiently as a team.	*	*

*The Intelligence Community budget is classified. Savings from these recommendations cannot be shown in this report.
cbe = cannot be estimated (due to data limitations or uncertainties about implementation time lines).
na = not applicable—recommendation improves efficiency or redirects resources but does not directly reduce budget authority.

Recommendation	Fiscal Impact, 1994-99 (Millions of Dollars)	
	Change in Spending	Change in Receipts
INTEL02 Enhance Community Responsiveness to Customers A 40-year emphasis on the Soviet Union allowed the Intelligence Community to develop a repertoire which was not dependent on a close relationship with its customers. That is no longer the case today, and NPR makes recommendations for improvements in this area.	*	*
INTEL03 Reassess Information Collection to Meet New Analytical Challenges The analytical issues the Intelligence Community faces are far more diverse and complex today, requiring new focus and new techniques to meet the intelligence needs of policymakers.	*	*
INTEL04 Integrate Intelligence Community Information Management Systems The Intelligence Community lacks the connectivity and interoperability in its information systems to do its job efficiently and effectively.	*	*
INTEL05 Develop Integrated Personnel and Training Systems This recommendation focuses on organizational development and training issues within the Intelligence Community.	*	*
INTEL06 Merge the President's Intelligence Oversight Board with the President's Foreign Intelligence Advisory Board The roles of these two oversight bodies are sufficiently similar that small savings and some efficiencies can be achieved by combining them.	*	*
INTEL07 Improve Support to Ground Troops During Combat Operations Numerous studies of intelligence support during the Gulf War focused on agency or service-specific support issues. This issue outlines a reinvention lab effort which proposes an integrated approach to studying support to ground forces during combat operations.	*	*
DEPARTMENT OF THE INTERIOR		
DOI01 Establish a Hard Rock Mine Reclamation Fund to Restore the Environment To address health and safety threats and environmental damage caused by toxic metal and chemical leaching from abandoned mines, the federal government should establish a hard-rock mine reclamation fund.	cbe	cbe
DOI02 Redefine Federal Oversight of Coal Mine Regulation To overcome organizational problems that inhibit an effective state-federal relationship, federal oversight of coal mine regulations should be redefined.	-28.0	0.0
DOI03 Establish a National Spatial Data Infrastructure By supporting a cross-agency coordinating effort, the federal government can develop a coherent vision for the national spatial data infrastructure (NSDI). (Spatial, or geographic, data refers to information that can be placed on a map.) This will allow greatly improved information analysis in a wide range of areas, including the analysis of environmental information and the monitoring of endangered animals and sensitive land areas.	36.0	0.0
DOI04 Promote Entrepreneurial Management of the National Park Service** The Park Service should be allowed to raise additional revenues from appropriate sources and to use a portion of the money for investment in park infrastructure. This proposal would increase selected park entry fees and would increase fees on park concessionaires.	332.0	993.0
DOI05 Obtain a Fair Return for Federal Resources The federal government should institute reforms to guarantee a fair return for federal resources such as livestock grazing and hard-rock mining. Some of the programs regulating the commercial sale and use of natural resources on federal lands operate at a loss to the taxpayers and fail to provide incentives for good stewardship practices. The administration should also develop a new fee schedule for communications sites on DOI and Department of Agriculture lands.	132.4	549.7

*The Intelligence Community budget is classified. Savings from these recommendations cannot be shown in this report.

**NPR recommends redirecting half of increased park income to investment in park infrastructure.

cbe = cannot be estimated (due to data limitations or uncertainties about implementation time lines).

na = not applicable—recommendation improves efficiency or redirects resources but does not directly reduce budget authority.

Recommendation	Fiscal Impact, 1994-99 (Millions of Dollars)	
	Change in Spending	Change in Receipts

DOI06 Rationalize Federal Land Ownership
DOI needs to reinvent the way it manages and acquires federal lands. Due to historical patterns of settlement and development of this country, adjoining federal lands often fall under the jurisdiction of several federal agencies. To the degree possible, this should be corrected based on the principle of ecosystem management.
na — na

DOI07 Improve the Land Acquisition Policies of the DOI
The Secretaries of Interior and Agriculture and the Director of OMB should modify the process for determining land acquisition priorities and procedures. The new system should reflect major objectives of federal land acquisition, including outdoor recreation resources, resource protection, and resource and cultural heritage protection.
na — na

DOI08 Improve Mineral Management Service Royalty Collections
Better management of DOI's royalty collection program would increase revenues and improve efficiency.
0.0 — 28.0

DOI09 Establish a System of Personnel Exchanges in DOI
A change in management philosophy is needed to address bureaucratic barriers at DOI. This recommendation outlines various approaches to this problem.
na — na

DOI10 Consolidate Administrative and Programmatic Functions in DOI
To manage its bureaus effectively, DOI needs to reduce duplicative services. By consolidating administrative and programmatic functions, DOI can improve customer service, promote efficiency, and reduce costs.
-17.5 — 0.0

DOI11 Streamline Management Support Systems in DOI
To create a quality management culture, the department should streamline its management support systems, including telecommunications, procurement, financial management, and paperwork control.
cbe — cbe

DOI12 Create a New Mission for the Bureau of Reclamation
The Bureau of Reclamation needs to redefine its mission toward new environmental priorities and clarify its role in water management. . The original mission to develop water resources and provide for economic development of the West—is almost complete.
-184.1 — 0.0

DOI13 Improve the Federal Helium Program
The federal government needs to reexamine its role in the federal helium program. The program can be run more efficiently, reducing outlays by federal helium customers and increasing revenue. To obtain maximum benefit from helium operations, the government should cancel the helium debt, reduce costs, increase efficiencies in helium operations, and increase sales of crude helium as market conditions permit.
-12.0 — 35.0

DOI14 Enhance Environmental Management by Remediating Hazardous Material Sites
The time is right to integrate skills across bureau boundaries in the remediation of DOI's hazardous materials sites. The high cost of remediation requires DOI to make maximum use of existing resources.
18.7 — 0.0

DEPARTMENT OF JUSTICE

DOJ01 Improve the Coordination and Structure of Federal Law Enforcement Agencies*
NPR recommends the designation of the Attorney General as the Director of Law Enforcement to coordinate federal law enforcement efforts. It also recommends changes in the alignment of federal law enforcement responsibilities.
-$187.0 — $0.0

DOJ02 Improve Border Management*
Federal border management should be significantly improved. NPR recommends a series of actions to be taken by Customs and INS to make these improvements.
cbe — cbe

DOJ03 Redirect and Better Coordinate Resources Dedicated to Interdiction of Drugs*
This recommendation outlines changes that can be made to better coordinate federal programs directed at the air interdiction of drugs.
na — na

*Issue corresponds to an identical issue in the Department of Treasury report; fiscal impact is for Justice only.

cbe = cannot be estimated (due to data limitations or uncertainties about implementation time lines).

na = not applicable—recommendation improves efficiency or redirects resources but does not directly reduce budget authority.

Recommendation	Fiscal Impact, 1994-99 (Millions of Dollars)	
	Change in Spending	Change in Receipts

DOJ04   **Improve Department of Justice Debt Collection Efforts**   cbe   cbe
This recommendation would make improvements in the Justice debt collection effort, including giving the department the ability to retain a small percentage of debts collected and allowing Justice to credit its working capital fund with a percentage of debt collections to be used for the creation of a centralized debt tracking and information system.

DOJ05   **Improve the Bureau of Prisons Education, Job Training, and Financial Responsibilities Programs**   0.0   13.8
NPR makes a series of recommendations for improving prison education, training, and inmate financial responsibility policies.

DOJ06   **Improve the Management of Federal Assets Targeted for Disposition***   cbe   cbe
Improvements are needed in the methods by which the federal government disposes of various assets.

DOJ07   **Reduce the Duplication of Drug Intelligence Systems and Improve Computer Security***   cbe   cbe
NPR recommends several changes to eliminate duplication in the federal drug intelligence system.

DOJ08   **Reinvent the Immigration and Naturalization Service's Organization and Management**   -48.0   0.0
NPR recommends a number of changes in INS organization and management processes to provide an improved management structure and a strategic vision for the agency.

DOJ09   **Make the Department of Justice Operate More Effectively as the U.S. Government Law Firm**   na   na
Justice should undertake several improvements in the way it manages its litigation functions to improve service to its customers and better manage its case load.

DOJ10   **Improve White Collar Fraud Civil Enforcement**   14.0   111.0
Civil fraud recovery should be established as a priority and the department should take steps to improve its white collar fraud enforcement.

DOJ11   **Reduce the Duplication of Law Enforcement Training Facilities**   cbe   cbe
Overlap and duplication in the provision of federal law enforcement training facilities should be examined. Multi-agency training needs should be accommodated through existing facilities in lieu of the construction of new facilities by individual agencies.

DOJ12   **Streamline Background Investigations for Federal Employees**   -60.0   0.0
The current method of completing background examinations on federal employees is time-consuming and inefficient. This recommendation outlines improvements to streamline the process without sacrificing thoroughness.

DOJ13   **Adjust Civil Monetary Penalties to the Inflation Index**   0.0   193.0
Civil monetary penalties have not been adjusted to keep up with inflation. Under this recommendation, a "catch-up" adjustment would be made and the need for additional inflation adjustments would be automatically reassessed every four years.

DOJ14   **Improve Federal Courthouse Security**   24.0   0.0
This recommendation is intended to address concerns of the U.S. Marshals Service concerning security at federal courthouses.

DOJ15   **Improve the Professionalism of the U.S. Marshals Service**   -36.0   0.0
U.S. Marshals should be selected based on merit by the Director of the U.S. Marshal Service and reduce some positions.

DOJ16   **Develop Lower Cost Solutions to Federal Prison Space Problems**   cbe   cbe
This recommendation describes approaches to solving existing prison space problems.

DEPARTMENT OF LABOR

DOL01   **Enhance Reemployment Programs for Occupationally Disabled Federal Employees**   -$125.7 $0.0
These recommendations would help occupationally disabled federal employees return to productive careers by expanding DOL's return-to-work program. This saves money by reducing long-term benefit costs to the government.

---

cbe = cannot be estimated (due to data limitations or uncertainties about implementation time lines).

na = not applicable—recommendation improves efficiency or redirects resources but does not directly reduce budget authority.

Recommendation	Fiscal Impact, 1994-99 (Millions of Dollars)	
	Change in Spending	Change in Receipts
DOL02 Develop a Single Comprehensive Worker Adjustment Strategy Improve services to the unemployed—and those at risk of dislocation—and make better use of resources available for assistance by developing a new worker adjustment strategy.	na	na
DOL03 Expand Negotiated Rulemaking and Improve Up-front Teamwork on Regulations DOL should provide administrative guidance more quickly and cheaply through negotiated rulemaking and a streamlined team approach to the rules development process.	cbe	cbe
DOL04 Expand the Use of Alternative Dispute Resolution by the Department of Labor The increased use of alternative dispute resolution could reduce litigation and produce significant long-term savings.	cbe	cbe
DOL05 Automate the Processing of ERISA Annual Financial Reports (Forms 5500) to Cut Costs and Delays in Obtaining Employee Benefit Plan Data Automating the filing and processing of annual financial reports required of pension and benefit plan administrators (ERISA Forms 5500) would reduce costs and delays.	-49.7	0.0
DOL06 Amend the ERISA Requirement for Summary Plan Descriptions The filing of summary plan descriptions by employee benefit plan administrators with DOL is intended to make the plans more readily available for participants and beneficiaries. Since requests for copies are received on only about one percent, the cost to maintain the system and the administrative burden on employers far outweighs the public benefit.	-0.6	0.0
DOL07 Redirect the Mine Safety and Health Administration's Role in Mine Equipment Regulation Shifting the Mine Safety and Health Administration's regulatory role from one of in-house testing to one of on-site quality assurance would provide increased economic benefits to the mining industry and would allow DOL to redirect resources.	na	na
DOL08 Create One-Stop Centers for Career Management Establishing one-stop centers for career management would create a customer-driven work force system, empowering Americans to make informed career choices and providing the means to achieve those goals.	cbe	cbe
DOL09 Create a Boundary-Spanning Work Force Development Council Because the greatest barriers to creating an integrated work force development system are the categorical nature of federal funds and structural fragmentation of various federal programs, this issue proposes to coordinate work force development efforts by convening a multi-agency Work Force Development Council and implementing "bottom-up grant consolidation" for states and localities.	na	na
DOL10 Refocus the Responsibility for Ensuring Workplace Safety and Health This recommendation proposes to shift responsibility for workplace safety and health to employers by issuing regulations requiring self-inspections and implementing a sliding scale of incentives and penalties to ensure safety standards are met.	cbe	cbe
DOL11 Open the Civilian Conservation Centers to Private and Public Competition A long-term reduction in costs is possible through expanded competition for contracts to operate Job Corps Civilian Conservation Centers.	cbe	cbe
DOL12 Partially Fund Mine Safety and Health Enforcement Through Service Fees Charge for services to put the mining industry on a comparable footing with other industries which bear the cost of their regulation. This proposes to partially fund enforcement of mine safety regulations through service fees.	-44.4	0.0
DOL13 Integrate Enforcement Activities within the Department of Labor Introduce greater coordination and flexibility in the DOL enforcement agencies to project a consistent message to customers and integrate approaches to common issues.	cbe	cbe
DOL14 Apply Information Technology to Expedite Wage Determinations for Federal Contracts Developing an electronic data interchange/data mapping system which is integrated into the Service Contract Act process should eliminate delays both in the delivery of wage determinations and in procurement when caused by determination delays.	0.1	0.0

cbe = cannot be estimated (due to data limitations or uncertainties about implementation time lines).

na = not applicable—recommendation improves efficiency or redirects resources but does not directly reduce budget authority.

	Fiscal Impact, 1994-99 (Millions of Dollars)	
Recommendation	Change in Spending	Change in Receipts

DOL15 Provide Research and Development Authority for the DOL's Mine Safety and Health Program
Granting the Mine Safety and Health Administration authority to procure services and goods directly would improve the mine safety program by expediting the acquisition process for new and improved technology.
na — na

DOL16 Increase Assistance to States in Collecting Delinquent Unemployment Insurance Trust Fund Contributions
This recommendation outlines ways of improving state collections of delinquent unemployment insurance contributions.
na — na

DOL17 Revise and Update the Consumer Price Index
The consumer price index has important consequences for both public and private decisions. This important measure should be updated to reflect recent inflation trends.
56.0 — 0.0

DOL18 Improve the Delivery of Legal Services by the Office of the Solicitor in the Department of Labor
The delivery of legal services by the Office of the Solicitor can be improved by using cooperative agreements, coordinated budgeting and better use of resources.
na — na

DOL19 Transfer the Veterans' Employment and Training Service to the Employment and Training Administration
The DOL can improve service delivery to veterans and save money by consolidating administration of this function.
-66.0 — 0.0

DOL20 Reduce Federal Employees' Compensation Act Fraud
Congress needs to amend several sections of the United States Code to enable DOL to eliminate benefits to persons who have been convicted of defrauding the program.
-22.6 — 0.0

DOL21 Change the Focus of the Unemployment Insurance Benefits Quality Control Program to Improve Performance
Re-examining the present mix of systems to shift the focus of this program from error measurement to a constructive use of the results would allow DOL to improve benefit payment quality and more effectively achieve the program's goals.
na — na

NATIONAL AERONAUTICS AND SPACE ADMINISTRATION

NASA01 Improve NASA Contracting Practices
This recommendation outlines several steps NASA can take to improve its contracting procedures, including greater use of performance standards, contracting out for data instead of hardware whenever appropriate, and using cooperative research agreements to more quickly exploit high performance computing techniques.
cbe — cbe

NASA02 Increase NASA Technology Transfer Efforts and Eliminate Barriers to Technology Development
NASA should expand its technology transfer efforts and promote the development of new technologies.
na — na

NASA03 Increase NASA Coordination of Programs with the U.S. Civil Aviation Industry
NASA should develop a closer relationship with the U.S. civil aviation industry to ensure industry input is received early and throughout the technology development process.
na — na

NASA04 Strengthen and Restructure NASA Management
NASA program management should be aggressively overhauled. This recommendation outlines a number of steps the agency should take, both in overall management and in the management of the space station program.
-1,982.0 — 0.0

NASA05 Clarify the Objectives of the Mission to Planet Earth Program
This recommendation suggests a number of steps needed to improve the management and performance of the Mission to Planet Earth program.
na — na

---

cbe = cannot be estimated (due to data limitations or uncertainties about implementation time lines).

na = not applicable—recommendation improves efficiency or redirects resources but does not directly reduce budget authority.

Recommendation	Fiscal Impact, 1994-99 (Millions of Dollars)	
	Change in Spending	Change in Receipts

NATIONAL SCIENCE FOUNDATION/OFFICE OF SCIENCE AND TECHNOLOGY POLICY

NSF01 Strengthen Coordination of Science Policy
NPR recommends modifying the current structure of the Federal Coordinating Council for Science, Engineering, and Technology (FCCSET) to strengthen its role in science policy. — na / na

NSF02 Use a Federal Demonstration Project to Increase Research Productivity
NPR recommends using a demonstration project structured between several universities and five federal agencies as a model for a program to reduce administrative overhead on research grants. — na / na

NSF03 Continue Automation of NSF Research Support Functions
NSF should push forward with efforts to implement advanced information technology in the proposal submission, review, award, and information dissemination areas. — na / na

SMALL BUSINESS ADMINISTRATION

SBA01 Allow Judicial Review of the Regulatory Flexibility Act
Allow access to the courts when federal agencies develop rules that fail to properly examine alternatives that will lessen the burden on small businesses. — cbe / cbe

SBA02 Improve Assistance to Minority Small Businesses
This proposal recommends a complete review of all federal minority business assistance programs and the establishment of a Small Disadvantaged Business Set-Aside program for civilian agencies to provide increased opportunities for minority small business. — na / na

SBA03 Reinvent the U.S. Small Business Administration's Credit Programs
Identify ways to improve SBA's credit programs to make SBA more responsive to those industries with the potential for creating a higher number of jobs, those involved in international trade, and those providing critical technologies. It will also enable the agency to operate more efficiently. — na / na

SBA04 Examine Federal Guidelines for Small Business Lending Requirements
The federal government should examine the guidelines bank regulators set for small business lending by financial institutions to ensure that capital is available without undue barriers while maintaining the integrity of the financial institutions. — na / na

SBA05 Manage the Microloan Program to Increase Loans for Small Business
Allowing SBA to guarantee loans made by banks to nonprofit intermediaries, who could, in turn, make small loans to low-income individuals, women, minorities and other small businesses unable to obtain credit through traditional lending sources would increase private sector participation and lessen administrative burdens linked to direct government lending. — na / na

SBA06 Establish User Fees for Small Business Development Center Services
Authorize Small Business Development Centers to charge a nominal fee for their services to reduce federal outlays and require the direct beneficiaries of the assistance to pay a share of the cost. — 0.0 / 102.0

SBA07 Distribute SBA Staff Based on Workload and Administrative Efficiency
Reallocating staff based on administrative efficiency and objective workload measures to allow the SBA to better serve its customers by shifting resources from its central and regional offices into its district offices. — na / na

SBA08 Improve Federal Data on Small Businesses
The quality of information made available to shape federal legislative and regulatory actions affecting small and large businesses will be increased if federal household and employer surveys include a "size of firm" question. — na / na

cbe = cannot be estimated (due to data limitations or uncertainties about implementation time lines).

na = not applicable—recommendation improves efficiency or redirects resources but does not directly reduce budget authority.

Recommendation	Fiscal Impact, 1994-99 (Millions of Dollars)	
	Change in Spending	Change in Receipts

DEPARTMENT OF STATE/U.S. INFORMATION AGENCY

DOS01 Expand the Authority of Chiefs of Mission Overseas
This recommendation proposes a pilot program to expand the management authority of Chiefs of Mission overseas in the allocation of fiscal and staffing resources.
cbe / cbe

DOS02 Integrate the Foreign Affairs Resource Management Process
NPR recommends specific reforms of the interagency foreign policy resource management process to improve coordination. The recommendation also covers specific improvements within the Department of State.
na / na

DOS03 Improve State Department Efforts to Promote U.S. Business Overseas
International trade is an important responsibility of U.S. missions overseas in the post-Cold War world. This recommendation outlines several improvements that can be made in State Department efforts in this area.
cbe / cbe

DOS04 Provide Leadership in the Department's Information Management
The Department of State should make significant changes in the way it manages information technology policy. Several improvements are recommended.
cbe / cbe

DOS05 Reduce Mission Operating Costs
Several recommendations are made for reducing U.S. costs to operate missions overseas, including eliminating certain facilities, reducing security costs and considering altogether new forms of overseas representation.
-57.8 / 0.0

DOS06 Consolidate U.S. Nonmilitary International Broadcasting
This recommendation supports the Administration's decision to consolidate U.S. international broadcasting under USIA and outlines ways of extending the benefits of this change.
na / na

DOS07 Relocate the Mexico City Regional Administrative Management Center
NPR recommends moving this administrative support office to the U.S. to save money and recommends examining the need for similar offices now in Paris and Bangkok.
-0.1 / 0.0

DOS08 Improve the Collection of Receivables
The State Department should do a better job collecting debts, such as medical expenses and others, owed to the department.
-9.8 / 0.0

DOS09 Change UN Administrative and Assessment Procedures
This recommendation outlines several changes in the U.S.'s fiscal relationship with the United Nations, including recommending an oversight office for the organization and tax law changes to reduce costs to the federal government.
-36.2 / 0.0

DEPARTMENT OF TRANSPORTATION

DOT01 Measure Transportation Safety
NPR recommends the development of common, government-wide measures of transportation safety.
na / na

DOT02 Streamline the Enforcement Process
NPR recommends pilot programs in the U.S. Coast Guard, the Federal Aviation Administration, and the Federal Highway Administration, designed to offer greater flexibility in enforcement methods.
cbe / cbe

DOT03 Use a Consensus-Building Approach to Expedite Transportation and Environmental Decisionmaking
DOT should conduct two demonstration projects to apply a problem-solving approach to transportation planning, development and decisionmaking as a means of reducing costs and improving the efficiency of agency decisionmaking.
na / na

DOT04 Establish a Corporation to Provide Air Traffic Control Services
NPR recommends development of a detailed action plan and statutory language for changes in air traffic control management to make it more business-like.
0.0 / 0.0

cbe = cannot be estimated (due to data limitations or uncertainties about implementation time lines).

na = not applicable—recommendation improves efficiency or redirects resources but does not directly reduce budget authority.

Recommendation	Fiscal Impact, 1994-99 (Millions of Dollars)	
	Change in Spending	Change in Receipts
DOT05 Permit States to Use Federal Aid as a Capital Reserve This recommendation would allow federal transportation grant recipients to use grant funds capital reserve to back debt financing to construct eligible transportation projects.	na	na
DOT06 Encourage Innovations in Automotive Safety NPR recommends allowing the National Highway Traffic Safety Administration to grant more exemptions from highway safety standards to develop new safety systems.	na	na
DOT07 Examine User Fees for International Over-Flights DOT should conduct a cost allocation study to determine whether foreign air carriers passing over U.S. air space are paying their fair share and whether direct user fees should be imposed.	0.0	9.0
DOT08 Increase FAA Fees for Inspection of Foreign Repair Facilities To ensure full cost recovery, increase the fees charged for certification and surveillance of foreign aircraft repair stations.	0.0	8.0
DOT09 Contract for Level I Air Traffic Control Towers NPR recommends converting 99 Level I (low-use) air control towers to contract operation and reviewing the remaining Level I towers for possible decommissioning.	-3.1	0.0
DOT10 Establish an Aeronautical Telecommunications Network to Develop a Public-Private Consortium FAA should pursue the creation of a public-private consortium under a cooperative agreement with industry to develop an Aeronautical Telecommunications Network.	na	na
DOT11 Improve Intermodal Transportation Policy Coordination and Management DOT should institute a strategic planning process to promulgate national, integrated transportation policies.	na	na
DOT12 Develop an Integrated National Transportation Research and Development Plan DOT should examine the nation's transportation-related research and development portfolio and develop an integrated national transportation plan that considers specific transportation research needs as well as intermodal transportation plans.	na	na
DOT13 Create and Evaluate Telecommuting Programs DOT should implement a telecommuting plan within the agency and should evaluate transportation-related behavior and other topics requiring research in this area.	na	na
DOT14 Improve DOT Information Technology Management The department should develop an information management strategy which will enable the sharing of data among its component agencies and reduce costs.	-224.5	0.0
DOT15 Provide Reemployment Rights for Merchant Mariners Guarantee reemployment rights to U.S. seafarers at their private sector jobs if called to serve during a war or national emergency.	na	na
DOT16 Establish an Independent Commission to Review U.S. Maritime Industry NPR recommends a detailed examination of the future of the maritime industry in the U.S. and the benefits derived by the taxpayers from maritime industry subsidies and related issues.	na	na
DOT17 Eliminate Funding for Highway Demonstration Projects Rescind funding for existing highway demonstration projects. These demonstration projects should compete at the state level for the limited highway resources available and not be singled out for special treatment at the federal level.	-7,853.0	0.0
DOT18 Reduce Spending for the U.S. Merchant Marine Academy As an economy measure, federal funding for the U.S. Merchant Marine Academy should be cut by half. The Academy should be given the ability to charge tuition to cover a portion of its operations.	-45.6	0.0
DOT19 Rescind Unobligated Earmarks for the FTA New Starts and Bus Program Rescind unobligated balances for fiscal year 1992 and prior earmarked funding under this FTA program that remain unobligated after three years.	-131.5	0.0

cbe = cannot be estimated (due to data limitations or uncertainties about implementation time lines).

na = not applicable—recommendation improves efficiency or redirects resources but does not directly reduce budget authority.

Recommendation	Fiscal Impact, 1994-99 (Millions of Dollars)	
	Change in Spending	Change in Receipts

DOT20 Reduce the Annual Essential Air Service Subsidies | -65.0 | 0.0
This recommendation would set new, more restrictive criteria for small airports to qualify for essential air service subsidies.

DOT21 Terminate Grant Funding for Federal Aviation Administration Higher Education Programs | -45.4 | 0.0
To reduce costs, eliminate federal grant funding of two FAA post-secondary education programs.

DOT22 Assign Office of Motor Carriers (OMC) Field Staff to Improve Program Effectiveness and Reduce Costs | cbe | cbe
OMC should develop a resource allocation model so that regional managers will be able to optimize geographic assignment of staff, schedule carrier reviews in an efficient manner, and eliminate unnecessary travel requirements.

DOT23 Automate Administrative Requirements for Federal Aid Highway Projects | na | na
NPR recommends improvements in the flow of information on Federal Aid Highway projects that will reduce paperwork and reduce staff time in completing certain forms and other current requirements.

DEPARTMENT OF TREASURY/RESOLUTION TRUST CORPORATION

TRE01 Improve the Coordination and Structure of Federal Law Enforcement Agencies* | $-92.9 | $0.0
NPR recommends the designation of the Attorney General as the Director of Law Enforcement to coordinate federal law enforcement efforts. It also recommends changes in the alignment of federal law enforcement responsibilities.

TRE02 Improve Border Management* | cbe | cbe
Federal border management should be significantly improved. NPR recommends a series of actions to be taken by Customs and INS to make these improvements.

TRE03 Redirect and Better Coordinate Resources Dedicated to the Interdiction of Drugs* | -186.6 | 0.0
This recommendation outlines changes that can be made to better coordinate federal programs directed at the air interdiction of drugs.

TRE04 Foster Federal-State Cooperative Initiatives by the IRS | cbe | cbe
Cooperative relationships between the IRS and state tax administrations, including joint filing of data, should improve taxpayer service as well as collection activity while reducing costs.

TRE05 Simplify Employer Wage Reporting | cbe | cbe
The administrative burden caused by our current employer wage-reporting requirements could be reduced while maintaining or improving the effectiveness of government operations by developing and implementing a simplified wage reporting system.

TRE06 Establish Federal Firearms License User Fees to Cover Costs | 0.0 | 132.5
The current fee for a retail dealer's firearms license (authorized in 1968) does not cover the cost of license processing and is low enough to encourage applications from individuals wishing to occasionally purchase firearms at reduced cost. Increased fees would recover the cost of operating the firearms program.

TRE07 Improve the Management of Federal Assets Targeted for Disposition* | cbe | cbe
Improvements are needed in the methods by which the federal government disposes of various assets.

TRE08 Reduce the Duplication of Drug Intelligence Systems and Improve Computer Security* | na | na
NPR recommends several changes to eliminate duplication in the federal drug intelligence system.

TRE09 Modernize the IRS | cbe | cbe
The IRS Tax System Modernization (TSM) initiative, currently in its initial stages, would ease taxpayer burdens due to manual return processing and inaccessible information, and enable IRS to provide a level of service comparable to private sector financial institutions.

---

*Issue corresponds to an identical issue in the Department of Justice report; fiscal impact is for Treasury only.

cbe = cannot be estimated (due to data limitations or uncertainties about implementation time lines).
na = not applicable—recommendation improves efficiency or redirects resources but does not directly reduce budget authority.

Recommendation	Fiscal Impact, 1994-99 (Millions of Dollars)	
	Change in Spending	Change in Receipts
TRE10 **Modernize the U.S. Customs Service** NPR recommends a number of changes in Customs' organization and management processes to provide an improved management structure and strategic vision.	0.0	450.0
TRE11 **Ensure the Efficient Merger of Resolution Trust Corporation into the FDIC** The merger of the RTC and the FDIC should ensure the transfer of RTC expertise not currently held by the FDIC in order to provide the most efficient administration of these asset-disposition functions.	na	na
TRE12 **Reduce the Duplication of Law Enforcement Training Facilities*** Overlap and duplication in the provision of federal law enforcement training facilities should be examined. Multi-agency training needs should be accommodated through existing facilities in lieu of the construction of new facilities by individual agencies.	cbe	cbe
TRE13 **Streamline Background Investigations for Federal Employees*** The current method of completing background examinations of federal employees is time-consuming and inefficient. This recommendation outlines improvements to streamline the process without sacrificing thoroughness.	cbe	cbe
TRE14 **Adjust Civil Monetary Penalties to the Inflation Index*** Civil monetary penalties have not been adjusted to keep up with inflation. Under this recommendation, a "catch-up" adjustment would be made and the need for additional inflation adjustments would be automatically reassessed by the government every four years.	0.0	126.0
TRE15 **Increase IRS Collections Through Better Compliance Efforts** NPR supports the current efforts of the IRS under Compliance 2000 to improve voluntary compliance and other efforts to collect taxes already owed to the federal government.	cbe	cbe
TRE16 **Improve Agency Compliance with Employment Tax Reporting Requirements** Many federal agencies do not fully comply with federal tax reporting requirements. Responsibilities for compliance should be more fully communicated and enforced.	cbe	cbe
TRE17 **Authorize Federal Tax Payment by Credit Card** Legislation should be enacted to allow certain taxpayers to make tax payments with a credit card.	cbe	cbe
TRE18 **Modernize the Financial Management Systems** NPR recommends several changes to improve financial management with Treasury, including consolidation of some operations, the improved use of technology, and other actions.	-41.1	0.0
TRE19 **Repeal Section 5010 of the Internal Revenue Code to Eliminate Tax Credits for Wine and Flavors** The wine and flavors tax credit should be repealed.	0.0	500.0
TRE20 **Amend or Repeal Section 5121 of the Internal Revenue Code Requiring Special Occupational Taxes on Retail Alcohol Dealers** This recommendation would increase federal income from alcohol dealers.	0.0	45.0

DEPARTMENT OF VETERANS AFFAIRS

DVA01 **Develop the Master Veteran Record and Modernize the Department's Information Infrastructure** Creation of a master veteran record for all VA programs and the improvements in the department's information technology will improve services to veterans and their families.	na	na
DVA02 **Modernize Benefits Claims Processing** Modernization of the VA benefits claims processing system will improve the quality of service and save taxpayer dollars over time.	na	na

*Issue corresponds to an identical issue in the Department of Justice report; fiscal impact is for Treasury only.

cbe = cannot be estimated (due to data limitations or uncertainties about implementation time lines).

na = not applicable—recommendation improves efficiency or redirects resources but does not directly reduce budget authority.

Recommendation	Fiscal Impact, 1994-99 (Millions of Dollars)	
	Change in Spending	Change in Receipts
DVA03 Eliminate Legislative Budget Constraints to Promote Management Effectiveness VA is covered by a number of special legislative requirements, including employment "floors" for certain programs. Reducing or eliminating some of these controls can reduce costs and improve service without sacrificing accountability.	cbe	cbe
DVA04 Streamline Benefits Claims Processing VA should examine the usefulness of a New York Regional Office approach to benefits claims processing that promises to streamline the process. It should also examine regional staffing.	1.8	0.0
DVA05 Consolidate Department of Defense and Department of Veterans Affairs Compensation and Retired Pay Programs DOD and VA should create a task force to jointly examine their disability compensation adjudication and disbursement processes.	cbe	cbe
DVA06 Enhance VA Cost Recovery Capabilities Revise VA policy to use a portion of cost recovery funds to defray debt collection costs and expand recoveries to save money.	0.0	486.5
DVA07 Establish a Working Capital Fund This recommendation would allow creation of a working capital fund using existing resources in the department to be used for certain selected needs.	na	na
DVA08 Decentralize Decisionmaking Authority to Promote Management Effectiveness NPR recommends that VA headquarters and field management work together to improve agency decisionmaking, including the delegation of some decisionmaking to field activity directors.	na	na
DVA09 Establish a Comprehensive Resource Allocation Program VA should design and develop a comprehensive, departmentwide, performance and needs-based resource allocation program to replace current approaches.	na	na
DVA10 Serve Veterans and Their Families as Customers This recommendation outlines several approaches for VA to improve its focus on veterans and their families as customers.	na	na
DVA11 Phase-Out and Close Supply Depots VA should convert its existing centralized depot storage and distribution program to a commercial just-in-time delivery system and close unneeded supply depots.	-168.0	0.0
DVA12 Improve Business Practices through Electronic Commerce VA should expand its use of electronic media to reduce paperwork and save money. It should seek to make greater use of electronic funds transfer of compensation and pension benefits.	-124.1	0.0
DVA13 Eliminate "Sunset" Dates in the Omnibus Budget Reconciliation Act of 1990 To achieve cost savings, extend certain cost savings measures that are due to expire in 1998.	-704.8	490.0
DVA14 Raise the Fees for Veterans Affairs' Guaranteed Home Loans As a cost savings measure, loan fees on veterans loans should be raised above the levels set in the Omnibus Budget Reconciliation Act of 1994.	-811.4	0.0
DVA15 Restructure the Veterans Affairs' Health Care System VA should reexamine its role and delivery structure after the issuance of the report of the President's National Health Care Reform Task Force and take actions to restructure the VA health care system.	0.0	0.0
DVA16 Recover Administrative Costs of Veterans' Insurance Program from Premiums and Dividends VA should be permitted to recover certain insurance program costs from insurance trust fund surpluses.	0.0	0.0
Grand Total	**$28,100**	**$8,300**

cbe = cannot be estimated (due to data limitations or uncertainties about implementation time lines).

na = not applicable—recommendation improves efficiency or redirects resources but does not directly reduce budget authority.

APPENDIX B

NATIONAL PERFORMANCE REVIEW
SUMMARY OF SAVINGS

Introduction

The NPR recommendations yield $108.0 billion in savings for the 5 year period, FY1995-1999. $36.4 billion result from the specific changes in individual agencies that were detailed in Appendix A. The remaining $71 billion result from governmentwide changes explained here.

This appendix provides the estimates of the governmentwide changes, and the assumptions underlying those estimates. Savings by major issue area are shown in Table B-1.

1. Streamlining The Bureaucracy Through Reengineering.

These estimates assume:

a. Agency reengineering will allow a 12% reduction of civilian personnel over 5 years.

b. Administrative and central control staffs and supervisors will be the primary areas for downsizing.

c. Attrition, enhanced severance, reassignment, relocation, outplacement and retraining will be the primary tools to accomplish the reduction.

d. Agencies will use other tools as necessary to accomplish the 12% reduction.

e. The 12% reduction includes and increases the Administration's previously established 4% personnel reduction goal for fiscal 1995.

f. Indirect costs associated with personnel, such as office space and expenses, travel and supplies, are not included in the dollar estimates.

2. Reinventing Federal Procurement

These estimates assume:

a. The General Service Administration's estimate that total annual procurement costs equal $200 billion (GSA Federal Procurement Report).

b. Savings can be generated by a variety of reforms in procurement systems, including simplified acquisition thresholds, labor law reforms, IT procurement reforms, shifting from government specifications to commercial items, expanded use of purchase cards, and electronic commerce.

c. Savings up to 12% of procurement spending may be achieved through these reforms (study by Defense Systems Management College). The NPR used 5% as a mid-range estimate.

d. To avoid double-counting, savings associated with reductions in procurement personnel are excluded from this "reinventing procurement" savings estimate.

3. Reeingeering Through Information Technology

These estimates assume:

a. A $25 billion baseline in information technology (IT) spending, based on obligations reported through OMB circular A-11 by executive branch agencies for acquisition, operation, and use of IT systems.

b. 30% savings in IT systems may be achieved through information infrastructure consolidation and standardization — this savings estimate is extrapolated from the "Defense Information Infrastructure Initiative" (December 1992, Resource Summary). Since Defense IT spending constitutes roughly one-half of total IT spending it is assumed that equal savings can be obtained from the IT budgets of civilian agencies.

c. Savings from electronic benefits transfer and from consolidation and modernization of the federal information infrastructure; offsetting costs result from consolidation and modernization of the law enforcement and safety mobile networks and a program to provide citizens with better access to government information.

d. Savings for electronic benefits transfer nationally may be extrapolated from pilot programs in the states of New Mexico and Minnesota.

e. Savings recommended for the Department of Transportation IT consolidation and modernization are subtracted to avoid double-counting.

4. Intragovernmental Administrative Costs.

Simplifying and reducing the federal government's reporting requirements will generate savings at the federal, state, and local levels. The estimate assumes that over 75% of the state and local governments will accept a fee-for-service option in place of existing cost reimbursement procedures from FY1995-1999 in return for greater administrative flexibility. Eliminating cost reimbursement procedures slows cost growth by 3% per year at the federal level.

Table B-1. Estimates of Savings from NPR Recommendations
(dollars in billions)

	Fiscal Year 1995	Fiscal Year 1996	Fiscal Year 1997	Fiscal Year 1998	Fiscal Year 1999	Total
1. Streamlining the Bureaucracy through Reengineering	5.0	5.8	7.4	9.5	12.7	40.4
2. Reinventing Federal Procurement	0.0	5.6	5.6	5.6	5.7	22.5
3. Reengineering Through Information Technology	0.1	0.5	1.2	1.6	2.0	5.4
4. Reducing Intergovernmental Administrative Costs	0.5	0.7	0.7	0.7	0.7	3.3
5. Changes to Individual Agencies (see Appendix A)	7.0*	6.2	7.0	7.3	8.9	36.4
Total NPR Savings	12.6	18.8	21.9	24.7	30.0	108.0

*FY95 column includes $0.5 billion in FY1994 savings.

APPENDIX C

NATIONAL PERFORMANCE REVIEW
MAJOR RECOMMENDATIONS
AFFECTING
GOVERNMENTAL SYSTEMS

Recommendations

CREATING QUALITY LEADERSHIP AND MANAGEMENT

QUAL01   PROVIDE IMPROVED LEADERSHIP AND MANAGEMENT OF THE EXECUTIVE BRANCH
The President should define a vision for the management of the government in the 21st century. To act on this vision, he should direct department and agency heads to designate chief operating officers and he should establish a President's Management Council, comprised of the chief operating officers, to oversee the implementation of NPR's recommendations.

QUAL02   IMPROVE GOVERNMENT PERFORMANCE THROUGH STRATEGIC AND QUALITY MANAGEMENT
Encourage all department and agency heads to lead and manage in accordance with the criteria in the Presidential Award for Quality. To begin this culture change, all executive branch employees—starting with the President and Cabinet—should attend appropriate educational sessions on strategic and quality management.

QUAL03   STRENGTHEN THE CORPS OF SENIOR LEADERS
Develop guidance to be used to determine the qualifications needed for selected senior political appointee positions, and provide adequate orientations for individuals upon their appointment.

QUAL04   IMPROVE LEGISLATIVE-EXECUTIVE BRANCH RELATIONSHIP
Improve communications between the executive branch, members of Congress, and congressional staff on key issues during and after program and policy development and implementation. Develop an agreed-upon approach for dealing with management failures, crises, and chronic program difficulties.

STREAMLINING MANAGEMENT CONTROL

SMC01   IMPLEMENT A SYSTEMS DESIGN APPROACH TO MANAGEMENT CONTROL
Redesign the existing collection of management control mechanisms for the executive branch, using a systems design approach, in order to create a well managed and cost-effective system.

SMC02   STREAMLINE THE INTERNAL CONTROLS PROGRAM TO MAKE IT AN EFFICIENT AND EFFECTIVE MANAGEMENT TOOL
Rescind the current set of Internal Control Guidelines and replace them with a broader handbook on management controls.

SMC03   CHANGE THE FOCUS OF THE INSPECTORS GENERAL
Change the focus of Inspectors General from compliance auditing to evaluating management control systems. In addition, recast the IGs method of operation to be more collaborative and less adversarial.

SMC04   INCREASE THE EFFECTIVENESS OF OFFICES OF GENERAL COUNSEL
Define clearly the clients of agency General Counsel offices as agency line managers. Train staff attorneys to understand the cultural changes they will need to undertake to operate in an environment where program results are important. Develop performance measures and "feedback loops" to ensure close cooperation with line managers.

SMC05   IMPROVE THE EFFECTIVENESS OF THE GENERAL ACCOUNTING OFFICE THROUGH INCREASED CUSTOMER FEEDBACK
Improve GAO's documentation of best practices and the use of feedback loops on its performance.

SMC06   REDUCE THE BURDEN OF CONGRESSIONALLY MANDATED REPORTS
Eliminate at least 50 percent of all congressionally mandated reports. Review new reporting requirements for management impact, and include a sunset provision.

SMC07   REDUCE INTERNAL REGULATIONS BY MORE THAN 50 PERCENT
Direct department secretaries and agency heads to reduce by at least 50 percent the number of internal regulations, and the number of pages of regulations, within 3 years.

SMC08   EXPAND THE USE OF WAIVERS TO ENCOURAGE INNOVATION
Establish a process for obtaining waivers from federal regulations and identifying those regulations for which this process should apply.

TRANSFORMING ORGANIZATIONAL STRUCTURES

ORG01   REDUCE THE COSTS AND NUMBERS OF POSITIONS ASSOCIATED WITH MANAGEMENT CONTROL STRUCTURES BY HALF
Cut management control positions over the next 5 years. Reinvest some of the savings in benchmarking, training, and investments in new technology. In addition to separation incentives (see HRM14), provide outplacement services to affected staff.

ORG02   USE MULTI-YEAR PEFORMANCE AGREEMENTS BETWEEN THE PRESIDENT AND AGENCY HEADS TO GUIDE DOWNSIZING STRATEGIES
Performance agreements with agency heads (see BGT01) should be used to identify progress toward agreed upon downsizing goals—not central management agency controls such as across-the-board cuts or ceilings on employment. In exchange, agencies will be supported with increased management flexibilities.

ORG03   ESTABLISH A LIST OF SPECIFIC FIELD OFFICES TO BE CLOSED
Within 18 months, the President's Management Council should submit a list to Congress of civilian field offices that should be closed.

Recommendations

ORG04 THE PRESIDENT SHOULD REQUEST AUTHORITY TO REORGANIZE AGENCIES
Congress should restore to the President the authority to restructure the executive branch.

ORG05 SPONSOR THREE OR MORE CROSS-DEPARTMENTAL INITIATIVES ADDRESSING COMMON ISSUES OR CUSTOMERS
The President's Management Council should identify and sponsor three or more cross-departmental initiatives in areas such as illegal immigration, debt collection, and the problems of the homeless.

ORG06 IDENTIFY AND CHANGE LEGISLATIVE BARRIERS TO CROSS-ORGANIZATIONAL COOPERATION
As cross-organizational collaborations become an integral part of government operations, barriers to ready collaboration and funding should be removed.

IMPROVING CUSTOMER SERVICES

ICS01 CREATE CUSTOMER-DRIVEN PROGRAMS IN ALL DEPARTMENTS AND AGENCIES THAT PROVIDE SERVICES DIRECTLY TO THE PUBLIC
Establish an overall policy for quality of federal services delivered to the public and initiate customer service programs in all agencies that provide services directly to the public.

ICS02 CUSTOMER SERVICE PERFORMANCE STANDARDS—INTERNAL REVENUE SERVICE
As part of its participation in the NPR, the Internal Revenue Service is publishing customer service performance standards. To speed the delivery of taxpayer refunds, the Secretary of the Treasury should delegate disbursing authority to IRS in 1993 and future tax seasons.

ICS03 CUSTOMER SERVICE PERFORMANCE STANDARDS—SOCIAL SECURITY ADMINISTRATION
As part of its participation in the NPR, the Social Security Administration is publishing customer service performance standards. SSA will also obtain customer opinions on all the goals and objectives of their strategic plan, using that input to revise the goals and objectives as needed, set priorities, and establish interim objectives.

ICS04 CUSTOMER SERVICE PERFORMANCE STANDARDS—POSTAL SERVICE
As part of its participation in the NPR, the U.S. Postal Service will expand its plans to display customer service standards in Post Office retail lobbies.

ICS05 STREAMLINE WAYS TO COLLECT CUSTOMER SATISFACTION AND OTHER INFORMATION FROM THE PUBLIC
For voluntary information collection requests directed at customers, OMB will delegate authority to approve such requests if departments certify that they will fully comply with Paperwork Reduction Act requirements. OMB will also clarify rules on the use of focus groups and streamline renewals of previously approved survey requests.

MISSION-DRIVEN, RESULTS-ORIENTED BUDGETING

BGT01 DEVELOP PERFORMANCE AGREEMENTS WITH SENIOR POLITICAL LEADERSHIP THAT REFLECT ORGANIZATIONAL AND POLICY GOALS
The President should develop performance agreements with agency heads, starting with the top two dozen. Agency heads should also use performance agreements within their agency to forge an effective team committed to achieving organizational goals and objectives.

BGT02 EFFECTIVELY IMPLEMENT THE GOVERNMENT PERFORMANCE AND RESULTS ACT OF 1993
Accelerate planning and measurement efforts to improve performance in every federal program and agency. Designate as pilots under the act several multi-agency efforts that have related programs and functions. Develop common measures and data collection efforts for cross-cutting issues. Clarify the goals and objectives of federal programs. Incorporate performance objectives and results as key elements in budget and management reviews.

BGT03 EMPOWER MANAGERS TO PERFORM
Restructure appropriations accounts to reduce overitemization and to align them with programs. Ensure that direct operating costs can be identified. Reduce overly detailed restrictions and earmarks in appropriations and report language. Simplify the apportionment process. Reduce the excessive administrative subdivision of funds in financial operating plans .

BGT04 ELIMINATE EMPLOYMENT CEILINGS AND FLOORS BY MANAGING WITHIN BUDGET
Budget and manage on the basis of operating costs rather than full-time equivalents or employment ceilings. Request Congress to remove FTE floors.

BGT05 PROVIDE LINE MANAGERS WITH GREATER FLEXIBILITY TO ACHIEVE RESULTS
Identify those appropriations that should be converted to multi- or no-year status. Permit agencies to roll over 50 percent of their unobligated year-end balances in annual operating costs to the next year. Expedite reprogramming of funds within agencies.

Recommendations

BGT06   STREAMLINE BUDGET DEVELOPMENT
Begin the President's budget formulation process with a mission-driven Executive Budget Resolution process
that will replace hierarchial budget development, delegate more decision making to agency heads, and promote a collaborative
approach to crosscutting issues. In the process, eliminate multiple requirements for detailed budget justification materials.
Negotiate a reduction in the detailed budget justification provided to Congress.

BGT07   INSTITUTE BIENNIAL BUDGETS AND APPROPRIATIONS
Submit a legislative proposal to move from an annual to a biennial budget submission by the President
Establish biennial budget resolution and biennial appropriation processes. Evaluate program effectiveness
and refine performance measures in the off-year.

BGT08   SEEK ENACTMENT OF EXPEDITED RESCISSION PROCEDURES
Pursue negotiations with the leadership of the House and Senate to gain enactment of expedited rescission authority.

IMPROVING FINANCIAL MANAGEMENT

FM01   ACCELERATE THE ISSUANCE OF FEDERAL ACCOUNTING STANDARDS
Issue a comprehensive set of federal financial accounting standards within 18 months. If all standards are not issued under the
present advisory board structure, create an independent federal financial accounting standards board.

**FM02   CLARIFY AND STRENGTHEN THE FINANCIAL MANAGEMENT ROLES OF
OMB AND TREASURY**
Develop a Memorandum of Understanding to clarify the roles of OMB and Treasury in financial management. Create a
governmentwide budget and financial information steering group to develop and provide guidance in implementing an
integrated budget and financial information strategic plan. Shift review of Financial Management Service budget to the OMB
Deputy Director for Management.

FM03   FULLY INTEGRATE BUDGET, FINANCIAL AND PROGRAM INFORMATION
Ensure that agency financial systems are in compliance with a revised OMB Circular A-127 , "Financial Management
Systems," by September 1996. Provide interagency funding for the joint development of financial systems.

FM04   INCREASE THE USE OF TECHNOLOGY TO STREAMLINE FINANCIAL SERVICES
Use electronic funds transfer to pay and reimburse expenses for all federal employees, to handle all interagency payments, to
make payments to state and local governments, and to pay for purchases from the private sector. Similarly, all payments to
individuals should be done electronically.

FM05   USE THE CHIEF FINANCIAL OFFICERS (CFO) ACT TO IMPROVE FINANCIAL SERVICES
Identify the set of financial management functions which should report to agency CFOs, and ensure that all financial
management personnel are fully-qualified when hired. Ensure that information being collected, disseminated, and reported on
is useful, objective, timely, and accurate for the benefit of program managers.

FM06   "FRANCHISE" INTERNAL SERVICES
The President's Management Council should encourage agencies to purchase common administrative services, such as payroll,
computer support, or procurement, competitively from other federal agencies that may be more responsive or offer better
prices.

FM07   CREATE INNOVATION FUNDS
Allow agencies to create innovation capital funds from retained savings to invest in innovations that can improve service and
provide a return on investment.

FM08   REDUCE FINANCIAL REGULATIONS AND REQUIREMENTS
Eliminate timesheets and timecards and use technology to enter payroll data only on an exception basis. Allow use of
commercial checking accounts instead of third-party accounts. Create a threshold below which it is not cost effective to resolve
audit findings.

FM09   SIMPLIFY THE FINANCIAL REPORTING PROCESS
Grant OMB the flexibility to consolidate and simplify over a dozen related statutory reports to Congress and the President.
Require agency heads to provide two reports annually, a planning report and an accountability report. Ensure that any future
financial management reporting requirements can be addressed in either the planning or accountability reports.

FM10   PROVIDE AN ANNUAL FINANCIAL REPORT TO THE PUBLIC
Provide a simplified version of a consolidated report on the finances of the federal government for distribution to the taxpayers
by June 1995. Develop a method of identifying and budgeting for the expected costs of contingent liabilities of the Federal
Government.

FM11   STRENGTHEN DEBT COLLECTION PROGRAMS
Propose legislation to allow debt collection activities to be funded by the revenues generated from collections and to allow the
agencies to keep a certain percentage of any increased collection amounts. Propose legislation to lift restrictions on the use of
private collection, and expand agency litigation authority for debt collection through the designation of special assistant U.S.
Attorneys.

Recommendations

FM12   MANAGE FIXED ASSET INVESTMENTS FOR THE LONG TERM

Establish a long-term fixed asset planning and analysis process, and incorporate it into the federal budget process. Ensure there is no bias in the budget against long-term investments.

FM13   CHARGE AGENCIES FOR THE FULL COST OF EMPLOYEE BENEFITS

Require all agencies to pay the full accruing cost of Civil Service Retirement and Pensions. OMB and the Office of Personnel Management should also research the possibility of charging agencies for civilian retiree health benefits.

REINVENTING HUMAN RESOURCE MANAGEMENT

HRM01   CREATE A FLEXIBLE AND RESPONSIVE HIRING SYSTEM

Authorize agencies to establish their own recruitment and examining programs. Abolish centralized registers and standard application forms. Allow federal departments and agencies to determine that recruitment shortages exist and directly hire candidates without ranking. Reduce the types of competitive service appointments to 3. Abolish the time-in-grade requirement.

HRM02   REFORM THE GENERAL SCHEDULE CLASSIFICATION AND BASIC PAY SYSTEM

Remove all grade-level classification criteria from the law. Provide agencies with flexibility to establish broadbanding systems built upon the General Schedule framework.

HRM03   AUTHORIZE AGENCIES TO DEVELOP PROGRAMS FOR IMPROVEMENT OF INDIVIDUAL AND ORGANIZATIONAL PERFORMANCE

Authorize agencies to design their own performance management programs which define and measure success based on each agency's unique needs.

HRM04   AUTHORIZE AGENCIES TO DEVELOP INCENTIVE AWARD AND BONUS SYSTEMS TO IMPROVE INDIVIDUAL AND ORGANIZATIONAL PERFORMANCE

Authorize agencies to develop their own incentive award and bonus systems. Encourage agencies to establish productivity gainsharing programs to support their reinvention and change efforts.

HRM05   STRENGTHEN SYSTEMS TO SUPPORT MANAGEMENT IN DEALING WITH POOR PERFORMERS

Develop a culture of performance which provides supervisors with the skills, knowledge, and support they need to deal with poor performers, and holds supervisors accountable for effectively managing their human resources. Reduce by half the time needed to terminate federal employees for cause.

HRM06   CLEARLY DEFINE THE OBJECTIVE OF TRAINING AS THE IMPROVEMENT OF INDIVIDUAL AND ORGANIZATIONAL PERFORMANCE; MAKE TRAINING MORE MARKET-DRIVEN

Reduce restrictions on training to allow managers to focus on organizational mission and to take advantage of the available training marketplace.

HRM07   ENHANCE PROGRAMS TO PROVIDE FAMILY-FRIENDLY WORKPLACES

Implement family-friendly workplace practices (flex-time, flexiplace, job sharing, telecommuting) while ensuring accountability for customer service. Provide telecommunications and administrative support necessary for employees participating in flexiplace and telecommuting work arrangements. Expand the authority to establish and fund dependent care programs. Allow employees to use sick leave to care for dependents. Allow employees who leave and then re-enter federal service to be given credit for prior sick leave balances.

HRM08   IMPROVE PROCESSES AND PROCEDURES ESTABLISHED TO PROVIDE WORKPLACE DUE PROCESS FOR EMPLOYEES

Eliminate jurisdictional overlaps. All agencies should establish alternative dispute resolution methods and options for the informal disposition of employment disputes.

HRM09   IMPROVE ACCOUNTABILITY FOR EQUAL OPPORTUNITY GOALS AND ACCOMPLISHMENTS

Charge all federal agency heads with the responsibility for ensuring equal opportunity and increasing representation of qualified women, minorities, and persons with disabilities into all levels and job categories, including middle and senior management positions.

HRM10   IMPROVE INTERAGENCY COLLABORATION AND CROSS TRAINING FOR HUMAN RESOURCE PROFESSIONALS

Establish an Interagency Equal Employment Opportunity and Affirmative Employment Steering Group under the joint chair of the Equal Employment Opportunity Commission and the Office of Personnel Management. Require appropriate cross training for human resource management professionals.

HRM11   STRENGTHEN THE SENIOR EXECUTIVE SERVICE SO THAT IT BECOMES A KEY ELEMENT IN THE GOVERNMENTWIDE CULTURE CHANGE EFFORT

Create and reinforce a corporate perspective within the Senior Executive Service that supports governmentwide culture change. Promote a corporate succession planning model to use to select and develop senior staff. Enhance voluntary mobility within and between agencies for top senior executive positions in government.

Recommendations

HRM12 ELIMINATE EXCESSIVE RED TAPE AND AUTOMATE FUNCTIONS AND INFORMATION
Phase out the entire 10,000 page Federal Personnel Manual (FPM) and all agency implementing directives by December 1994. Replace the FPM and agency directives with automated personnel processes, electronic decision support systems and "manuals" tailored to user needs.

HRM13 FORM LABOR-MANAGEMENT PARTNERSHIPS FOR SUCCESS
Identify labor-management partnerships as a goal of the executive branch and establish the National Partnership Council.

HRM14 PROVIDE INCENTIVES TO ENCOURAGE VOLUNTARY SEPARATIONS
Provide departments and agencies with the authority to offer separation pay. Decentralize the authority to approve early retirement. Authorize departments and agencies to fund job search activities and retraining of employees scheduled to be displaced. Limit annual leave accumulation by senior executives to 240 hours.

REINVENTING FEDERAL PROCUREMENT

PROC01 REFRAME ACQUISITION POLICY
Convert the 1,600 pages of the Federal Acquisition Regulation from a set of rigid rules to a set of guiding principles.

PROC02 BUILD AN INNOVATIVE PROCUREMENT WORKFORCE
Establish an interagency program to improve the governmentwide procurement workforce. Provide civilian agencies with authority for improving the acquisition workforce similar to that of the Defense Department's.

PROC03 ENCOURAGE MORE PROCUREMENT INNOVATION
Provide new legislative authority to test innovative procurement methods. Establish a mechanism to disseminate information governmentwide on innovative procurement ideas.

PROC04 ESTABLISH NEW SIMPLIFIED ACQUISITION THRESHOLD AND PROCEDURES
Enact legislation to simplify small purchases by raising the threshold for the use of simplified acquisition procedures from $25,000 to $100,000 and raise the various thresholds for the application of over a dozen other statutory requirements that similarly complicate the process. To ensure small business participation, establish a single electronic bulletin board capability to provide access to information on contracting opportunities.

PROC05 REFORM LABOR LAWS AND TRANSFORM THE LABOR DEPARTMENT INTO AN EFFICIENT PARTNER FOR MEETING PUBLIC POLICY GOALS
Enact legislation to simplify acquisition labor laws such as the Davis-Bacon Act, the Copeland Act, and the Service Contract Act. Improve access to wage schedules through an on-line electronic system.

PROC06 AMEND PROTEST RULES
Change the standard of review at the General Services Board of Contracts Appeals to conform to that used in the relevant courts. Allow penalties for frivolous protests. Allow contract negotiation to continue up to the point of contract award, even though a protest has been filed with the General Services Board of Contract Appeals.

PROC07 ENHANCE PROGRAMS FOR SMALL BUSINESS AND SMALL DISADVANTAGED BUSINESS CONCERNS
Repeal statutory limitations on subcontracting and substitute regulatory limitations to provide greater flexibility. Authorize civilian agencies to establish small disadvantaged business set-asides.

PROC08 REFORM INFORMATION TECHNOLOGY PROCUREMENTS
Increase the delegation of authority to agencies to purchase information technology. For purchases less than $500,000 for products, and $2.5 million for services over the life of a contract, eliminate indepth requirements for analyses of alternatives. Pilot-test alternative ways of buying commercially available information technology items.

PROC09 LOWER COSTS AND REDUCE BUREAUCRACY IN SMALL PURCHASES THROUGH THE USE OF PURCHASE CARDS
Provide managers with the ability to authorize employees to purchase small dollar value items directly using a government purchase card. Require internal government supply sources to accept this card.

PROC10 ENSURE CUSTOMER FOCUS IN PROCUREMENT
Revise Procurement Management Reviews to incorporate NPR principles such as "focusing on results" for the line managers.

PROC11 IMPROVE PROCUREMENT ETHICS LAWS
Create consistency across the government in the application of procurement ethics laws.

PROC12 ALLOW FOR EXPANDED CHOICE AND COOPERATION IN THE USE OF SUPPLY SCHEDULES
Allow state and local governments, grantees, and certain nonprofit agencies to use federal supply sources. Similarly, allow federal agencies to enter into cooperative agreements to share state and local government supply sources.

PROC13 FOSTER RELIANCE ON THE COMMERCIAL MARKETPLACE
Change laws to make it easier to buy commercial items. For example, revise the definition of commercial item. Revise governmentwide and agency regulations and procedures which preclude the use of commercial specifications.

PROC14 EXPAND ELECTRONIC COMMERCE FOR FEDERAL ACQUISITION
Establish a governmentwide program to use electronic commerce for federal procurements.

Recommendations

PROC15   ENCOURAGE BEST VALUE PROCUREMENT
To recognize other factors besides price, define "best value" and provide regulatory guidance to implement a program for buying on a "best value" basis. Issue guide on the use of "best practices" source selection procedures.

PROC16   PROMOTE EXCELLENCE IN VENDOR PERFORMANCE
Establish an interagency Excellence in Vendor Performance Forum that would develop policies and techniques to measure contractor performance for use in contract decisions. Establish an award for contractor and government acquisition excellence.

PROC17   AUTHORIZE A TWO-PHASE COMPETITIVE SOURCE SELECTION PROCESS
Authorize the use of a two-phase selection process for certain types of contracts so that an offeror does not incur a substantial expense in preparing a contract proposal.

PROC18   AUTHORIZE MULTIYEAR CONTRACTS
Authorize multiyear contracts and allow contracts for severable services to cross fiscal years.

PROC19   CONFORM CERTAIN STATUTORY REQUIREMENTS FOR CIVILIAN AGENCIES TO THOSE OF DEFENSE AGENCIES
Repeal requirements for commercial pricing certificates and authorize contract awards without discussions, where appropriate. Maintain the $500,000 threshold for cost and pricing data requirements for the Defense Department and establish the same threshold for civilian agencies.

PROC20   STREAMLINE BUYING FOR THE ENVIRONMENT
Develop "best practice" guides on buying for the environment. Encourage multiple award schedule contractors to identify environmentally preferable products. Provide energy efficiency information in government catalogs and automated systems.

REINVENTING SUPPORT SERVICES

SUP01   AUTHORIZE THE EXECUTIVE BRANCH TO ESTABLISH A PRINTING POLICY THAT WILL ELIMINATE THE CURRENT PRINTING MONOPOLY
Give the executive branch authority to make its own printing policy that will eliminate the mandatory printing source. Develop a new executive branch printing policy for the 21st century.

SUP02   ASSURE PUBLIC ACCESS TO FEDERAL INFORMATION
Give the executive branch agencies responsibility for distributing printed federal information to depository libraries. Require agencies to inventory the federal information they hold, and make it accessible to the public.

SUP03   IMPROVE DISTRIBUTION SYSTEMS TO REDUCE COSTLY INVENTORIES
Permit customer choice in sources of supply. Compare depot distribution costs with commercial distribution systems. Take away the Federal Prison Industries' status as a mandatory source of federal supplies and require it to compete commercially for federal agencies' business. Increase the use of electronic commerce for ordering from depot systems.

SUP04   STREAMLINE AND IMPROVE CONTRACTING STRATEGIES FOR THE MULTIPLE AWARD SCHEDULE PROGRAM
Eliminate the use of mandatory supply schedules. Make the supply schedule system easier to use by reducing the administrative burden for acquisitions under $10,000. In addition, eliminate the announcement requirements and raise the maximum order limitations for the purchase of information technology items listed in supply schedules.

SUP05   EXPAND AGENCY AUTHORITY AND ELIMINATE CONGRESSIONAL CONTROL OVER FEDERAL VEHICLE FLEET MANAGEMENT
Update vehicle replacement standards. Increase emergency repair limits to $150. Eliminate the monopoly on disposing of agency-owned vehicles.

SUP06   GIVE AGENCIES AUTHORITY AND INCENTIVE FOR PERSONAL PROPERTY MANAGEMENT AND DISPOSAL
Provide incentives to agencies to dispose of excess personal property. Automate the process and eliminate the monopoly on personal property disposal.

SUP07   SIMPLIFY TRAVEL AND INCREASE COMPETITION
Increase choices for federal travelers and automate the travel process. Pilot-test a tender system for airfares.

SUP08   GIVE CUSTOMERS CHOICES AND CREATE REAL PROPERTY ENTERPRISES THAT PROMOTE SOUND REAL PROPERTY ASSET MANAGEMENT
Give agencies greater authority to choose their sources of real property services. Create competitive enterprises within the government to provide real property services on a fee basis, and encourage federal managers to seek the best available source. Create an ownership enterprise for the sound management of federal real property assets. Establish a governmentwide policy for real property asset management. Manage the Federal Buildings Fund in a manner comparable to the commercial sector.

SUP09   SIMPLIFY PROCEDURES FOR ACQUIRING SMALL BLOCKS OF SPACE TO HOUSE FEDERAL AGENCIES
Simplify the procedures for acquiring small amounts of leased space under 10,000 square feet.

Recommendations

SUP10   ESTABLISH NEW CONTRACTING PROCEDURES FOR THE CONTINUED OCCUPANCY
OF LEASED OFFICE SPACE
Simplify the procedures for renewing leases.

SUP11   REDUCE POSTAGE COSTS THROUGH IMPROVED MAIL MANAGEMENT
Encourage postage savings through the implementation of mail management initiatives.
Allow line managers to manage their own postal budgets.

REENGINEER THROUGH THE USE OF INFORMATION TECHNOLOGY

IT01   PROVIDE CLEAR, STRONG LEADERSHIP TO INTEGRATE INFORMATION TECHNOLOGY INTO THE
BUSINESS OF GOVERNMENT
Create a Government Information Technology Services working group to develop a strategic vision for the use of government
information technology and to implement NPR's information technology recommendations.

IT02   IMPLEMENT NATIONWIDE, INTEGRATED ELECTRONIC BENEFIT TRANSFER
Design an integrated implementation plan for the use of electronic benefit transfer for programs such as Food Stamps and for
direct payments to individuals without bank accounts.

IT03   DEVELOP INTEGRATED ELECTRONIC ACCESS TO GOVERNMENT
INFORMATION AND SERVICE
Use information technology initiatives to improve customer service by creating a one-stop "800" calling service, integrated
one-stop service "kiosks," and a governmentwide electronic bulletin board system.

IT04   ESTABLISH A NATIONAL LAW ENFORCEMENT/PUBLIC SAFETY NETWORK
Establish a national law enforcement/public safety data network for use by federal, state, and local law enforcement officials.

IT05   PROVIDE INTERGOVERNMENTAL TAX FILING, REPORTING, AND PAYMENTS PROCESSING
Integrate government financial filings, reporting, and payments processing, and determine ways to eliminate the need for
filing routine tax returns.

IT06   ESTABLISH AN INTERNATIONAL TRADE DATA SYSTEM
Develop and implement a U.S. Government International Trade Data System in the Treasury Department.

IT07   CREATE A NATIONAL ENVIRONMENTAL DATA INDEX
Organize the implementation of a national environmental data index in the Commerce Department.

IT08   PLAN, DEMONSTRATE, AND PROVIDE GOVERNMENTWIDE ELECTRONIC MAIL
Improve electronic mail and messaging among federal agencies.

IT09   ESTABLISH AN INFORMATION INFRASTRUCTURE
Develop a Government Information Infrastructure to use government information resources effectively and support electronic
government applications. Consolidate and modernize government data processing centers.

IT10   DEVELOP SYSTEMS AND MECHANISMS TO ENSURE PRIVACY AND SECURITY
Establish a Privacy Protection Board. Establish uniform privacy protection practices and generally
acceptable implementation methods for these practices. Develop a digital signature standard for sensitive, unclassified data by
January 1994.

IT11   IMPROVE METHODS OF INFORMATION TECHNOLOGY ACQUISITION
(see PROC 08, PROC09, PROC14, SUP04, and FM06)

IT12   PROVIDE INCENTIVES FOR INNOVATION
Retain a portion of agency information technology savings to reinvest in information technology. Promote performance-based
contracting for information technology. Establish a governmentwide venture capital fund for innovative information
technology projects

IT13   PROVIDE TRAINING AND TECHNICAL ASSISTANCE IN INFORMATION TECHNOLOGY TO FEDERAL
EMPLOYEES
Establish a program to train non-technical senior executives and political appointees in information technology. Require
managers of information resources to meet certification standards. Promote collegial assistance in using information
technology. Include training costs as part of all information technology purchases.

RETHINKING PROGRAM DESIGN

DES01   ACTIVATE PROGRAM DESIGN AS A FORMAL DISCIPLINE
The President's Management Council should commission the development of a handbook to help federal managers
understand the strengths and weaknesses of various forms of program design.

DES02   ESTABLISH PILOT PROGRAM DESIGN CAPABILITIES IN ONE OR TWO AGENCIES
Test the usefulness of the program design handbook and the value of program design as a useful discipline.